EVERYTHING

IS NORMAL

THE LIFE AND TIMES

OF A SOVIET KID

SERGEY GRECHISHKIN

Published by Inkshares, Inc., Oakland, California
www.inkshares.com

Edited by Matt Harry

Cover design by CoverKitchen | Interior design by Kevin G. Summers

ISBN: 9781942645900
e-ISBN: 9781942645917
LCCN: 2017955464

First edition

To my children: Mike, Alex, and Zoya

NOTE ON IMPERIAL VS. METRIC MEASURES:

- 1 meter = 3.28 feet = 39.4 inches
- 1 kilometer = 0.62 miles = 1,093 yards
- 1 liter = 33.8 fluid ounces
- 1 kilogram (or kilo) = 2.2 pounds

- 1 foot = 0.3 meters
- 1 mile = 1.6 kilometers
- 1 pint = 0.56 liters
- 1 pound = 0.45 kilograms

NOTE ON SOVIET PRICE LEVELS IN THE EARLY '80S:

Money in:
- *40 rubles/month – university student scholarship*
- *120–200 rubles/month – typical salary, whether for a janitor, an engineer, or a ballerina*
- *600 rubles/month – salary of a government minister or senior Communist Party official*

Money out:
- *1 kopeck – box of matches; glass of soda water without syrup; pencil; slice of bread*
- *2 kopecks – local call on a pay phone; newspaper; monthly Komsomol membership dues; glass of tea with sugar; twelve-page school notebook*
- *3 kopecks – glass of soda with syrup or glass of kvass; tram ride*
- *5 kopecks – subway ride; children's paperback; pretzel*
- *10 kopecks – glass of tomato juice; 1 kilo of salt; 1 kilo of potatoes; one amusement park ride; cinema ticket (child)*
- *12 kopecks – bar of children's soap; 1 kilo of carrots*
- *15 kopecks – one game on an arcade machine*
- *20 kopecks – 1 liter of gasoline or milk; ballpoint pen; taxi fare for 1 kilometer; ticket to public baths; loaf of rye bread*
- *22 kopecks – cream pastry from Sever bakery*
- *27 kopecks – bottle of Soviet lemonade*
- *40 kopecks – haircut (child); 1 kilo of rice*
- *45 kopecks – bottle of Pepsi-Cola*
- *50 kopecks – lottery ticket; packet of Bulgarian cigarettes; packet of Soviet chewing gum*

- *90 kopecks – 1 kilo of sugar; ten eggs*
- *1 ruble – bottle of Troynoy cologne; rental of bed linen on a train*
- *1.10 rubles – 1 kilo of bananas*
- *1.50 rubles – monthly landline phone charges; packet of Marlboro cigarettes*
- *2 rubles – 1 kilo of beef, pork, chicken, or mutton; 1 kilo of zefir candy*
- *2.90 rubles – 1 kilo of sausages*
- *3 rubles – Kiev cake; 1 kilo of cheese; hardback book; monthly electricity bill; pair of Soviet-made pantyhose*
- *3.60 rubles – 1 kilo of butter*
- *4.70 rubles – 0.5-liter bottle of vodka (Andropovka)*
- *5 rubles – two hours of private tutoring; foreign-made plastic shopping bag with a Marlboro logo (black market); packet of foreign-made cigarettes (black market)*
- *10 rubles – foreign-made audio cassette; Moscow–Leningrad train ticket; monthly rent for an average apartment*
- *20 rubles – 1 kilo of roasted coffee beans*
- *35 rubles – plain gold ring; Soviet-made calculator*
- *45 rubles – Soviet-made vacuum cleaner; Soviet-made skateboard*
- *96 rubles – Soviet-made folding bicycle*
- *100 rubles – a Bible (black market)*
- *155 rubles – Soviet-made cassette tape recorder*
- *200 rubles – foreign-made brand-name jeans, e.g., Lee, Levi's (black market)*
- *250 rubles – foreign-made brand-name sneakers, e.g., Reebok, Nike, Adidas (black market)*
- *700 rubles – Soviet-made color TV*
- *7,200 rubles – Soviet-made car (Lada VAZ-2106)*

Anekdot

n.: the most popular form of Soviet humor, a short story or dialogue with a punch line, often politically subversive. "Being simultaneously independent from and parasitically attached to mass cultural production and authoritative discourse, the anekdot served as a template for an alternative, satirical, reflexive, collective voice-over narration of the Soviet century."

Many of the *anekdots* under this book's chapter headings were once punishable in the USSR by up to ten years of forced labor under article 58 of the criminal code ("Anti-Soviet Propaganda"). This article was used freely to put critics of the Soviet government behind bars. Today, of course, things are very different in Russia. Now it's article 282.

*Seth Benedict Graham, "A Cultural Analysis of the Russo-Soviet Anekdot" (PhD diss., University of Pittsburgh, 2003).

August 19, 2011

I got the call at 7:18 a.m.

My career in finance in London had turned me into a miserable early bird. Vacation or no vacation, 7 a.m. found me sorting through emails.

At the time, I was sitting on the edge of the infinity pool at our Tuscan vacation house. My wife and kids were still asleep upstairs, so I was free to dangle my feet in the water and quietly survey the hills and vineyards surrounding me.

In spite of the view, my heart was uneasy. Back in Saint Petersburg, Russia, my grandmother was ailing. The home attendant who I had hired for her a few years ago had been reporting a steady decline in her health for the past several weeks.

I was working through the avalanche of work emails that had inundated my Blackberry overnight when suddenly the screen flashed the name of Grandma's home attendant.

I knew it right away.

The conversation lasted only a minute or two. As predictable as the news was, it still managed to shake me. On one hand, I had spent my entire childhood in anxious dread of Grandma's death. Some small, subconscious part of me must have still expected her to remain in my life forever. And yet another, more disquieting part of me felt liberated.

After hanging up, I sat there with my legs in the cool water.

Out of nowhere, a memory came back to me, as vivid as though it had happened the other week.

It was Friday, January 11, 1980, the second day of school after the winter break. At four in the afternoon, it was already getting dark in Leningrad. Grandma and I were standing in deep snow and waiting for trolleybus number fifteen at the stop on Tchaikovsky Street.*

Grandma, a daughter of a tsarist admiral, always knew exactly what to do, and when to do it, and to whom things should be done. Her appearance matched her clout. A tall, somewhat heavyset woman, she never used any makeup and she wore her hair short—as she said, "à la Deanna Durbin." She had blue eyes and a prominent nose, which held up a pair of large, thick-framed spectacles.

It was freezing cold, but I was snug in my lambskin coat and *ushanka* fur hat. It was a proper hat, with earflaps made of rabbit fur. When I was in kindergarten, the only hat I owned looked like a girl's bonnet. I was small for my age and really looked like a girl, so this was even more distressing. To make me feel better, Grandma had taken a metal and enamel army officer's badge—wheat sheaves framing a red star and the Soviet hammer and sickle—and sewed it to the front of the hat. But this new *ushanka* didn't need any badges—it was a proper big boy's hat.

The next day I was turning nine. That made me practically a grown-up. I would have a party, and all my friends would come over—at least all the ones Grandma deemed "admissible" into the house, by virtue of their good breeding and manners. We would eat pastries from the Sever bakery, play with Konstruktor construction blocks, and

*A trolleybus is an electric bus with "horns" that attach to power lines.

watch diafilms—colored filmstrips with pictures and captions that we projected onto a wall.

Grandma and I were waiting for the number fifteen to take me to the Rauchfuss Pediatric Hospital. Last week, I had surgery there, and they needed to remove my dressings.

The surgery had been an unpleasant surprise. Right before New Year's Eve—surely the worst possible moment for such an announcement—Grandma had informed me that I was to be circumcised.

When I asked what that meant, she told me a piece of skin on the tip of my willy had to be cut off.

"What for?" I had asked, going cold all over.

"If we don't do it, you might end up an invalid," she said without elaborating.

To me, invalids were people without legs or arms who begged passersby for change at train stations. Even assuming that some of them were also missing parts of their willies, mine was intact and functioned quite as expected. But I knew better than to press Grandma for explanations. In our house, children were expected to leave the thinking to adults and not ask any questions or voice any opinions.

But I'd already started to get the sense that adults didn't always know what they were doing. For instance, last week during the surgery, the anesthesiologist didn't put the mask properly over my face, so it took me ages to fall asleep as my eyes wandered the room restlessly. After the surgery, I had spent five days in the hospital, in a huge room filled with cots occupied by twenty other bandaged convalescents. Whoever did my bandaging also did a piss-poor job—literally, in my case, because it had been incredibly painful to go to the bathroom. I cried every time.

Later I learned that Grandma had asked the surgeon to perform the circumcision in such a way that it "wouldn't look like a Jewish one." It was bad enough, she must have thought, that I looked Jewish while fully dressed, with my brown eyes, dark curly hair, and protruding ears. This way, at least I'd have the option of refuting the accusation by dropping trou.

The trolleybus was late. I skimmed the fresh issue of the *Komsomol Pravda* newspaper pasted to the side of the bus shelter. It quickly bored me. *Pravda* never printed anything interesting—just tedious policy speeches made by various Communist Party officials and reports about how some textile factory had increased its output by 24.8 percent this quarter. Occasionally there were also glowing profiles of some milkmaid or tractor driver being decorated with the order of Hero of Labor in return for fifty years of hard work at a local collective farm.

Last week's surgical ordeal was not my first. When I was six, Grandma decided that my recurring respiratory infections were caused by my adenoids and that I should have them removed. Through some back channels, she got me a spot in the city's inpatient otorhinolaryngological hospital—which proved to be utterly inhospitable. I stayed there for four days, all alone. Visiting patients, however small they were, was discouraged. But worst of all was the procedure itself.

My surgeon must have been some kind of luminary, because the operation was observed by a bunch of her students. There I was, all alone, surrounded by a crowd of aloof adults in white coats and hats. The surgeon poked me with a needle, reached into my throat with a metal wrench, and cut something out of me. Then she took out the piece of flesh, all goopy with blood and pus, and presented it to her students on a stainless-steel plate, like an hors d'oeuvre at a cannibal soiree.

Still waiting for the number fifteen, I turned my thoughts to the future. Not my birthday party, or next week's schoolwork, or even the upcoming summer, when the USSR would be hosting the Olympics, but the very distant future. It was 1980, the start of a new decade—my first year with an 8 in front of it. It had been "the '80s" for only eleven days, but everything already felt somehow futuristic and space-agey. And in twenty years it would be a brand-new century, and I would be an old man, about to turn twenty-nine.

I tried to picture myself as a grown-up, with long hair and a mustache. (All the coolest grown-ups I knew had long hair and mustaches, like the front man of the popular band—or, to use the official Soviet lingo, "vocal-instrumental ensemble"—Pesnyary.)

Twenty years felt like an unfathomably long time. By then we would have built Communism in the Soviet Union. At school, we were told that Communism would be just like normal Soviet life, except everyone would be morally upstanding and diligent, and all the stores would be full of food, clothes, and toys, free to anyone who needed them. We were told that every family would have a separate apartment to live in, with every person getting a room to themselves. I had also bet that in the year 2000 we would all go on vacations to outer space, maybe to Mars, but if not, then at least for sure to the moon.

All of this seemed to be just over the horizon, not nearly as hard to imagine as myself with long hair and a mustache.

Little did I know that my actual future would be much like my circumcision—unexpected, twisted, and ill-advised.

Back in Tuscany, I picked up my Blackberry again. Without taking my legs out of the pool, I purchased a plane ticket to Saint Petersburg for that evening. I was composed. I had, after all, been preparing for this day for a very long time. Then I got up and went back to the house, where my wife, Ira, was already preparing breakfast for our children—Mike, Alex, and Zoya—and for all the guests who were staying with us.

CHAPTER 1

A NORMAL SOVIET CITIZEN

A woman is taking a bath in a communal apartment and notices a man's face watching her from behind frosted glass.

"What's the matter with you?!" she yells.

"Oh please, like you've got something I've not seen before," he says. "I'm just making sure you're not using my soap!"

IF I WERE to describe my Soviet childhood in one word, that word would be *normal*.

I had a normal family. We lived in Leningrad, today's Saint Petersburg, in an apartment that the Soviet government had confiscated, as it was wont to do, from a church. We did not own our apartment. All Soviet buildings belonged to the government; residents simply rented them in perpetuity. Since demand for apartments far outstripped supply, people waited on lists for years or even decades to be allotted a new *zhilploschad*—a mouthful meaning "living area." Because of this, most people continued to live with their parents well into young adulthood, often even after marriage.

The most frequently encountered residential arrangement in Leningrad in the 1970s was a *kommunalka*, a communal apartment. These were very large, once-opulent residences that the Soviet government had confiscated from their wealthy former owners after the 1917 Revolution and then divided between multiple families. The bigger the apartment, the more people were crammed into it, usually one household per room.

In January 1971, one such communal flat became my first home. Grandma, Mom, and little brand-new me were pretty well off; we had two connecting rooms to ourselves. Our *kommunalka* was not very big: besides us, there were only seven other families in it, about twenty people altogether. Still, that meant twenty people squeezing past each other through the narrow hallways, arguing over who got to use the phone next, jostling each other in the kitchen over multiple stoves with pots on permanent boil, and fidgeting in line for the single, continuously used toilet.

Dad did not live with us, but this was not unusual. In fact, my parents' marriage was a perfectly normal Soviet story from start to finish. Mom and Dad had attended the same school for ten years without saying a word to each other. They were in the same grade but in different homerooms, so they didn't have any classes together. In tenth grade, they began dating. When they finished school and turned nineteen, they got married. When they turned twenty-two, they had me.

Dad's name was Sergey, just like his dad's and like mine.* He was tall and slim, well mannered, extraordinarily erudite, a talented poet, and a great dancer. As a team captain on a popular local TV quiz show, he was often recognized in the street. It

---

*If it's starting to seem like all Russian men are named Sergey, it's not that far from the truth. Between 1950 and 1981, Sergey was the second-most popular name for boys in the Soviet Union, topped only by Alexander (Sasha). More than 10 percent of boys born in those decades ended up named Sergey.

was easy to see why Mom fell for him. Grandma also thought him very handsome. Her friends used to joke that she let him marry her daughter only because he was too young for her to marry herself. But looks and charm alone were not enough to hold the young family together, and my parents divorced when I was two.

My very first memory is from that time, and it is not a happy one. I am lying in my bed back in our communal apartment. Next to me is a large green plastic crocodile. I am distraught because Grandma has just told me that the crocodile swallowed my favorite pacifier. This inauspicious beginning set the tone for most of my early childhood. Grandma's unmerciful ruse to wean me from my pacifier awakened me to the fact that the world around me was fundamentally dreadful.

After my parents' divorce, Grandma decided two things. Firstly, I would be living with her from now on. And secondly, a communal flat was not "hygienic" enough for her delicate little Sergey. So she armed herself with the newspaper *Exchange* and began to search the classifieds section. Since all apartments were government-owned, when people wanted to move, they had to find other people who wanted to move and trade residences with them. They'd do this by placing an ad in a newspaper, describing their place and what sort of a home they wanted in return. Having piped hot water and a bathtub merited separate mention. When the apartments were of clearly unequal value, one of the parties would also kick in some money, even though this was illegal. After intense comparison shopping, Grandma found a studio in Peterhof, about twenty miles out of Leningrad. Deciding it would do, she exchanged residences with its owner, giving them her two rooms in the communal apartment.

Peterhof, Dutch for "Peter's Court," is the Russian take on Versailles. Resplendent with parks and palaces, this summertime countryside residence of the tsars did double duty; besides sheltering the royal family in style, it impressed upon visiting Western dignitaries and heads of state that Russians were civilized and European, and had money to burn.

In the '70s, Peterhof, with its residential neighborhoods and university buildings, was remote enough from the city that moving there almost qualified as retirement to the countryside. Leningrad was half an hour away by commuter train, and those trips were dreary. On this route, there were no pretty dachas with orchards and gardens. This was not the train people took in anticipation of a fun weekend of foraging in the forest for wild mushrooms or pottering in their vegetable gardens. All stops along this line served the postwar bedroom communities, buildings hastily assembled out of cheap concrete paneling. The train took people to and from work in the city only. One look instantly told one that its miserable passengers had already accomplished everything they were going to achieve in life, which didn't add up to much. They were never going to travel abroad. They were never going to own cars. They were never going to be allowed to start their own businesses, and they were never going to own their own houses or land. Their horizons were bereft of opportunities.

One particular trip brought this home to me. One day when I was four years old, Grandma and I were returning from Leningrad to Peterhof with a distant relative of ours. She had married a man from Sudan and now mostly lived abroad. She got me an awesome present: a piece of chewing gum. Had I been given such a thing several years later, I would have squirreled it away to share with my friends on some meaningful occasion or to trade it to a schoolmate for some other valuable object, perhaps a toy soldier. But I was still naive in the ways of the world, so I opened it immediately. Inside the outer wrapper was an inner one, with a picture of some Western animated character on it. The rarity and value of this souvenir were entirely lost on me. I popped the pink gum into my mouth and began chewing with gusto. It was my first piece of gum ever, and it tasted like nothing I'd ever had before—a mixture of strawberry, banana, and vanilla! The only thing I was told was not to swallow it under any circumstances, so I kept on chewing and looking out the window as the train chugged along.

The party in my mouth brought into sudden contrast the dreariness of the view outside. It was early spring; the winter snow was already melting into slush and mud, but there were no flowers or grass yet to gladden the eye. There was nothing but sickly naked trees, distant industrial factory chimneys, and endless squat rows of grim apartment buildings, all the same height and shape. Everything looked dreary, grimy, and gray.

I turned my attention to my fellow passengers. They, too, looked bleak. The seat across from me was taken by a middle-aged man, clad in a blue waterproof jacket. He sat quietly, holding a newspaper but not reading it or solving the crossword. He was also staring out the window, clearly thinking the same uncharitable thoughts about the backdrop.

Later, these existential doldrums began finding me at home in our tiny Peterhof flat. I would spend hours by the balcony window, watching smoke rise from the power station chimneys on the horizon and listening to the suburban trains chug by in the distance. Most of my memories of that time coalesce into a sense of timeless boredom. But after my first taste of bubble gum, something new began to mix with my malaise: jealousy of the kids in faraway countries who could chew such gum every day.

* * *

My mom was a known beauty in Leningrad in her youth. She had striking, refined southern European features, thick brunette hair, bright blue eyes, and something very prized in the USSR: an enigmatic French name, Vera Brosset. When filling out official forms, she wrote "Russian" for her ethnicity and "white-collar workers" in the section asking about her family's class origins. But that was all a lie. Mom was actually mostly French and Greek, and even more damningly, before the Revolution, her family had belonged to the nobility. Having either foreign or upper-class roots in the USSR was problematic, and having both was downright unwise. Therefore, like many others in her situation, my mother lied on her forms. Lying to the government was quite normal, too.

Officially, Mom lived with Grandma and myself at the Peterhof apartment, meaning she was registered as a resident at that address. Every Soviet citizen was subject to address registration, and free movement within the Soviet Union was restricted. If, for example, you lived in the village of Shitka in the Irkutsk area of Siberia, you couldn't just wake up one day, pull up stakes, and move to Moscow. You would need to have a relative in the city willing to let you register as a resident at their address. This would be an act of great trust on their part, because it would give you certain legal rights to their abode. This did not stop many people from moving to various cities illegally, so to make sure places like Moscow and Leningrad didn't get overrun by folks from the countryside, the police were empowered to stop anyone at any time, and anywhere, and demand to see their address registration papers. If the papers weren't in perfect order, the person could be ordered to leave town or even thrown in jail.

So even though Mom was registered at our address, she lived with her then-boyfriend and my future stepdad, Tolya. Tolya was a member of the Communist Party and had a promising university career as a professor, and would later become vice dean of Leningrad State University. He was a tall, balding blond man eight years older than Mom.

Grandma and I remained in Peterhof for two years. In all that time, I remember my mother visiting us only once. She came and took me with her to the grocery store. As we walked, she held my hand and told me that I would soon be meeting a little brother or sister. I was excited, but also somewhat baffled. Where would this new baby come from? Come to think of it, where did babies come from at all? While we're at it, where is Dad? And who is this new Tolya character? But neither Mom nor Grandma volunteered any explanations, and I was already learning—it must've been in the very air we all breathed—that it was best not to ask questions. Everything was normal. Everything that I needed to know, I would be told. If I wasn't told something, then it was none of my business.

*   *   *

Because of a chronic real estate shortage, marriage in the USSR often meant the merging of old households rather than the formation of a new one. Everyone would move in together: the happy couple, their parents, their grandparents, their siblings, children from previous marriages, and so on. This merger of family residences after a marriage was called a *s'ezd*, which translates handily as "congress," same as what the Communist Party did every five years.

After Tolya and Mom got married, Tolya and Grandma traded in both of their apartments for a bigger one in the very heart of Leningrad, and a new Soviet family unit was forged: Mom and Tolya, Grandma, myself, and my brand-new brother, Alyosha. Though we were half brothers, we looked very different. He looked Scandinavian—pale skin, light eyes, and messy light-blond hair without a hint of a curl—whereas I took after my mom's swarthy Mediterranean side of the family. When friends or relatives commented on our complete lack of resemblance, Grandma, a former English professor, would say in English, "I call those two 'Black and White.'"

Even after the family "congress," Grandma continued to have complete control of my upbringing. She was the one who fed and clothed me, checked my homework, and arranged my scheduled Saturday meetings with Dad. However, she did not do any of these things for Alyosha. When he was born, Grandma declared that one child was enough for her, and that Mom would have to raise the new baby herself. And that's how it was from then on: Alyosha belonged to Mom, and I continued to be cared for by Grandma. She and I lived largely on her retirement pension and child support payments. The fact that these payments were being made not by my father to my mother but by my paternal grandfather to my maternal grandmother seemed normal at the time.

So this way, I had two dads. Devious relatives often asked me which one of them, Dad Sergey or Dad Tolya, I loved more. I learned early on that it was best to short-circuit the interrogation by answering, "The same." Luckily, it happened to be true.

* * *

Our new home was on Kalyaeva Street. Before the Revolution, it had been called Zahar'evskaya Street, after the Church of

Saints Zachariah and Elisaveta, which used to be located there. The Soviet government renamed it in 1923 to honor Ivan Kalyaev, the terrorist who assassinated one of the sons of Tsar Alexander II with a homemade explosive. The Soviet government had its own naming priorities.

With the church now gone, a new landmark dominated the neighborhood: Bolshoi Dom—literally, the "Big House." That was what everyone called (in hushed voices) the local KGB headquarters. The Big House was a large, ugly building designed in the Constructivist spirit of the early '30s, aggressively rectangular, with a canary-yellow facade framed by reddish bricks. Its windows were vertically elongated in a way that instantly suggested prison bars. People said that its six stories actually sat on top of another six stories of prison cells below ground. They also said that it was the tallest building in town, because from any of its windows, one could "see all the way to Magadan."* In dissident circles, the words *Kalyaeva Street* elicited a frisson of terror. My brother and I would often watch cars pull up to the gates of the Big House as we walked hurriedly by. Little did we know that future president of the "Russian Federation" Mr. Vladimir Putin was walking its halls as an up-and-coming KGB agent.

Our apartment building stood three stories tall, with thick brick walls and cavernous fifteen-foot-high ceilings. It was built in 1812 as a boardinghouse run by the church, so unlike many other buildings dating from that time, it had been designed much more for function than form. But plain or not, it had everything I needed, namely a large courtyard with a

*An isolated port town on the far eastern side of Russia and the center of many forced-labor mining operations, Magadan was one of KGB's favorite places to send undesirables, like freethinking writers, artists, religious activists, and other citizens with "anti-Soviet" views.

playground, a dozen tall trees, and a curious construction that resembled a colossal doghouse but was actually a subway vent.

Our apartment was the only non-communal residence in the building. It had been carved out of a larger set of rooms that had once belonged to the curiously named Church of All the Afflicted. The church itself still occupied the larger part of our building, but services were no longer held there. Instead, the space now housed a museum devoted to the history of Leningrad trade unions. When it wasn't hosting what I assume were truly electrifying exhibitions, it mostly stood locked and empty.

This unusual provenance gave our apartment a very odd layout. By Soviet standards, it was rather large, with three rooms and a kitchen. I say "rooms" rather than "bedrooms" because the idea of a dedicated living room where no one slept at night was absurd. Our living room doubled as the master bedroom. My brother and I had a room that was just over two meters wide and eight meters long—basically, a long, narrow hallway with a window at one end and an old dark green stove covered in glazed tiles in the opposite corner. It shared a wall with the interior of the former church. The third and smallest room was Grandma's.

The apartment had piped cold water; a massive gas water heater, which adults needed to ignite with matches every time warm water was needed; and, very unusually, a combined bathroom (i.e., the bathtub, bathroom sink, and toilet were all in the same place). Although common in the West, this was practically unheard of in the USSR. Another oddity was a working fireplace in the living-room-slash-master-bedroom, which lent the place a decidedly European air of refined coziness.

As with most Soviet families, the hub of our life was the kitchen. It was where we ate all our meals, where Grandma and Mom had their never-ending arguments, and where Tolya smoked, since he was not allowed to do it anywhere else in the apartment. It was also permanently festooned with ropes strung with assorted multicolored linen, which dried day in and day out beneath the high ceiling. Walking to the dinner table usually meant a cautious stalk through a jungle of moist sheets and underpants clouded by cigarette smoke.

Although we lived on the second floor, the peculiar layout of the house gave the apartment a shallow basement. A trapdoor in the kitchen led to a dreadfully grimy vault that extended under the entire length of our apartment. We used this marvelous fluke of architecture to store all our junk. As I discovered some years later, if one braved the dust and the peril of hitting one's head on the three-foot-high ceiling, the basement would lead the adventuring soul backwards through time, all the way through the Soviet era and into the nineteenth century, yielding ever-older, ever-dustier belongings abandoned by the apartment's previous occupants. Who were all these people? What had happened to them? Were they arrested and deported? Did they die in World War II, starving during the Siege of Leningrad? Or did they emigrate in haste after the Revolution broke out, leaving behind everything they couldn't pack into several suitcases and take onto a steamship? I half suspected it was the last explanation. This made their old belongings doubly fascinating. To my mind, anyone who'd managed to escape the USSR must have been a truly remarkable person.

CHAPTER 2

ALL KIDS ARE EQUAL

A teacher in a Soviet kindergarten tells her class, "Unlike in the capitalist countries, in the USSR, children have plenty to eat and nice clothes to wear. They live in large apartments, and they have lots of wonderful toys to play with."

In the back row, a little boy starts to cry. "I don't want to live here anymore!" he says. "I want to live in the USSR!"

THE VERY FIRST thing I learned how to write, around the age of four, was the acronym CCCP (USSR). It must've been an early manifestation of my love of effortless solutions. Three identical crescents, then a smaller one facing backwards with a stick next to it, and voilà: you had a genuine word. No need to struggle with lines of varying lengths and unpredictable connections, as in *mama*.

Once I got the motion down, I started signing all my drawings with "CCCP" in a large, swaggering scrawl. It became my calling card, my *particularité*. Whatever I was drawing—a family of humanoid cephalopods, a wet splotch of gouache titled

"Buket" (bouquet), a multicolored cloud representing the epic panorama of some Soviet-Nazi tank battle (my favorite)—the top right corner of the picture was hallmarked with those four letters.

At a later stage of my artistic development, I turned my attention to the political map of the world that hung next to my stepfather's desk. I was inordinately proud of the fact that my country was the biggest in the world, and secretly nursed a grudge against the two American continents for being bigger if considered together. But the map could still use some improvement. And improve it I did, by proudly scribbling "CCCP" in blue marker across most countries as well as on large swaths of the world's oceans. As far as I was concerned, it behooved both the workers and the whales of the world to unite.

* * *

Steadfast though it seemed, my love for my homeland did not survive my first direct run-in with its government—namely, kindergarten.

The kindergarten where I ended up was a little unusual: it had a boarding group for kids whose parents worked particularly long hours. These unfortunate children were dropped off on Monday and only picked up Friday evening or even on Saturday morning. For some reason, I was assigned to that group even though I got picked up every day. This made me the object of much envy.

There were about twenty of us in the group, overseen by one teacher and one nanny. We spent most of our days playing, both indoors and outdoors in the kindergarten's courtyard playground. We also got taken on long walks through the Tavrichesky Sad, or Tauride Garden, a large park that had once belonged to a private estate but was "gifted to the children" by Vladimir Lenin after the Revolution—or at least that's what we were told.

In my first year, we were taught little songs like this:

> Let there always be sunshine,
> Let there always be blue skies,
> Let there always be Mommy,
> Let there always be me!

In my second year, the songs got longer and more morally ambiguous:

> A little grasshopper sat in the grass,
> A little grasshopper sat in the grass,
> Just like a little cucumber,
> He was quite green.

> He ate nothing but grass,
> He ate nothing but grass,
> He was friends with all the bugs,
> And never hurt a fly.

> But then a frog came along,
> But then a frog came along,
> Frog the Gluttonous Belly
> And ate the grasshopper up.

> He never thought or reckoned,
> He never thought or reckoned,
> He never, ever expected
> To meet such an end!

As one can see, all the basics were covered: life is pointless, good deeds are meaningless, there is no justice in the world, and the weak are ever at the mercy of the strong.

We were not taught to read, write, or count. All that would begin in first grade. Of course, many of us got a head start at home. Grandma had taught me the alphabet by the time I was four, so when I started school, I could already read with ease.

I hated kindergarten. The worst thing about it was getting dressed in the morning. Most days of the year, Grandma made me put on cotton tights, which were considered a unisex article of clothing for young children in the USSR. But my budding comprehension of gender norms could not be fooled; I knew deep in my heart that tights were girly. Every morning, I would go through all the stages of grief with these tights, first declining to put them on, then fighting back like a cornered animal, then offering Grandma all kinds of deals to avoid wearing them, then bawling, and then finally, dispirited, allowing Grandma to put them on me. Somehow, those tights traumatized me even more than the tiny sliver of soap that, following folk wisdom, Grandma would shove up my behind whenever I failed to have a bowel movement for more than a day.

The second-worst thing about kindergarten was the food. I was a picky eater, and government fare—boiled carrots, revolting milk soup, and lumpy rice porridge—was highly unappetizing. Thankfully, we weren't always pressured into cleaning our plates, or else I might've puked.

The third-worst thing about kindergarten was nap time. I don't recall ever sleeping through even one of those state-mandated siestas. As far as I was concerned, nap time was a waste of a perfectly good hour and a half of daylight. To avoid going insane from boredom, I would stare at the ceiling and invent stories in my head. One of them involved a cat and a dog who dug tunnels under Leningrad and chased each other through them. Another frequent subject was a family who moved from the city to a village called Romashkino (Daisy Farm) and had to adjust to rural life. Years later, I would tell these stories to my own kids at bedtime.

There was one way to temporarily escape the hell of a forced nap: raising your hand and whispering to the nanny that you had to go potty. Thus, I would often find myself sitting on the restroom windowsill and looking out the window, to avoid returning to the hated bed. I came to know every aspect of that view intimately: the trees in the street, the trucks usually parked under the windows, the people walking their dogs after lunch, the cadets making their way in and out of the military school across the street. I would watch it all and ponder the pointlessness of existence. The world-weariness I discovered on the train from Peterhof didn't go away; it just got better regimented. Any other time of day, I was a perfectly normal, easygoing child, but nap time was for ennui.

I did not know this at the time, but I had inadvertently discovered the zeitgeist of the 1970s—or perhaps it discovered me. Its name was *zastoy*: "stagnation." There is an academic definition of this term, which tells us that *zastoy* was the period under the leadership of Leonid Brezhnev, lasting roughly from the late 1960s to the early 1980s, which saw no economic growth, no improvements in people's lives, a slow-down of liberalization reforms begun under Nikita Khrushchev, and an increase in repressive pressure on artists, writers, and thinkers. But this was a matter for future academics. For five-year-old me, it simply meant a profound awareness that the dreary world around me was never going to change in any way.

The USSR stretched, huge and mighty and utterly permanent, across one-sixth of the world's surface. Life was dull and unvarying, like morning buckwheat porridge without butter or salt. Every year resembled the one before it. The same Communist Party leaders spoke the same boring and meaningless words on TV and the radio for decades on end. It was an epoch bereft of passion and energy. The best minds of the generation lost all hope of progress in their country in any sphere, be it politics, art, or every science not harnessed to the military-industrial complex. Some of them were lucky enough to emigrate to the West. Many of those who stayed behind, left with no creative outlet for self-actualization, spiraled into alcoholism and mental illness. My father was to become one of them. But I didn't know any of this yet. I just stared out at the small, grimy, fly-dotted kindergarten toilet window and was excruciatingly bored.

At five in the afternoon, Grandma would come to pick me up, and my ordeal would be over. On Fridays she collected me even earlier, to spare me the torture of nap time. On our way home, we would stop at a local café called Kolobok, on the corner of Chernyshevsky Avenue and Tchaikovsky Street. Kolobok is the title character from the Russian version of "The Gingerbread Man" children's story. Almost everything is the same as in the Western version: Kolobok is baked by a childless old couple and then proceeds to run away from them and a number of other characters with the mocking singsong: *"I've run away from the old woman, I've run away from the old man, and I can run away from you, too, I can!"* The only difference is that instead of a man made out of sweet gingerbread, the Russian fairytale character is a ball of sourdough. But just like his Western counterpart, our yeasty whole-wheat hero eventually meets an ignoble end in the jaws of a fox, all because of his prideful disobedience of his grandparents. Perhaps Grandma's choice of venue was a subtle attempt at neurolinguistic programming.

At the café, Grandma always got us both what Russians call by the French name *café glacé*: two scoops of ice cream with syrup or grated chocolate, with a cup of coffee. She saw nothing wrong with my having the occasional coffee, even as a kindergartener. In the USSR, tea was ubiquitous, and coffee was expensive and hard to find in stores. Both Grandma and Mom loved coffee, and they always drank it with a vaguely rebellious air, as if ceremonially emphasizing their ethnic and cultural non-Sovietness. I was allowed to drink coffee (with milk, at first) from age six, on Fridays at the café and on Sunday mornings. It was Grandma's way of slowly drawing me into her world, which was somewhat out of alignment with that of the rest of the state.

In June 1977, Grandma stepped up her game.

* * *

Our family had no house in the countryside. At least not by the time I was around. Back in the 1910s, when Grandma was a little girl, her father, a senior officer in the navy, had built a manor house in the Pskov region, some two hundred miles south of Saint Petersburg. The estate was located near an old village that used to be called Bolshiye Strugi—Big Strugi. The word *strugi*, a plural of *strug*, is not one I've ever encountered anywhere else, so I have no idea what they are. Several years later, the Communists took over, and the village was given a more politically correct name: Krasniye Strugi, or Red Strugi. It's likely that the authorities in charge of the renaming also didn't know what *strugi* were and just settled on making them sound more Communist.

Three years after the estate was finished, the 1917 Revolution rolled in and Soviet authorities confiscated the manor and turned it into a club and library for the village. However, even though the house was gone, Grandma and her siblings continued to spend their summers at Red Strugi for years to come, usually renting a room in the log cabin of the estate's former carriage driver and his young wife, who used to be a kitchen maid. It was far from the oddest thing in this brave new upside-down world they found themselves in.

However, by the time I was born, all that was far in the past. When summer came, bringing with it an exodus of children from the city, my parents had no place to ship me off to. (Most parents, not unreasonably, considered hot summer city air, with its dust, pollen, and industrial exhausts, an unhealthy environment for extended outdoor play.)

One day in early June 1977, after Grandma picked me up from kindergarten, she didn't get me ready for bed by half past eight. In fact, she did not get me ready for bed at all.

At some point in the evening, a tremendous amount of luggage began to pile up in her room. For a while, I watched as Grandma hauled all the suitcases and bags we owned out of various closets. The amount of stuff going into them was astounding. Wherever she was going, most of the apartment seemed to be coming with her.

I counted the bags.

"Why do you need seven bags?"

"Seven places," corrected Grandma.

"What?" I asked, puzzled.

"Seven places means seven items of luggage," she explained. "When you're traveling by train, a piece of luggage is called a 'place.' Here, take your backpack." She picked up my small backpack from the pile and handed it to me. "Our train leaves at midnight."

When we left the house, it was still light outside. In the weeks surrounding the summer solstice, Leningrad, which is located at 59°57' N latitude, experiences what we locals call "white nights." The sun hangs low on the horizon, only dipping below around eleven o'clock at night and then reemerging several hours later. In late June, it stays light enough all night to read newspapers outdoors.

Since I was always sent to bed by 20:30 (the USSR lived on military time), I had never experienced a white night before. My mind boggled. Then it boggled again when a taxi pulled up to our door: a yellow Volga with a black checkered pattern on the side.

The driver and Grandma loaded our luggage—all the "places" except for my backpack and my little plastic bucket with a plastic shovel. (I was promised a beach, and I was coming prepared.) And then we were off.

The taxi was another first. Even setting aside my young age, it was rare for Soviet citizens to cruise around in taxis. At twenty kopecks per kilometer, they were not a cheap ride. I drank in the pungent smell of gasoline, tobacco, and worn leather, watched the twilit houses fly by outside, listened to the huge round mechanical meter click on the dashboard, and all but shivered with anticipation of boarding our midnight train.

Railways and trains in Russia have always been much more than just pragmatic modes of getting from point A to point B. For a Russian soul, a never-ending train journey across the empty vastness of its land is a state of mind, a meditation, an existential reflection on life itself. One might also argue that Russia, the largest country on earth, is essentially built around a sprinkling of train stops on a single-track railway constructed by the tsars in the late nineteenth century. And then one might ponder whether the Russian national character stands in opposition to the American frontier spirit of personal freedom and yearns to submit to the train driver and his predetermined itinerary, however long he might take and wherever he should choose to stop along the way. (But that is a subject for a study by some esteemed psychoanalyst from a serious research establishment somewhere in Vienna or Heidelberg.)

Despite the fact that the USSR was supposed to be a classless paradise of absolute equality, Soviet trains had three travel classes. First class, or SV, had sleeper cars with two-person compartments. For people with less money to spend, there were the *kupe*: four-person compartments with two high bunks and two low. And finally there were the *platzkarta*: cars packed with three levels of bunks without any privacy dividers.

Grandma and I rode in the four-person compartment with two other passengers. She took a low bunk, and I took a high one, which was at least a meter and a half off the floor. At midnight, as promised, the train got underway.

For a while, I watched the shadowed trees rush by outside, then I fell asleep, lulled by the clatter of train wheels. When I woke up the next morning, we were already well south of Moscow.

As the hours passed and the train chugged ever southward, the temperature outside and inside crept up notably. (The train was not air-conditioned, because nothing in the USSR was air-conditioned.) The landscape changed from spruces and sickly birches to wide open steppes. The people at the train stops also changed, becoming more open and hospitable. (Oddly enough, southern hospitality is as much a cultural quirk in Russia as it is in America.)

Every few hours, the train stopped for ten or fifteen minutes at a town or a village. Tula, Orel, Kursk, Kharkov . . . Wherever we stopped, local grannies were waiting on the platform with delicious eats: home-cooked potatoes with dill, pickles, sunflower seeds roasted in the shell, local fruit. Occasionally, there would even be an ice cream kiosk.

Every foraging excursion out to the platform meant a heart-pounding countdown: Would I make it back to the train on time? Or if Grandma was the one to leave the train, would she make it back? What would happen if we got separated? What if I got left behind literally in the middle of nowhere, all alone with no money, no ticket, and no way to contact Grandma? Hands filled with baggies of sunflower seeds or pastries, I dashed back into the train, swimming in adrenaline and delighted at having gotten away with it—this time.

All this was so new and so fun that the two days flew by before I knew it. When I woke up on the second morning, we were in the sunny Crimea.

* * *

Before the 1917 Revolution, the Crimea had been the Riviera of the Russian Empire. It was the favored domestic resort of artists and poets as well as the wealthy bourgeoisie and aristocracy. Even the royal Romanov family wintered there. In my time, summers in the Crimea were probably the peak of the Soviet experience. Koktebel was a sort of poor man's Cannes: everyone around was if not rich then at least famous, and dressed to the nines—or to the extent Soviet circumstances permitted it, so probably more like fours or fives. There were alfresco cafés, a thing almost never seen in the USSR. At night, there were open-air film screenings, and singing cicadas, and, most unusually for northerners like me, summer sunsets. Quite early in the evening, the sun would suddenly fall into the sea, leaving behind inky-black starlit skies instead of milky twilit ones. Everything around was sea and sun and mountains, and life was manifestly wonderful. If not for the generally shabby surroundings and street names like Ulitsa Desantnikov

(Paratrooper Street), one could almost forget they were in the USSR.

In Koktebel, Grandma and I rented a little room in a private house close to the Writers' Union's members-only beach. Over the next three months, I would spend many happy hours constructing elaborate sandcastles there. I also made some new friends, like small children do on beaches the world over. For instance, I met a very nice girl named Masha. Little did I know that Masha was the daughter of the celebrated author Vasily Shukshin and famous actress Lidiya Fedoseeva. But I was too young to appreciate all the Soviet celebrities sunbathing and mingling on the beach. Google tells me that Masha has now also made it in the world of TV and film. I thought about dropping her a line, but I doubt she remembers me, despite my strikingly good looks and superior sandcastle-building skills.

* * *

My Crimean summer was filled with firsts. For instance, it was where I saw my first snake, a huge gray viper slithering with gut-churning speed through the grass patch where I was picking flowers for Mom's visit. There was also the first time I ever peed myself in public. I was playing with a friend I met on the beach. He had found a tube of some sort and decided, quite logically, that it would be hilarious if he peed through it. He was right: it was hilarious. So much so that I peed myself with laughter right along with him.

I also saw a movie on the big screen for the first time. A theater in town was showing *The Golden Voyage of Sinbad*, a foreign fantasy film from the UK. In retrospect, it was an unexpected treat. Very few films from the capitalist West made it to Soviet movie screens in those days. Unfortunately, it was not an auspicious start to my life as a moviegoer: all the giants, centaurs, and cyclopes scared me so much that after twenty minutes, I was begging Grandma to take me home.

And when Dad came to visit us, I saw my first dolphins, at a dolphin habitat. It was open only to scientific researchers, but Dad was friends with the guy in charge. He took us around the sanctuary, and I watched dolphins swim around in closed-off pools in the Black Sea. A few years later, I found out that the head of the sanctuary had killed himself. As Dad explained it, military programs were displacing scientific ones in the sanctuary, and he couldn't stand the fact that his dolphins were now getting trained to deliver explosives to ships.

At the end of August, we said farewell to the deep blue sea, abundant greenery, and bright southern flowers and took the train back to my bleak and rainy Leningrad. On the taxi ride home from the train station, I listened to the giant mechanical meter click and looked out the window to see if the city had changed in my absence. On one corner, a new watermelon stand had been set up; on another corner, a new tobacco kiosk. But something else was different, too: here and there, signs appeared in store windows advertising school supplies. They must've been there every August, but I had never paid attention to them until now.

Memories of three months spent among sunshiny colors, green mountains, and bright flowers, which our cold climate lacked even in the summer, were already growing bittersweet in my mind. Surely, I thought, there must be a way to live in a place like that, where it's always sunny and green, and there are always cafés and outdoor movies, and the ocean, and sandy beaches, and lots of friends?

A week later, on August 30, 1977, Grandma took me to enroll at my future school.

CHAPTER 3

WELCOME TO SCHOOL NUMBER 185

"What are the key aspects of the Soviet educational process?"

"First, we teach our children to speak. Then, we teach them to keep their mouths shut."

MY CITY—WHICH AT different points in its history has been called Saint Petersburg, Petrograd, Leningrad, and finally Saint Petersburg once more—was founded in 1703, after Peter the Great decided that Russia ought to throw its lot in with Europe rather than Asia. In the long term, his efforts were only partially successful. To this day, Russia remains unsure of its own cultural affiliation, occasionally making valiant efforts toward establishing a society based on European values, but then drifting back listlessly toward its addiction to strongmen rule. But Leningrad has always had a rather European air. Geographically, it's much nearer to Europe than most people realize.[*]

---

[*] *For example, Berlin is closer to Saint Petersburg than to Madrid.*

My future school, elegantly named Leningrad City Secondary School Number 185 with In-Depth English Language Instruction, was located a stone's throw away from the Bolshoi Dom KGB headquarters. It was a long, squat, yellow-gray box of four stories, sandwiched between two even longer and even squatter residential buildings from the nineteenth century. An arch with a wrought-iron gate led into a small gravel courtyard with no trees and several stinking trash cans in the corner, where stray cats copulated relentlessly. In other words, it was a normal Soviet school building.

Soviet children started school at age seven. In my case, despite the prevailing family opinion that I was not the sharpest pencil in the box, I was deemed mature enough to start at six and a half.

All incoming first graders had to undergo a medical examination on the premises, as well as a short interview to determine his or her homeroom assignment. Grandma and I showed up early, and I had the pleasure of being the first in line—the first and possibly last time that's ever happened to me. A second boy soon came to stand behind me. We got to talking. His name was Vova. He was a bit taller and stockier than me and had messy brown hair and a cheeky squint. While more and more kids queued up behind us, the two of us covered many topics of interest to Soviet boys, such as which toy soldiers were the best and what were our favorite movies about Nazis. Although it wasn't about Nazis, I told him that I had just seen *The Golden Voyage of Sinbad*, omitting the fact that I'd lasted only twenty minutes before fleeing from the theater in terror. In return, Vova told me all about his summer at his family's village house.

"I made a fishing weir across our river, with five hooks, and then I put five live frogs on them! Next morning, I pulled out three huge catfish, at least three kilos each! All the villagers came to see them!"

I suspected this was a fisherman's tale, but I didn't want to start our friendship with an argument.

By the time they called me into the medical office, there was a line of about fifty kids, and the foyer was crowded with moms and grandmas meeting one another and making friends, just like their children. (So many Soviet friendships and even families have been formed while standing in lines.)

Inside, a nurse measured me, weighed me, and noted down my hair and eye color for my official school medical chart, while two female teachers watched and bombarded me with questions.

"What's your name, boy?"

"Where do you live?"

"Have you got brothers or sisters?"

"What sort of things do you like to do?"

"Can you read?"

"Can you count to a hundred?"

They conferred briefly. Then one of them said, "All right, I'll take this one."

I left the office, let in Vova, and stood aside to wait for him. When he walked out again and we went to the foyer together, we discovered that our grandmas were deep in conversation. Apparently, they had sat next to each other on the same bench.

That was how all four of us left the school: Vova and I ran ahead, picking up where we'd left off in our debate about which Nazi tank was the best, and our grandmas brought up the rear, also deep in conversation, though probably about much less exciting things.

* * *

A few years ago, I saw a home movie of the traditional First Bell ceremony on our first day of school, September 1, 1977. It was shot by the father of my classmate Vasilina, who was fortunate enough to own a movie camera. Even thirty-five years later, that silent, grainy, monochrome footage brought back vividly my terror on that day.

There we were, a group of fifty or so ex-kindergarteners standing in our first *linejka* (lineup) in the school yard in our oversized school uniforms—the boys buttoned up to the chin in blue suits, the girls in tights and short brown dresses with white aprons over them. All of us held bouquets of gladioli and dahlias practically as tall as ourselves, some vertically and some diagonally, like riflemen in an inspection parade. The momentousness of the occasion was visibly crushing us.

The school's principal came out to stand before us and launched into a pompous spiel—something about our new responsibilities as future Communist citizens of the Soviet state, our school, our parents . . . I wasn't listening. I was preoccupied by my brand-new uniform. It was freaking itchy.

Then several older kids, fourth or fifth graders—though they looked practically like grown-ups to me at the time— carried out the Young Pioneers' red flag and vowed in unison to study diligently and serve the Soviet Union. After that, we were ordered to separate by homeroom. I looked for the lady teacher who'd picked me during my medical examination. Her name was Ekaterina Alexandrovna, and she would be my homeroom teacher for the next three years. When all her new charges had gathered around her, we followed her into the school, clutching our flowers. We were still strangers, but we were about to become classmates.

Classmate meant far more in the USSR than in the West. In my time, Soviet schooling lasted between eight and ten years. All those years were spent in the same building, with no relocation or reshuffle of any kind between elementary, middle, and high school. Once you were assigned to a homeroom, you stayed in it until the end. A homeroom had all its classes together, year in and year out. This meant that on your very first school day, you met the twenty or so people who would be your constant companions all the way to adulthood. The person you sat down next to on the first day of first grade would often be the same person who rose with you on your last day ten years later. Your homeroom was usually where you met your best friend for life and was often where you met your future spouse.

The only boy I knew in my homeroom was Vova. So the very first day, he and I hung out at recess and then got picked up by our grandmas after school and walked home together. Then we did it again the next day, and the next, and the next. Soon, we were no longer Sergey Grechishkin and Vladimir Nadezhdin: we were Grechishkin-and-Nadezhdin. From the earliest days, classmates and teachers talked about us as though we were Siamese twins: "Grechishkin-and-Nadezhdin's homework is late," "Grechishkin-and-Nadezhdin are quite good at math," "Grechishkin-and-Nadezhdin went to the movies."

Vova's family was very similar to mine. He was also being raised by his grandma. By an odd coincidence, his parents' names were also Vera and Sergey. They were also divorced, and his mother had remarried. However, unlike me, Vova was not in touch with his dad. And although both of us had lost our maternal grandfathers, mine had passed away long before I was born, and Vova's had died recently. He had been a professor of some kind, and he used to spend a lot of time with his little grandson. As a result, even in first grade, Vova already knew a lot about subjects that went completely over our heads, such as archaeology, astronomy, and military history. He was also a good seven centimeters taller than me. Was I happy with this? Not bloody likely!

* * *

The homeroom teacher covered all our subjects through third grade, hence the huge bouquets heaped on them on September 1; it paid to start off on the right foot. These first three years were quite restricted in their scope compared with schools in America or the UK today. The only subjects we had in grades one to three were math, Russian, English, art, singing, and PE. No history, no social studies, no geography, and no science of any kind at that point.

Classroom rules were simple and easy to follow. You only had to remember these four things:

1) Stand up when a teacher enters the room.
2) Only speak after being called upon.
3) When not called upon or writing, sit with your eyes on the teacher and your arms folded one over the other in front of you, palms flattened.
4) Everything else is prohibited.

Our schedule was not exceptionally punishing. The day started at nine o'clock, but one had to come a bit earlier to allow time for changing shoes; for most of the school year, the weather was so inclement that one had to come to school in an overcoat and outdoor boots, remove them in the changing room, and put on indoor shoes or slippers. First and second graders had four to five classes a day and were home free by one o'clock.

There was no lunch, but there was a scheduled snack time after third period. Everyone would pile into the lunchroom to eat a small pastry or a bread roll with jam and drink some milk or apple juice. Snack times were not free; our parents paid four rubles a month for them. That worked out to just under twenty kopecks per snack, which wasn't cheap. Outside of school, twenty kopecks could buy you two scoops of the best ice cream, twenty matchboxes, two children's tickets to a movie, four metro or bus rides, two amusement park rides, or six glasses of soda water with syrup (or twenty without syrup). In short, snack time was a total rip-off.

Schools had a six-day week. Every day except Sunday was a full school day. Naturally, we all considered this extremely unfair. On Saturdays, kindergartens were closed, adults were off work, and only we schoolchildren had to suffer. The unfairness of it was particularly hard for me to swallow back when my brother, Alyosha, was still in kindergarten and could sleep in. The only positive side of having one single day off was the pleasure of coming home Saturday afternoon and getting all homework out of the way. The weekend ahead—all the next day and what was left of the first one—seemed to stretch into glorious infinity.

I soon got used to my new uniform: navy-colored pants and a matching jacket with huge aluminum buttons and little military-style shoulder straps with buttons instead of insignia. One of my jacket sleeves had a soft plastic emblem glued to it: an open book with the sun rising behind it. The patch quickly got grimy and scratched up. Many boys peeled theirs off altogether, but some (me included) only did it along one side and turned it into a secret pocket for crib sheets.

Girls got the short end of the uniform stick. They were stuck wearing brown woolen dresses to the knee with aprons over them: black aprons for regular days, white aprons for special occasions. No jewelry or makeup was allowed. On the whole, they looked less like the future builders of Communism and more like nineteenth-century scullery maids.

There were no lockers. Everyone carried all their stuff with them from class to class: books, notebooks, and PE gear. To be fair, Soviet textbooks were substantially smaller and lighter than their Western counterparts. They had mostly small-print text, with very few pictures. All textbooks were given out to students for free, not sold. This wasn't so much an expression of Communist ideals as a measure to counterbalance paper scarcity. They were basically treated like library books, issued to kids in the beginning of the year and then collected at the end. Predictably, this led to an accumulation of scribbles and doodles, as generations of bored schoolchildren left their surreptitious mark on the system that was slowly crushing their spirits with verb conjugations and algebra. And of course, the answers to all the exercises were often also filled in by previous owners. This was inconvenient, as there was no way of knowing if the person who wrote the answer was a reliable source, or whether they were just passing their ignorance down to future generations. At my school, however, since there were only about fifty kids per grade level and all grade levels were in the same building, you sometimes knew the person who had had the book before you and could try to make your own judgment call. I had rotten luck in this respect; I was able to identify my textbooks' prior owners only twice over the course of my school career, and both times the other kids were renowned dumbasses.

We were graded on a scale from 1 to 5, with 5+ being the highest possible mark and 3 a squeaker pass. The standard failing grade was 2. To score a 1 (colloquially *kol*, meaning "stake"), one would have to really go all out and aggravate incompetence with insolence. A *kol* was not so much a grade as a statement about your general hopelessness as a person.

Grades were recorded in a *dnevnik*, or "diary," a grade book carried by every student. It dominated one's school years from the first class bell to the last. To this day, when I close my eyes and visualize the upcoming calendar week, I see three days on one side and three on the other, because that's how they were laid out in a *dnevnik*. (Sunday was, naturally, omitted.) Each day had a column for the various classes, which we filled out according to the changing schedule: for instance, 09:00–09:45, Russian; 10:00–10:45, math; et cetera. Whenever a teacher asked you to come up to the blackboard and answer questions, you brought your diary along and handed it over. The teacher would evaluate your performance, fill in your grade, and occasionally also make notes about your behavior for your parents. It was often something along the lines of, "Your child conducted himself reprehensibly during music class today," or the even more worrying, "Parents, you are to come to school immediately to discuss your child with the principal!"

The *dnevnik* had to be signed by our parents every week. One could write volumes on all the tricks Soviet kids came up with to avoid this. *Dnevniks* got lost; grades were altered (3s into 5s, usually); pages got accidentally glued together. Faking parents' signatures was practically an industry. Two grades above us, there was a boy named Vitalik who was a master of artful handwriting forgeries. His services were in great demand all over the school. I sometimes wonder what he's up to now. A man of his talents must have surely achieved great things in life.

I never bothered with any of this. I got decent grades, and besides, my family somehow didn't expect great things from me. Grandma was of the opinion that intelligence and talent "skip a generation," and my dad was very gifted both academically and artistically. It was therefore assumed that nature, to use a Russian turn of phrase, "took a break" while shaping me. Whatever grades I brought home, I was neither praised nor criticized.

It did not take me long to get my first 2, after completely blanking on a pop quiz. It was a terror unlike anything I had experienced up to that point in my life. I cried and begged Ekaterina Alexandrovna not to put the offending mark in my diary, but, alas, in vain. It took me a while to work up the nerve to tell Grandma and my parents about this shame, but finally I did it, steeling myself for their well-deserved outrage. Imagine my surprise when all they said was that it was going to be okay and not to worry so much. The advice fell on deaf ears; I was too deeply mired in self-loathing. So I went to the courtyard and, wallowing in my profound sadness, watched from a bench as other kids ran around and played.

"Look at how happy they are," I thought. "Bastards."

* * *

A few weeks after we started school, Vova and I discovered a fun activity to do together: roof climbing. We would meet after school, pick one of the old nineteenth-century buildings, and run up the stairs to the very top. The back entrances and stairways, used by servants and deliverymen before the Revolution, usually had a door out into the loft. The attics were supposed to stay locked, but we knew that in many cases the access doors were left open, or the locks on them were busted. From the attic, we would then climb out onto the roof. Since the houses of old Saint Petersburg were built very close together, each building adjoined its neighbor from the foundation to the weathercock, and we were able to walk from one roof onto the next without much effort.

Lest you think we did this in secret, my parents knew about this new hobby. One day, Vova and I climbed out onto the roof of the building across the street from ours. It was three stories high, with five-meter-high ceilings. Had we fallen from that roof, it would've been curtains for us. I looked down into our kitchen window, which had the drapes drawn back, and saw my mother. She was busy with something by the stove. I yelled hello to her from across the street. She heard me, looked out and up, waved at me, and went back to doing whatever she was doing.

On reflection, it's a miracle neither of us ever got hurt. The only time things got dicey was when one grumpy resident, tired of listening to us stomping above his head, emerged from his lair and chased Vova and me away to another roof. When he had left, we lay low for a while, then crept back cautiously and tried the attic door. But the man had locked it from the inside. The neighboring building's attic door was also locked. Thus, we set out on a quest, wandering from roof to roof and trying every attic door on the street until we finally found one that was open. It took a few hours.

Other boys soon joined us on our expeditions. I remember one spot in particular that only the daredevils of our group ventured to approach. It was the roof edge of a tall building that promised a vertical fall of thirty meters or so. It had no border or railing of any kind. The bravest of us would lie down on our bellies and crawl forwards to stick our heads out over the edge for a look below.

In retrospect, I was just practicing for leaning over another dangerous abyss, though this one would be cultural.

CHAPTER 4

SPORT IS LIFE. THE REST IS JUST DETAILS.

Brezhnev is reading a speech from a typed copy:
"Oh . . . Oh . . . Oh . . . Oh . . . Oh!"
An aide comes up to him and whispers in his ear,
"Comrade Brezhnev, that's the Olympic ring logo!"

MOST OF MY life between the ages of seven and nine was spent in breathless anticipation of the 1980 Summer Olympics.

It wasn't just that Moscow was to host an event of worldwide importance. And sure, there were government placards everywhere promoting the Olympic spirit, but by the age of nine I was already used to ignoring government placards. No, my earnest excitement was driven mostly by the fact that foreigners from all over the world were coming to the USSR. It was as though we were finally being welcomed into the global community. Finally, we'd have a chance to interact with people from around the world!

So imagine what a massive disappointment it was for all of us when almost no one showed up to the party! Sixty-five countries skipped the Moscow Olympics after the USSR's invasion of Afghanistan. Hardly anyone from Western Europe came, and only about half of the Middle Eastern and African states did, plus a few more from South America.*

The Soviet reporting on the global boycott was awkward. The government could not admit that the boycott was a reaction to the invasion of Afghanistan, because then it would have to acknowledge that there was an invasion, when all along they'd been describing it as limited military aid being sent to some Communist brothers in need. So instead, it offered a number of rationalizations for why Western countries were really boycotting the Games. It was suggested that the Americans were just trying to sabotage Moscow's success as the Olympic host out of spite, and that President Carter initiated it as a rallying call to save his sinking popularity. The Soviet Union also announced that the boycott violated the Olympic Charter, the Helsinki Accords, the United Nations Charter, and the Amateur Sports Act of 1978, not to mention the United States Constitution, since it infringed on the rights of its own athletes. In conclusion, the government announced that despite the United States' being a literal spoilsport, the 1980 Games would be the most glorious of all time.

Regardless of the boycott, a few Western renegades did show up. Some of them even went on Soviet television, where they excoriated the White House and the Pentagon for cheating athletes out of their chance to compete for political reasons. I watched them on TV in great puzzlement. How on earth, I wondered, did all these people manage to leave their countries if their governments didn't want anyone to participate in the Moscow Olympics?

---

*Curiously enough, Britain, America's "most loyal lapdog," delivered a Brexit-style surprise and decided to participate.

In the USSR, no one could leave the country without an exit visa, a special permission document issued by OVIR, the Department of Visas and Registrations. Getting such a visa required multiple background and character checks, in-person interviews, and the appointment of a travel group "companion" from the KGB to follow you around and make sure you didn't embarrass yourself (and by extension, the entire Soviet Union). For those lucky Soviet citizens who were allowed to cross the border, any sort of misbehaving while abroad or giving the slightest hint at being unhappy with the Soviet workers' paradise would mean no more trips anywhere except to camping locations in eastern Siberia.

* * *

In preparation for the Olympics, the authorities decided to clean up Moscow and Leningrad, both literally and metaphorically. Many known dissidents—troublesome artists and other unreliable types—were temporarily deported "beyond the 101st kilometer," (i.e., forbidden to enter within 100 kilometers of Moscow or Leningrad). Black market dealers, prostitutes, and habitual drunkards prone to public misbehavior were also rounded up and either locked away or kicked out of town.

To my utter shock, they did the same to all the children.

About six months before the opening ceremony, Ekaterina Alexandrovna, like all homeroom teachers in Moscow and Leningrad, held a special PTA meeting. She had received "instructions from above" that no children would be allowed in either Moscow or Leningrad for the duration of the Games. All parents had to notify the authorities within two weeks as to where their children would be staying.

A worried hubbub arose in the parental crowd.

"Where are we supposed to send them?" asked Sasha Lesman's mom, voicing the concern of the baffled many. "We don't have a dacha! We don't have any grandparents in some village! And you know how hard it is to get a spot at a summer camp!"

"Don't worry," said Ekaterina Alexandrovna confidently. "They will make room in the camps for everyone."

(This was probably the most truthful thing ever spoken by a Soviet authority figure.)

But our family was not going to surrender Alyosha and myself to any summer camps, no matter how suspiciously accommodating. We might not have had a dacha, but Tolya's parents did. They took in Alyosha. As for me, Grandma knew exactly where I was going.

"The Games are mostly happening in Moscow, anyway," she consoled me. "We are only hosting soccer here in Leningrad. You and I will get to see something better."

"Kids aren't allowed in Moscow, either," I said glumly.

She smiled. "We're not going to Moscow. Do you know what a regatta is?"

I did know. In fact, I had just finished watching a hilarious new cartoon series called *The Adventures of Captain Vrungel*, which had become an instant classic among boys of my age. It was a Baron Munchausen-style tale about the amazing—and, with every episode, increasingly improbable—voyage of a renowned nineteenth-century professor of naval tactics who signs up for a race around the world to save his career and train his hapless apprentice. But of course, I would have known anyway. After all, my own great-grandfather had been a renowned professor of naval tactics.

We were going to see a boat race.

* * *

Sunshine and beaches might not be the first thing that pops into one's mind when one thinks about Estonia—if anything, in fact, pops into one's mind at all. But sunshine and beaches are there, and they are amazing, if predictably cooler and milder than along the Black Sea's coast.

Grandma and I had already been to the Estonian resort town of Pärnu twice. After I finished first grade, she decided to take me someplace other than the Crimea. So instead of heading south, we headed west. This time around, the train ride lasted just a day.

Grandma liked it in Pärnu so much that we ended up spending the next five summers there. After the first couple of years, we started taking Vova and his grandma with us. And at the end of each summer, the rest of my family would join us for a few weeks, until it was time to return home at the end of August. Grandma rented one room for herself and me in a private house; Mom, Tolya, and Alyosha rented another room. As always, this arrangement seemed completely normal.

Pärnu is a lovely Estonian medieval town with a long, contentious history. It was founded in the thirteenth century and has been an apple of contention ever since. Teutonic knights, Livonian knights, Poles, Russians, Swedes—everyone wanted to control Pärnu and its port, which doesn't freeze in the winter. In 1939, the Nazis ceded Estonia, along with Latvia, Lithuania, and eastern Poland, to Stalin under the Molotov-Ribbentrop Non-Aggression Pact. The Soviets wasted no time: they rigged elections throughout the region and set up a bunch of puppet regimes, then began arresting people in huge numbers. Any Estonians at all involved in the political or cultural life of their country were deemed "anti-Soviet" and deported to Siberia or

Kazakhstan. Consequently, when the Nazis invaded Estonia again in the summer of 1941, some people initially greeted them as liberators. Then the Nazis killed every Jew in the country. The only ones to survive were, ironically, those whom the Soviets had deported to Siberian labor camps the year before. After the Nazis were once more repelled, Estonia remained in the Soviet bear hug until 1991.

Geographically speaking, Pärnu is only as far from Leningrad as Boston is from Philadelphia, but culturally, it was a world away. In fact, all three Baltic republics were quite different from the rest of the Union. They were a sort of West-lite. When I was a child, they had only been a part of the USSR for less than four decades, and the Procrustean bed of Sovietization had not yet stripped them of everything European. Unlike the rest of the country, they had cheery houses with shingled roofs instead of apartment blocks made up of prefabricated concrete panels; they also had little cafés with outside seating, and small Continental-style bakeries. All Soviet movies set in the West were filmed there, on the medieval cobblestone streets of Tallinn or Riga or Vilnius, with Baltic actors playing Westerners. Everything was better in the Baltics: the food, the shops, the climate—even their accents were so cool.

Because of this quasi-Western glamour, the Baltic republics were a popular travel destination for the Soviet intelligentsia. While party officials and the working class, especially people from very cold regions like Siberia, usually preferred to vacation by the Black Sea, the cooler, windier, and more subdued Baltic coast attracted a more refined crowd.

For some reason, there were many *otkazniks*, people who had tried and failed to emigrate from the USSR. Sometimes they were denied permission because they had secret clearance, which was almost universal among engineers and scientists.

Sometimes they were unable to secure exit visas for their families to come along with them. And often, they were simply denied and given no particular reason. Understandably, they were a very pro-Western crowd. Many of them had relatives who had already emigrated abroad, so they were more plugged into the world beyond the Iron Curtain than your average Soviet citizen.

Lenya, a friend I made in Pärnu, had a grandmother who was an actual, honest-to-goodness American. She had come to the USSR in the 1920s as part of a small but spirited cohort of progressive leftists, eager to help build the first state run by workers and peasants. However, what looked so rosy from halfway around the world became a flower of a different color up close. Once these helpful folks had entered the USSR, the state of workers and peasants that welcomed them refused to let them leave. Some of them were deported to labor camps; some were exiled to remote areas in Siberia or Kazakhstan; and some, like Lenya's grandmother, settled down and tried to cope.

I was very envious of Lenya and his sister, because their grandmother always spoke to them in English. That was impressive. Fluent English speakers were as rare in the USSR as Amur leopards, for broadly similar reasons.

Grandma, too, made some friends on the beach. One of them was a tall old lady with a shock of absolutely white hair. Every other day, this woman would hold court on the beach, where she'd recline in her long chair, surrounded by other beachgoers, and share her memories of life in America. She talked about prewar New York and life in Europe in the 1950s. Many people in her audience were preparing to leave the country, fighting to leave the country, or often simply dreaming of leaving the country, so they soaked up her stories like sponges. I was never quite clear on who she was. The wife of a diplomat? The daughter of immigrants from the West? The widow of a

KGB or GRU officer who did not get to come in from the cold? All of the above, perhaps? A Russian's life story in the twentieth century was often stranger than fiction.

* * *

The regatta Grandma had promised me was happening in Estonia's capital, Tallinn. Grandma watched it with tremendous excitement, but I was rather underwhelmed; from the shore, the boats were just dots in the distance. While the adults peered through binoculars and cheered, I sat in anticipation of something truly thrilling: the souvenir shops.

All the shops in Estonia were flooded with knickknacks showcasing the 1980 Olympic mascot, a smiling cartoon bear cub wearing a belt with the five Olympic rings for a buckle. (Why he needed a belt was unclear; the bear wore no pants.) There was an abundance of posters, key fobs, and T-shirts, and they weren't just for foreigners: regular Soviet citizens could buy them, too! My materialistic soul was in paradise. I got a blue T-shirt and a cap with "Olympics-80" on it, and a mega-cool key chain with the Olympic bear. All in all, I spent over five rubles of my birthday present money. Grandma approved of my purchases. In fact, she rather approved too much. The key chain, she said, was far too nice to use every day, and if I were to take it to school, someone was sure to steal it from me. It would be best, she said, to keep it in a special drawer in her room, with other valuable toys that I was allowed to play with only on special occasions. I relented and surrendered my treasure to her.

But the biggest and most memorable surprise of the Olympic summer awaited me back in Leningrad. Upon returning home, I discovered that in my absence, the city had acquired Pepsi-Cola kiosks. Bright, colorful, and totally out of place on our bleak Leningrad streets, they were put up especially for the Olympics, and they still sold real American Pepsi-Cola!

What had happened was this. The Soviet government gave PepsiCo permission to sell their cola in the USSR in exchange for the rights to sell Stolichnaya vodka in the United States. Of course, since the distribution chain was still Soviet—i.e., fundamentally inefficient—one could buy Pepsi in only a few select locations, mostly in Moscow and Leningrad. Whenever those pricey forty-five-kopek bottles appeared on the shelves, they sold out within hours. Curiously, although Pepsi was now officially sanctioned, Coca-Cola was still considered the quintessence of rotting Western decadence.

The first thing that struck the Soviet mind about the new soft drink was its unusual packaging. Our own fizzy drinks and lemonades were sold in ugly stout green half-liter bottles topped with metal caps lined with cork. The same bottles were used to package sunflower oil, beer, and even vodka. But the Pepsi bottles were different: elegant, elongated, and made of clear glass. They made all our domestic soft drink bottles look positively dowdy by comparison.

Yes, the USSR had soft drinks, too. And, plain packaging aside, they were pretty delicious. My favorite was called Baikal, after the famous Siberian lake. It was made with water, sugar, citric acid, and a whole array of aromatic herbs and essential oils: eucalyptus, licorice, Siberian ginseng, bay laurel, black tea, and St. John's wort. Food chemistry was not particularly advanced in the USSR, so if a product was advertised as containing certain herbs, no one doubted it. It would have cost the government much more in terms of R & D to concoct a synthetic chemical mimicking that herbal taste than to hire people to forage for the actual herbs in the wild. Baikal was considered more of a dessert drink than a refreshment; it was pricey and hard to find.

In the spring, a highly seasonal and thoroughly Russian drink appeared in stores: birch juice. It was gathered in April, immediately after the thaw but before the appearance of leaf buds. One found a suitable birch tree, made an incision in the bark, and deployed a jar or bottle to collect the thin, slightly sweet sap. You could buy birch juice at the store, but many people, including me and my friends, made special trips to the countryside to harvest their own.

And then there was *kvass*, a true Russian institution. The national love of *kvass* remains unshakeable across centuries, time zones, geopolitical upheavals, and economic crises. The drink is made from fermented bread, looks a bit like cola, and tastes somewhat like weak barley beer, though its alcohol content is pretty negligible. Like beer, *kvass* is drunk chilled, so the appearance of carts with *kvass* barrels on the streets meant that summer was nigh. *Kvass* was one of the great pleasures of a Soviet kid's life, alongside ice cream and elusive bananas. One could buy a half-liter mug for five kopecks or bring a huge three-liter glass jar, fill it up for thirty kopecks, and drink oneself stupid at home.

But Pepsi was something else entirely. The soft drink brought with it another innovation to the USSR: kiosks that served cola in disposable plastic cups. This was a pleasant surprise, for two reasons. For one, *kvass* was served in actual glass mugs that got only a brief rinse between customers. Grandma would often tell me, "You should never drink from those communal glasses. Who knows what sort of germs are on them?" and, more puzzlingly, "Alcoholics drink from those glasses, too, you know!"

Now, we got a free gift with our soda purchase! Who would throw away a perfectly reusable plastic cup? Not any Soviet person, that's for sure. Those cups still had long and productive lives ahead of them as drinking vessels, ashtrays, seedling pots, containers for bolts and nails, et cetera.

My first sip of Pepsi out of this soft white plastic cup was a revelation. An explosion of entirely unknown flavors lit up my taste buds. Everything about this drink was new: its sweetness, so thick it was almost chewy; its beautiful, glaring dark color that you could not see through; and its powerful bubbles that hissed in your mouth and tickled your nose before gradually disintegrating under your tongue . . .

Imagining that there were kids in far-off lands who could quaff this magic potion whenever they pleased was beyond comprehension. It was my first gulp of a faraway world, and I immediately knew I wanted more.

CHAPTER 5

EAT, DON'T PRAY, LOVE LENIN

The USSR developed a new brand of boiled sausage and decided to send it to a laboratory in America for independent testing. Three weeks later, they received the reply: "There were no parasites identified in this stool sample."

THE SUMMER AFTER the Olympics, still haunted by the taste of Pepsi, I joined the Young Pioneers, the Communist youth group.

Ideological indoctrination began early in the USSR. In kindergarten, we learned that all of us kids had a special "grandpa" named Vladimir Ilyich Lenin, who in his youth used to be called Volodya Ulyanov. He led the October Revolution, which meant we had him to thank for the wonderful country we lived in. What made him our grandpa was unclear, but a benevolently smiling, crinkle-eyed portrait of him, balding and with a pointy goatee, hung in every classroom. In fact, portraits of Lenin hung in all official Soviet establishments, only differing in execution: smiling Lenin in kindergartens; hopeful, forward-gazing Lenin in schools; and neutral or solemn Lenin in municipal establishments.

The first chapter book one read in school was usually an abundantly illustrated and heavily sanitized biography of Lenin, largely focused on his idyllic relationship with his mother and siblings. For more advanced readers, there were books about his valiant and ingenious struggles against the tsarist regime, and finally his eventual martyrdom for the Soviet ideals: Lenin's official cause of death was "overwork," although in reality it was probably syphilis.

For all intents and purposes, Lenin was the secular messiah of the Soviet Union. His family was regarded much like the Holy Family, with a minor cult of personality springing up around his mother. However, whereas Catholic children learned all about where Jesus came from in the catechesis, the question of where Lenin came from remained obscure. Even after I learned how babies were made, it was downright impossible to imagine the virtuous, buttoned-up progenitors of the Ulyanov family getting down to this filthy business, which logic dictated they must have done fairly regularly, since the courageous future leader of the world proletariat had seven siblings.

All first graders over the age of seven had to join the Children of October youth group. Newly inducted *Oktyabryata* were lined up, and older kids pinned little enamel stars to their uniforms: five pointy red rays around the chubby, cherubic, curly-headed face of baby Lenin. From that point onwards, an October Child was not supposed to take the star off their uniform under any circumstances. Children of October had few obligations, most of which focused inward: keep yourself and your clothes neat, study hard, obey your parents, and help others.

In third grade, October Children "graduated" to become Young Pioneers. This meant new lapel pins—another red star, this time with a grown-up Lenin in its center, engulfed in symbolic flames—and also red neckties. Young Pioneers had more community-oriented responsibilities: tutoring underperforming peers, assisting the elderly, and collecting metal or paper for recycling. If you think they sound rather like old-fashioned Boy Scouts, you're right. After the October Revolution, the Young Pioneers basically displaced the older Scout organization, which had been Western oriented and anti-Bolshevik.

Young Pioneers were also required to march in celebratory parades on May 1 and November 7.

May 1 was the Day of Workers' Solidarity. It was a huge open-air saturnalia of red flags and absurd banners. All adults were "strongly encouraged" to participate, at least to the extent of attending and waving a small red flag at the marchers. Hoisting a small child on one's shoulders to have them wave the red flag for you counted. Less fortunate souls were impressed into carrying vast banners with slogans like "Peace, Labor, May!" and "Lenin lived, Lenin lives, Lenin will live on!" or "The people and the party are one"—a gem that could rival a Zen koan in its inscrutability.

The November 7 parade commemorated the start of the 1917 October Revolution. The reason October Revolution Day was celebrated in November was that before 1918, Russia followed the Julian calendar, which incorrectly assumed that there were precisely 365.25 days in the year. Meanwhile, the rest of Europe had switched from the Julian calendar to the Gregorian one, which was shorter by 0.002 percent. By the beginning of the twentieth century, Russia's calendar was thirteen days behind that of the rest of the world. Travelers coming to Saint Petersburg from Berlin would not just have to adjust their pocket watches by two hours, but also their calendars by almost two weeks! Finally, in January 1918, the Council of People's Commissars issued a decree that January 31 of that year was to be followed directly by February 14. This finally brought the country up to speed, at least in that one sense.

On November 7, everyone once more piled out into the streets with the same idiotic banners and red flags. Everything was the same as on May 1 except for the weather. The dank gloom of frosty, windy, rainy, and sometimes snowy late fall definitely put a damper on the outdoor fun.

While I didn't think much about the politics, I enjoyed the parades themselves. At the very least, each one was an outing. Plus, there was always a chance of getting a spot in the parade flow next to a friend or a girl you fancied.

(Side note: when the USSR fell apart in 1991 and October Revolution Day was abolished as a national holiday, all Russians grumbled—even those who hated Communists. Seventy years under Soviet rule had accustomed everyone to having a day off in late fall to get appropriately shit-faced. To appease the populace, Putin's government invented a new holiday in 2005: National Unity Day. It was scheduled for November 4 to commemorate a certain minor military victory against Poland sometime in the seventeenth century. But no one really cared what was being celebrated. The important thing was having the day off and spending quality time with assorted combustible beverages.)

By the time I joined the Young Pioneers in 1980, all the revolutionary fervor was long gone from the movement. On the surface, the propaganda remained as flashy and pompous as ever, but it was entirely hollow. Unlike the American Boy Scouts, who overflow with sincere Old Glory patriotism, the Young Pioneers understood that they were part of a sham. Everyone knew our drums and red flags were just pageantry for the sake of pageantry. We marched because we were instructed to do so by the teachers, not because we were genuinely excited by the advent of Communism. And the teachers made sure we did it not because they wanted to mold us into good

Communists but because they didn't want a visit from the city district officials.

All-encompassing systemic hypocrisy aside, becoming a Young Pioneer was a significant coming-of-age milestone for a Soviet kid. New Young Pioneers were admitted every year in several stages. If you were a good student with no disciplinary strikes against your name, you got in with the first cohort. It was not a high bar to clear, so about half of my class made it in, including Vova and myself. This first group got to wear the new lapel pin and the red tie right away. The second group, on the other hand, had to keep wearing their Child of October star until they were admitted later that year. A few of our friends were held back in this way, for various reasons. At the time, none of us found this passive-aggressive shaming irritating.

My classmates and I were initiated into Pioneerhood, appropriately enough, at the Young Pioneer Palace, a youth center for hobbies and recreation situated in a lavish old building on Nevsky Prospect. Our initiators were once again older kids, this time members of Komsomol, the Communist Youth Union. They were the next developmental form of the future adult Communist, teenagers of fifteen or sixteen. They tied red ties around our necks and then their leader bid us in a stirring voice, "Pioneer, be prepared for the fight for the cause of the Communist Party of the Soviet Union!"

"Always prepared!" we responded in chorus, extending our right arms forwards and upwards, crooking it slightly at the elbow. (It was almost the perfect average of a Nazi heil and a Mexican flag salute.)

That red tie turned out to be the thing I hated the most about being a Young Pioneer. It was made from a kind of synthetic silk that was very unpleasant to touch and creaked when tied in a knot. I hated it, and so did all of my friends. We had to wear them to school from the day they were tied around our necks right up until we joined Komsomol. For five years, we had to observe the precept, "When you put the tie on, take good care of it, for it shares its color with the red banner." (In Russian, this inanity rhymes.) In my darker moments, I liked to imagine that my tie was literally the result of someone going at a big red Soviet flag with giant scissors.

After our initiation ceremony, Vova and I were taken by our grandmas to the nearby Sever restaurant. It used to be a grand establishment, dating from the pre-Revolutionary days, and was similar to the opulent halls one sees in movies about the Prohibition-era Mafia: an enormous stage for performers, extensive space for dancers, round tables in recessed shadowy alcoves, velvet drapes on high windows, and potted flowers.

This time, of course, there were no dancers or gangsters. In fact, there was no one at all except for the four of us and a couple of lazy, poorly shaved waiters. The grandmas ordered us all chicken soup with little meat pies, followed by beef stroganoff with roasted potatoes, and ice cream for dessert. For two Soviet nine-year-olds, this was the peak of opulence. Of course, in the depth of our hearts, both Vova and I would have preferred to leave the grandmas to enjoy their lavish meal in peace without us, and to sod off to climb some roofs.

This was the only time I had ever eaten at a restaurant in Leningrad as a child. Our family ate all our meals at home. So did practically everyone else in the USSR, where there were no fast-food outlets or chain restaurants. There was nowhere to turn to for fast and cheap calories, mainly because Soviet calories were neither fast nor cheap: we were always in bigger danger of being underfed than overfed.

On the occasions when people did eat out, there were only three types of establishments on offer. Firstly, there were workplace cafeterias. These had no names, only numbers, same as shops, schools, health clinics, and prisons. In theory, our cafeterias didn't differ much from their Western counterparts: they had the same kind of serving counters, rails, trays, and limited but filling entrée options. This was not surprising, since Khrushchev borrowed this setup from America after his historic two-week visit in 1959. But in practice, they were a shambles. The selection was pitiful, the portions scant, and the quality subpar because the cafeteria staff usually took all the best groceries home with them. The true ingredient list of many dishes could only be guessed at.

Secondly, there were cafés. These mostly sold pastries, ice cream, and coffee, so as far as us kids were concerned, they were the nutritionally vital places. Some of the cafés had names, like the aforementioned Kolobok. Still, as with the cafeterias, the only stuff offered for sale to the general public was also what the employees hadn't had the inclination to steal. And as for sanitation standards . . .

Once, I was enjoying an ice cream and coffee at Kolobok when a young woman sat down across from me. She had a plate of macaroni and meatballs. When she broke the first meatball open with her fork, she said with mild surprise, "Whoops, a cockroach."

Indeed, a shiny little bugger had been baked right into the meatball. Undaunted, the lady carefully picked it out with her fingers, set it on the edge of her plate, just like people do with olive pits, and calmly ate her lunch.

Finally, there were restaurants. These establishments were very rare and always had proper names, not numbers. They were considered hotbeds of luxury and excess. To eat at a restaurant, one had to be a touring artist, a criminal, or a party big shot—or, once in a blue moon, a spoiled nine-year-old whose grandma had decided to celebrate his induction into the ranks of future Communists in style.

* * *

Had I known what food in the West was really like, I would have been so jealous. Many foodstuffs Westerners take for granted didn't exist in the Soviet universe even as a concept. There was no such thing as breakfast cereal, peanut butter, or ready-made heat-and-eat meals of any kind. We had never heard of yogurt, burgers, french fries, marshmallows, tea bags, popcorn, cookies with fillings, or a hundred other delicious items honed by the invisible hand of the market to entice consumers.

My usual breakfast was fairly meager: a small plate of *kasha* (porridge), usually buckwheat, though sometimes rice or oatmeal, chased down with a cup of hot tea.

The Soviet version of lunch usually happened somewhat later in the day than it does in the West. A normal lunch was supposed to have three courses: soup with bread and butter, a meat entrée with a starch side, and dessert with tea. Soup was considered imperative for proper digestion. Lunch without soup didn't count as a proper meal at all. Out of the pantheon of Soviet soups, two stand out: *shchi* and borsch, cabbage and beetroot soup, respectively. They were cooked with or without meat, according to one's means and inclinations, and always served with sour cream and dill. Tens of millions of Soviet people ate one of these two soups for lunch practically every other day. The second course was usually chicken and potatoes or macaroni and meatballs. Sometimes it was boiled frankfurters. Tradition also called for dessert, but sweets and pastries were hard to find. In our house, dessert usually took the form of a slice of white bread with butter and jam, and sometimes simply water or tea with some jam stirred into it.

The evening meal, taken around seven or eight o'clock, was supposed to be light, which meant no soup and usually no meat. Most days we ate *makarony*—i.e., pasta. Pasta was one of the few items one could almost always find for sale in the shops, so it had a reputation for being the poor man's staple. Urban legend had it that factories producing *makarony* in Russia were strategically important, because in wartime they could be swiftly retooled to produce AK-47 bullets, since both items were 7.62 millimeters in diameter.

Besides pasta, we often ate what would be considered "breakfast food" in the West. Sometimes Mom made blini, Russian-style crepes; or *syrniki*, thick fried pancakes made from cottage cheese, flour, and eggs. And sometimes she made omelets or—my favorite due to its foreign associations—French toast.

When I was a kid, most adults around me had lived through actual famines. Unsurprisingly, food to them was never a matter of aesthetics or even taste. The only thing that mattered was its nutritional content. The more calories, the better.

Everything that's considered bad for you today was decidedly good for you when I was a kid. The very notion of any food being "bad for you" would have seemed nonsensical. Sugar was great, fat was wonderful, and bread was altogether sacred. The only thing parents warned kids away from was cheap caramels, because they were bad for the teeth. When Grandma poured me tea, she would stir four teaspoons of sugar into the cup. She "improved" vegetable soup by throwing large hunks of butter into it. She referred to low-fat milk as "milk *rejecta*." When the family was fortunate to acquire cream, Alyosha and I were given it to drink instead of milk.

There was, however, one thing Grandma did consider dangerous to put in your mouth: a toothbrush with plastic bristles. As far as she was concerned, a proper and "natural" toothbrush was one made of horse hair. She also considered tooth powder to be healthier than toothpaste. Tooth powder was sold in flat, round tins, into which a moistened toothbrush was dunked. Getting your teeth clean with tooth powder took ages, because it did not foam. The day I was finally allowed to start using toothpaste was a red-letter day indeed. Leningrad stores had only one kind of it, called Zhemchug (Pearls); naturally, it was white. When, as a teenager, I saw blue-colored toothpaste for the first time, it looked like an alien artifact. And when I first beheld toothpaste with stripes, I realized deep in my bones that the Soviet system had totally failed us.

All cooking was done in bulk. On Sundays, Mom and Grandma made enough buckwheat porridge, soup, and meat to last the family the whole week. Then they would ration the food out to us, day by day, with a strict eye to equality of portions. One never simply set a large plate with meatballs in the middle of the table and let everyone help themselves. That sort of largesse was reserved only for New Year's Eve or birthday celebrations. All other days, portions were tightly controlled.

Grandma and Mom often quarreled over whether Alyosha and I were receiving equal rations. Grandma represented my interests while my mother advocated for my brother. Tolya always maintained a diplomatic silence, hiding behind cigarette smoke and the sports page. A typical dinnertime argument between Grandma and Mom went something like this:

"Vera, come here," Grandma would say. "Look at this plate. You know that Serezha likes breast meat. Why are you giving him a drumstick and the breast to Alyosha?"

"Mama, I'm giving them different pieces in turn. It's Serezha's turn to eat the drumstick."

"This drumstick is too small for him! He is going through a growth spurt; he needs to eat more!"

"Mama, I am just being fair! And by the way, I didn't say a single word yesterday when you gave Alyosha a blackened apple and Serezha got a perfectly ripe one. So don't start with me now!"

"Don't you argue with me! An apple is an apple; they are all the same! And by the way, you better tell Elena"—this was Tolya's mother—"that if she ever wants to come to this house again, she needs to bring more than just one banana for Alyosha! There are two children living in this house!"

"Why don't you just tell her yourself? And while you're at it, explain to her why you were so opposed to me having a second child at all!"

This could go on for hours.

Leaving anything on your plate was highly inadvisable. Your parents would just put the food back in the fridge and make you finish it tomorrow, when it was even less appetizing. The idea of throwing food away was anathema to all adults.

In the colder seasons, the pot with a week's worth of soup was kept not in the fridge but on a ledge outside the window. Leningrad winters were a serious business, and naturally the soup was always frozen solid. Every day, Mom or Grandma would thaw it out for lunch, dish it up, then put the remainders back outside. Halfway into the week, Grandma would often "improve" the soup, as she called it, by adding a new ingredient. For instance, on a Wednesday, when half the pot would already be gone, she might decide to upgrade the leftovers with cabbage or potatoes. This meant she would add the fresh vegetables, pour in more water, and reboil the whole thing, reducing the previous contents to unappetizing mush.

My mother could be a good cook when the occasion called for it, but most of the time her approach to food was utilitarian. Thankfully, Tolya was easy to please. His favorite dish was meat dumplings, which were sometimes available in frozen packages. If you bought them in the summer, they usually thawed while you walked home and resolidified into a single large brick in the freezer. Mom approached this brick as Alexander the Great approached the Gordian knot: by chopping it into chunks, which would then be boiled into a sort of nasty stew that looked like it had already been eaten once. Still, I can't recall Tolya ever grumbling about it. Food was food.

Teenage rebellion in the USSR often started with food. After being instructed, cajoled, and ordered to clean one's plate all of one's life, one eventually reached a breaking point. At some point, it dawned that guzzling *shchi* or borsch happily was as uncool as listening to censor-sanctioned Soviet pop music.

Once, I went to visit my friend Sasha Lesman at his room in a communal apartment. His grandmother told me that he was eating and couldn't go out and play until he cleaned his plate. Sasha was not a good eater. To keep him in line, his grandma sat on the sofa opposite the dining table and watched him put away spoon after spoon of meatball-and-noodle soup.

"Eat, eat," she repeated, watching him. "You are skin and bone!"

Sasha, a master actor, seemed to be putting away his soup with great enthusiasm. What his grandma couldn't see was that he really was putting it away—into a plastic bag on his knees.

After two minutes of watching him make enraptured faces at his grandma while spitting out the contents of his bowl into that bag mouthful by mouthful, I had to leave the room. I was afraid that if I stayed a moment longer, I would burst out laughing and ruin the whole caper. Which is why I missed the climactic moment when Sasha, after handing his empty bowl to his proud granny, surreptitiously tossed the now-full bag out the window of their sixth-story communal apartment into the courtyard, where it plopped loudly, scaring babushkas, pigeons, and stray cats.

CHAPTER 6

HUNTING AND GATHERING

In a Soviet grocery store, a customer asks the shop assistant, "Excuse me, can you slice me two hundred grams of salami?"

"Of course we can. Feel free to bring it over anytime."

ONE REASON WHY Soviet cuisine was so dull was that produce in the USSR was seasonal. Except for potatoes, carrots, and onions, which were available all year long, vegetables only appeared in stores when they ripened, and they did not stick around for long. It was the same with fruit, which was also only available during the harvest months of late summer and early fall. Winter and spring saw spikes in kids' being diagnosed with vitamin deficiencies.

Fruit imported from overseas only ever made it to Moscow and Leningrad. Outside of major metropolitan areas, it was practically unknown. When I was nine, Grandma took me for a short holiday to a village on the Karelian Isthmus, not far from Leningrad. The old woman with whom we stayed told us that life was getting better in her village.

"They were selling oranges in our local store the other day!" she said. "I bought some. What a nasty thing, these oranges, so bitter when you bite into them. But they do seem to get better the more you eat. . ."

It was a similar story with bananas. People in most places never laid eyes on them. But they did occasionally appear for sale in Leningrad. All bananas were sold green—not yellow green, to ripen over the course of the week, but solid green and hard as wood. Whenever Grandma managed to get some, she wrapped each one in newspaper and stashed them away like heirlooms in one of the drawers built into her bed. Every day, she would open the drawer and carefully check which bananas had ripened and which needed more time. The ripe ones were divided, with meticulous socialist fairness, between my brother and myself.

One day, when I was eight, I was on my way home from school and passed the vegetable store on the corner of Chernyshevsky Avenue. (The sign above the door read, "Fruit and Vegetables," but since there was almost never any fruit for sale there, everyone just called it "the vegetable store.") A huge line stretched out its door and around the block. I asked someone in line what was for sale. Miracle of miracles, it was bananas! One ruble ten kopecks a kilo, limit of two kilos per customer.

I couldn't see the person who was weighing out the bananas; the line was too long. There was a buzz of excited anticipation, the kind one might hear in the West in lines for the latest Air Jordans or the newest iPhone. I queued up and opened *The Life and Adventures of Robinson Crusoe*, which I was carrying in my schoolbag to read during boring classes, and settled in for the long haul. If nothing else, the USSR taught even its youngest citizens the joy of delayed gratification.

I stood in line for three hours or maybe more. Bananas were not packaged, and it was taking a long time for a sole shop assistant to measure two kilos for each customer in the queue. Eventually, the middle-aged man in synthetic socks and sandals in front of me bought his two bunches of bananas, and it was finally my turn. Or it would've been, except the salesman said, "That's it, all gone."

And he went back inside the store.

It was painful. But what hurt the most wasn't that I was going home empty-handed. Bananas were scarce, and a lot of people had been in line ahead of me, so I knew there was a risk of this. It wasn't even that I had wasted three hours standing in line. Standing in lines was something everyone did, every day. It was that the salesman didn't even offer to check if there were any bananas left out the back. I would've been happy with a few bananas, or even just one. But Soviet reality was not big on customer satisfaction, or being nice to children. Or being nice at all.

Had I been older, I might have gone home muttering to myself about what a miserable life we all live in this dump of a country, but I was eight, so I just walked on home and cried. Eventually, though, I felt hurt and disappointment slowly giving way to anger. Why was everything around me like this? I wondered. Not that I could articulate exactly what "like this" meant yet. All I knew was that "this" was perfectly exemplified by the sheer frustrating pointlessness of wasting three hours in a line for bananas only to have them snatched away from your waiting hands at the last second.

And I also knew, deep down, I did not want to live "like this."

* * *

Of course, it's not like I had a choice in whether to continue living like this. As the Russian saying goes, "We're in a submarine; where exactly are you fixing to go?"

Scarcity accompanied every Soviet citizen every step of the way from the cradle to the grave. The key word for Soviet shoppers was *defitzit*. If an item was in deficit, that meant it almost never appeared for sale in stores. So many food items were *defitzit* that it's easier to say what wasn't: potatoes, bread, pasta, salt, and canned fish. Those were the only items you could always count on finding in the stores.

To illustrate what life was like with most things being constantly in deficit, consider coffee. Coffee was our family's drink of choice—which was unusual in Russia, where most people preferred tea. Since it was next to impossible to find in stores, it was considered a somewhat decadent drink, favored by intellectuals and bohemians.

There were only two kinds of coffee: "in beans" and "instant." Roasted beans cost an arm and a leg: a kilo went for twenty rubles. Considering that a normal Soviet engineer—the Soviet equivalent of the American "Joe Six-Pack," with respect to both social standing and salary—made just over a hundred rubles a month, it was a substantial chunk of change. Unroasted green coffee beans were cheaper and somewhat easier to find. They were Tolya's favorite coffee option. He roasted them himself in a frying pan, a handful at a time, on a very low fire, stirring every few seconds. When he was at it, the apartment filled up with thin, eye-watering smoke, and we had to open all the windows, even if it was the dead of winter.

The hands-down consumers' choice of coffee was the instant. We didn't have international brands like Nescafé or Maxwell, naturally, just a Soviet version: a very fine powder sold in tall metal cans. The containers were tan and gold, were decorated with stylized coffee beans, and were imaginatively branded "Coffee Natural Dissolvable." When mixed with hot water, the powder yielded a great number of lumps. Still, walking into a grocery store and taking a can of instant coffee off the shelf was something one could only imagine happening in the very bright but very distant Communist future. In the '70s and '80s, it had to be traded for favors, obtained through special connections, or procured through a sophisticated system of special orders. If none of that worked, one could always hope to receive some as a present.

In our household, Grandma and Mom each had their own personal can of "Natural Dissolvable." On Sundays, when Alyosha and I came to the kitchen to enjoy our morning coffee allowances, I would take my spoonful from Grandma's can, and Alyosha would take his from Mom's. This arrangement was not restricted to coffee. Grandma and Mom kept all their foodstuffs in separate cupboards and fridges like two untrusting roommates on a tight budget. As always, it seemed totally normal.

* * *

Paradoxically, empty stores often meant full pantries. Since no one ever knew when any particular item might appear in stores, everything even remotely useful was bought on sight, regardless of whether it was actually needed. This went for food as well, making constant shortages a self-fulfilling prophecy.

In our house, the cupboards were always bursting with various flours, grains, and legumes. Unfortunately, there weren't enough well-sealed containers to hold them all. Every few years, Mom and Grandma would inspect their food supply and invariably have to throw out most of it, because it was infested with little multilegged black vermin known under the generic term *zhuchki*, or "bugs." Then they'd buy more fresh flour and grains. It was a vicious cycle without end.

Insects infested every nook and cranny of Soviet life. Liberally strewn with poorly covered dumpsters, Leningrad was a genuine fly paradise. As soon as the weather warmed up, every home became filled with a low drone of fly patrols. Most of the time, the only weapon in the war against these flying terrorists was a rolled-up newspaper. Swatting flies was an art. One didn't just swing willy-nilly; strategy was paramount. Tolya's method was to stalk the fly until it landed somewhere, and then observe it closely. If the fly was making rubbing, hand-washing motions with its front legs, that meant it was relaxed and would not react to a surprise hit quickly. This was the best time to strike. And strike he did. Although mangled fly corpses were collected and disposed of promptly, forensic evidence of Tolya's heroics would often remain, especially on light-colored wallpaper.

But the prize for most omnipresent pest went to the cockroach. We lived in an old building, full of cracks and holes in the walls. Also, all the other apartments around us were communal and overcrowded. Naturally, our cockroaches were legion. Moreover, they were a hospitable bunch, often entertaining visiting delegations. If you got up at night, walked into the kitchen, and turned on the lights, you would likely witness entire cockroach families breaking up their picnic in the middle of the room and hastily escaping into holes in the walls.

* * *

Scarcity meant that running a Soviet household demanded endless improvisation. Our parents didn't have the slightest clue about modern conveniences like trash bags, wet wipes, paper handkerchiefs, disposable diapers, shaving gel, and tampons (or any other types of female sanitary products). Until the mid-1970s, there wasn't even such a thing as deodorant. (Just try to imagine rush hour on a crowded public bus in the middle of summer! On second thought, don't.) There was no such thing as either sunscreen or soothing aloe gel, so when kids came home sunburned, they were smeared with sour cream. The universal solution to minor external abrasions, from skinned knees to hemorrhoids, was marigold ointment.

There were only three kinds of soap: "hand soap," used for washing people; "children's soap," used for washing babies; and "household soap," used for everything else—cleaning floors, countertops, clothes, and dishes, which of course had to be washed by hand. Household soap was made of brownish-gray lye, and it smelled terrible.

And then there was baking soda. That stuff was practically magic.

Need to get a stain out of anything?

Baking soda.

Need a facial scrub, shampoo, or acne-ridding face mask?

Baking soda.

Whitening your teeth?

Baking soda.

Sore gums? Sore throat? Sore stomach? Sweaty feet?

Baking soda.

Sick of this list?

Induce vomiting with baking soda.

Nothing made in the USSR was disposable. Planned obsolescence was not a part of the planned economy. In this way, household items were similar to foodstuffs; one never knew when the government was going to start or stop producing something, and goods were acquired based on their availability rather than need. It was safer to buy something you didn't need than to let the opportunity pass.

A typical Soviet apartment of those days looked like it belonged to hoarders. Nothing was ever thrown out, not even things that were hopelessly broken. After all, a broken thing might still get fixed someday, or at least used for scrap parts. So, families stockpiled rubbish—worn-out shoes, parts of broken furniture, punctured bicycle tires, et cetera—in their already cramped apartments, filling cluttered balconies, basements, and sometimes entire rooms with items left to gather dust and await the day, usually in vain, when they would be fixed or repurposed.

Hoarding was so prevalent that no one ever remarked on its absurdity. The parents of my classmate Vasya Bazanov finally got a new apartment after huddling for many years in a single communal apartment room. And yet, one of their two hard-won bedrooms was immediately consigned to storing old furniture, clothes, and other junk. The mother of the family simply couldn't bear to throw anything out, even the things no one had used in years.

It was a very Marxist understanding of the world: every material object produced with human labor was considered to have intrinsic value, quite regardless of whether it was actually in demand, or ever would be.

Our family was no different. We kept everything, including scraps of wrapping paper and plastic bags, which were not given out at stores with every purchase like they are today. Even when a plastic bag had been used to store something odorous and perishable, like fish, it just got washed carefully with "household soap" and hung out to dry.

This fretfully frugal attitude created a culture of reusing and recycling far beyond that achieved by any country in the West even after decades of environmentalist activism. Not that anyone cared about the environment; we were just poor and cheap.

*   *   *

The very act of shopping in the USSR was a perpetual exercise in frustration.

Most shops were simply called by the name of the product each sold. Dairy stores had a sign above the door that said, "Milk"; bakeries were called "Bread"; there were also stores called "Meat," "Fish," "Clothes," and "Household Items." Although if they had been called according to what they really sold rather than pretended to sell, most of those stores would've been named "Nothing Much," "General Disappointment," and "Fuck Off."

There were also a few nonspecialized grocery stores, which were called gastronoms and were numbered Gastronom #1, Gastronom #2, and so on. Shopping there was a fairly byzantine process. Let's say you needed three hundred grams of butter. Let's say also that they actually had some for sale. Here's the typical quest you'd have to complete to take it home with you:

Step 1. Stand in line for the butter itself. Bring a book—it might take a while.

Step 2. When your turn comes, ask the saleslady to weigh out three hundred grams of butter.

Step 3. Almost invariably, she will ask, "Is 285 okay?" Approve the amount or risk her ire.

Step 4. Wait for her to calculate the price using an abacus. (Soviet sales staff relied on these archaic devices for lack of electronic calculators.) She will then say out loud, "One oh three," meaning one ruble and three kopecks. Remember that number. The butter remains in her possession.

Step 4. Now get in the line for the dairy department checkout. This is important. If you accidentally get into the wrong checkout line, say for meat or for alcohol, you will have to leave it and find the right one.

Step 5. It's been another while, but you get to the cashier. Hurray! Tell them what you're buying and what you owe for it. (You didn't forget your total, did you?) "One oh three for butter." The cashier will take your money and give you a receipt.

Step 6. You've paid! Now return to the original line for the dairy department saleslady.

Step 7. When your turn comes, retrieve your wrapped package of butter. There are no grocery bags, either paper or plastic, so let's hope you remembered to bring your own.

Step 8. Leave the store feeling like a conquering hero.

Step 9. After walking two blocks, remember that you were also supposed to buy milk, too.

Shopping was convoluted enough on regular days, but when a store actually had something unusual and desirable in stock, like salami or hot dogs, everything suddenly got ludicrously chaotic. Lines got longer, passions ran higher, and the sales staff grew even more irritable.

Grocery shopping was the first chore most people were entrusted with growing up. I started getting sent out for bread, butter, or milk when I was about seven. Shopping for milk was my favorite, because I got to carry an enameled metal milk canister. Before going home, I would stop in our courtyard and, with the air of a world-famous prestidigitator, demonstrate the centrifugal effect to the neighbor kids by taking the lid off the filled canister and whirling it over my head.

Buying bread was less fun. A typical bakery had huge wooden shelves heaped with baked loaves of all kinds. None of the bread was packaged in anything—it just sat there. Also on the shelves were some large forks attached to chains. People used them to spear their chosen loaves, so as not to touch them with dirty hands. Since the bread was baked without preservatives and sat in the open air, it started going stale the second it was set out for purchase. People would always poke several loaves with the fork, to find the softest one.

The most fun was to be had at the vegetable store. Usually, I was sent there to buy some ungodly quantity of potatoes, like ten kilos. Potatoes got weighed out on huge scales behind the counter. The massive amounts of dirt on them weighed down the scales substantially, especially if the potatoes were wet. Mom and Grandma always warned me, "Watch that they don't give you too much dirt." At the counter itself, there was a hole with a metal drainpipe. After weighing the potatoes, the salesperson would press a button, and the spuds would roll down the pipe into the customer's bag, which they had hopefully set in time to catch them all. If you've never heard a sack of potatoes being emptied down a metal pipe, it sounds rather like muzzled machine-gun fire.

The only thing I was never sent out to buy was meat. Locating and purchasing meat products was an understated art form. In our family, the artist in charge was Mom. She maintained and managed a complex web of relationships with butchers at a multitude of meat stores in our neighborhood and beyond. Some of the relationships were friendly, even flirty; others were more tit-for-tat, with the butcher charging extra for setting good pieces aside for her. In the social pantheon of the USSR, meat shop salesmen and butchers outranked just about anyone else in usefulness, and finessing them was a skill one honed over one's entire lifetime.

* * *

In America, if you live in Manhattan and get a craving for a Philly cheesesteak, you don't actually have to go to Philadelphia to enjoy one. At any given moment, a dozen restaurants will be serving them within walking distance of you. That's the beauty of capitalism: someone is always ready to monetize your whims. It's an efficient mechanism for connecting people with the objects of their desire. Soviet citizens had no such accommodating mechanisms. If a family from Leningrad wanted to enjoy a cake from Kiev, they had to send someone to Ukraine to pick one up.

This isn't hyperbole, by the way. The Ukrainian city Kiev was famous for a specific type of cake, baked at the local Karl Marx Confectionery Factory. It had several layers of meringue with hazelnuts, chocolate glaze, and buttercream filling. It was phenomenally popular all over the USSR. Whenever anyone visited Kiev, their family expected them to bring back one of these iconic cakes. Whenever Tolya went to Kiev on business, he dutifully brought back a cake for the family.

Beyond being a delightful dessert, Kiev cakes opened all doors and solved all problems. Any government official would attend to your problem. Any doctor would see you. A Soviet person brought face-to-face with a Kiev cake felt like a Hamelin rat, who instead of the Piper's flute suddenly heard the "Triumphal March" from *Aida*. And since the confectioners of the Karl Marx Confectionery Factory refused to either disclose the recipe or let anyone else manufacture their creation, regular citizens were stuck making 650-mile bakery runs. But that just made the cake taste all the better. That was the other side of the scarcity coin: the harder you had to work for something, the better it tasted.

Leningrad also had a pastry with some claim to fame, though not to the same extent, of course. It was made in a bakery called Sever (North). Before the Revolution, the bakery had French owners and was called Nörd, but the government nationalized and renamed it. Just like its name and the ownership, the bakery's interior got "Sovietized" over time: wall paint peeled, the marble tiles cracked, tablecloths faded. Eventually the place looked like any other shabby Soviet establishment. Sever's pastries, however, remained very good. Its bestseller was called *kartoshka* (meaning "potato"), and it was made of cookie crumbs, condensed milk, and cocoa powder. It became widely imitated all over the USSR. They also made excellent oatmeal cookies, currant buns, and a pastry called, without the slightest hint of adult humor, "cream-filled tubes."

If most items were in deficit, many others were constantly overproduced, far in excess of real demand. This was done to satisfy *pyatiletki*, or "five-year plans," which set production goals for various factories. These goals tended to grow from year to year, quite regardless of whether anyone wanted or needed the item in question. As a result, the produced goods piled up in stockrooms.

To resolve instances of oversupply—shortages were far trickier—the government came up with the concept of *nagruzka* (literally, "load" or "burden"). It meant compulsory purchase of hard-to-move stock. For instance, if you were lucky enough to find some tangerines, the store might only sell them to you if you also bought several cans of kelp. The same went for stuff like clothes. If something wonderful was suddenly "tossed out" at a store (that's what we called it when rare items went on sale), customers would also have to buy something else that was collecting dust on the shelves. The two items would usually be completely unrelated. Want a pair of Romanian-made shoes? Enjoy your new ironing board!

Because laws of supply and demand did not apply, and shortages were permanent, the only way to procure many items was through *blat*. *Blat* meant knowing a guy, or knowing a guy who knew a guy. Knowing the right guy could provide you with access to hard-to-find desirables, like high-heeled shoes, a leather jacket, or a pair of jeans. Conversely, if your job placed you close to the right distribution network, then you were the guy! If you could get people a sheepskin coat or a regular supply of good cuts of meat, then you'd be able to leverage those favors for other favors: quality medical care, a spot at a Black Sea resort, university placement for an underachieving child, or even the papers necessary to avoid a military draft.

But not all retail was under strict government control. There were *rynki*, farmers markets, where ordinary people were allowed to sell produce that they had grown themselves. Farmers markets were the realm of the well heeled; many things that were perpetually absent from government stores could be found there, and with no limits per customer, but they all cost a pretty penny. Someone from a well-off family was said to be "raised on market food," and "to shop at the market" was a byword for living in a state of utter decadence.

When I got to be old enough to shoulder the responsibility, I started getting sent to the market to shop for family festivities. It made me feel very extravagant and posh. I would wander through the cornucopia of apples, dairy canisters, and slabs of meat that one never saw in any grocery store, and sometimes the vendors even let me taste their produce. Farmers markets were a window into a world of extraordinary abundance. Ironically, they looked the most like the Communist future described to us at school. Or what I presumed the capitalist West might look like—only if I were in the West, I would surely have more money to spend there.

But farmers market prices were nothing compared to "speculator" prices.

Since the USSR's planned economy couldn't, by its very nature, respond to the pressures of consumer demand, the authorities had to be on the constant lookout for speculators. Speculation—i.e., private citizen-to-citizen resale of goods—was illegal. It was nothing new: a vibrant black market had existed in the USSR practically since its inception. For a young entrepreneur, getting busted for even the most minor capitalist shenanigans could have consequences ranging from being thrown out of Komsomol with a permanent black mark against his or her name, to being expelled from university, to spending several years in prison.

Still, the practice thrived. In Leningrad some people actually made a good off-the-books living by secretly buying things like jeans and music albums off visiting foreigners and reselling them. A typical transaction went down something like this: a Finn would bring to Leningrad a suitcase crammed with blue jeans or pantyhose. He would then sell them to a speculator for a mind-boggling number of rubles and use said rubles to buy a mind-boggling amount of vodka. The vodka was then taken back to Finland for enjoyment and further resale. A gross market inefficiency could thus turn a pair of humble Levi's into twenty large bottles of top-quality Stoli.

Blue jeans were easily the most sought-after black market item. One of Grandma's former university colleagues had a job assignment in Norway teaching Russian for a few years. When I was twelve, Grandma asked her to bring me back a pair of jeans, a denim jacket, and Puma sneakers, all of which were impossible to buy in the USSR. This outfit instantly made me the coolest kid in the class. I wore my Puma sneakers to school every day until they literally fell apart at the seams.

But that was a one-off. Most of the time, coveted Western items were beyond my limited means. However, just because I couldn't buy something doesn't mean I couldn't find a way to get it.

A huge part of our recess time at school was devoted to trading. Adults dealt with the scarcity of cool stuff in stores by the means of a black market; we kids preferred to barter. Trading stuff among ourselves was a huge part of our lives. Whenever anyone saw a friend playing with some interesting new object, the first reaction was usually to ask what the lucky owner would trade for it, even if one had no immediate intention to trade. It was sort of like a price check.

My main focus through my primary school years was 3-D toy soldiers. I was always on the lookout to add more to my collection. Most Soviet-made plastic or tin toy soldiers were entirely flat; they stood upright only because their feet were melted into their horizontal stands. But there was one factory in Donetsk that manufactured sets of real 3-D soldiers—Romans, cowboys, Indians, pirates, Vikings, frontiersmen, and cavemen. Each set had six figurines (which were actually poured from molds designed by an American toy manufacturer called Louis Marx and Company—was it the owner's name that predisposed Soviets to use his designs?). These 3-D soldiers were nothing like the fancy G.I. Joes found halfway around the world. They were monochrome, either blue or brown, and not articulated. But they were still the best thing around, and the most Western, and I coveted them beyond all measure. On paper, they cost seventy-five kopecks per set. In reality, you could only get your hands on them through special connections. They were the envy of everyone in school and the one thing I was always ready to trade for.

Another particularly coveted object for barter was Donald bubble gum—the very same that had blown my mind back on that bleak commuter train when I was a preschooler. Boys whose parents traveled to work in exciting overseas places like Bulgaria or Iran would often bring back this colorful delicacy. On the black market, it went for one ruble a piece. The gum itself was mouthwateringly pink and had a captivating scent that resembled no fruit we'd ever eaten. And then there were the paper inserts! Each gum had a second, inner wrapper with small pictures detailing some episode from a Disney character's life. We could only guess as to the stories behind all those strange creatures—Mickey Mouse, Minnie, Goofy, Pluto, and Donald Duck—but we treasured the wrappers all the same simply for being artifacts from a world so foreign as to be practically alien. They also continued to retain the wonderful smell of the chewing gum for months afterward. These wrappers were a universal exchange currency for other hard-to-get toys. Since both the gum and the toy supplies remained steadily meager, their exchange rates likewise remained stable: three inserts were worth one foreign pencil with an eraser, or one 3-D soldier.

Real cash did not enter our exchanges. In general, money played a rather small part in our lives. For one thing, almost everyone was equally poor. Secondly, the most important things—housing, medical care, education—were practically free. Americans, who usually spend about 25 percent of their salary on rent, might be surprised to learn that their Soviet counterparts usually paid less than 5 percent. And finally, the thing that *really* mattered to material well-being in the Soviet universe was not money but connections or the ability to travel West. The last two usually went hand in hand. So, growing up, we never thought much about money beyond what we needed for the occasional ice cream cone or a movie ticket, or a rare big-ticket item like a bike.

I don't think I ever gave any thought to which of my friends were poorer or wealthier than myself until I was a young adult. If someone said about some kid, "His parents are rich," we wouldn't know what to make of it. If they had said, "His mom is a director of a gastronom," *that* would've been something! That kid probably ate ham and bananas every day, like the big shots in the Kremlin.

* * *

In sixth grade, a golden opportunity for scoring Western goodies opened up on my horizon: I was made president of the International Friendship Club.

It was a great racket. In our school, heading this club was a greatly sought-after post of substantial responsibility. As part of our duties, we were cleared by the authorities to receive foreign visitors, as part of their carefully shepherded tours of the "real life" of the Soviet Union. My main task as president of the club was to socialize with our foreign guests. I was picked for the job because I spoke English well and, even more importantly, the principal knew my family well. Grandma had been her English professor at university, and Tolya by then headed the physics department of Leningrad State, where her son was enrolled. (Leningrad may have been a city of four million, but the downtown intelligentsia lived in their own bubble.) So the principal could be confident that, as a reliable child from a good family, I would be on my best behavior and would not embarrass her, the school, or our motherland. I made sure not to betray her trust. However, in the grand tradition of Soviet nepotism, my first order of business was making Vova my vice president.

Our foreign visitors were not regular tourists. They were usually representatives of Western leftist organizations or correspondents from Communist newspapers, in town for some ideologically sound purpose rather than idle amusement. Naturally, many of them were eager to see a "normal" Soviet school. Ours was normal enough. Sure, our teaching staff was thoroughly vetted for ideological conformity, the kids spoke English unusually well, and almost everyone came from a "respectable" intelligentsia family. But all that aside, we were a school like any other. The visitors asked us about classes, our families, and our hobbies. By mutual unspoken agreement, politics were not brought up.

In general, Russians are the first to deride their own living standards, history, political leaders, weather, et cetera. But as soon as anyone of a different nationality chimes in to agree, we are apt to do a 180-degree turn and start defending everything Russian in the next breath, with the exact same level of passion. Whenever speaking about Russia, we always use the first-person plural *we* as shorthand for Russians or Soviets, even if the events in question took place decades or centuries ago. "Remember when we kicked out the Mongolian Golden Horde?" "Remember when we invaded Afghanistan?" "Remember when we shot down that Korean Boeing?" Even people who detest the Russian government retain this habit, as do people who have long emigrated and settled in other countries. The umbilical cord connecting us all to Mother Russia never drops off. (It took me a decade of living in the West to suppress the instinct of immediately taking offense whenever someone non-Russian criticized Russia.)

The International Friendship Club was the best extracurricular activity anyone could wish for. First of all, I could ask to be excused from almost any class at any time, and my arguments were ironclad: I had foreign guests to welcome. Surely it was in everyone's best interests for me to sacrifice a little class time to show them around our school and improve my English in the process?

Secondly, and more importantly, foreigners almost always brought presents, such as postcards, small souvenirs, or items of stationery. These school supplies were out-of-this-world exciting to us: round pencils with mysterious cartoon characters, strawberry-scented erasers, colorful stickers—all sorts of things we'd never seen before.

One day, I was chatting with a bold and ball-bellied visitor in a bright red sports T-shirt (an odd choice of attire for the snowed-in Leningrad). He was a journalist from the British Communist newspaper *Morning Star*. This guy was from Manchester, and his accent was so strong that I barely understood him. But he gave me something altogether amazing: an English football club pennant emblazoned with the words "Manchester United" and a picture of a running footballer. I knew nothing about English football clubs, but I did understand English grammar, and that phrase made no sense to me. I hung the pennant over my bed and often contemplated it as I fell asleep at night. What on earth could it mean? Was the city of Manchester united in supporting football? Was this only one of a pair of pennants, with half of the words in the slogan missing? Eventually, I decided that it must be a reference to some kind of trade union for northern English football players.

Gifts were the most valuable aspect of heading the International Friendship Club; my childhood aspirations were mostly material. There was practically no end to my material desires, stifled as they were by Soviet austerity. I didn't nurture hopes of my parents getting back together, like other children of divorce. I yearned not for academic honors or sports trophies. I didn't dream of becoming a cosmonaut. I had no hope of any abstract freedoms, like being able to read whatever book I wanted in peace without the KGB breathing down my neck.

I just wanted lots and lots of foreign pencils and erasers and stickers. I wanted our family to have a car. I also wanted my own room, and a color TV, and of course, lots and lots of toy soldiers—not the flat plastic ones but the awesome 3-D ones. And sweets, oh my God: cake, chocolate, Pepsi, some of that Donald chewing gum. And bananas. I would have killed for bananas.

It was too bad foreign guests were not allowed to feed the animals at the Communist zoo they were visiting.

CHAPTER 7

ENEMY VOICES, BOMBS, AND OTHER HOBBIES

A little boy is standing alone and crying in the middle of a large store. A security guard comes up to him and tries to console him.

"Don't worry, we'll announce on the radio for your parents to come pick you up."

The boy stops crying and says, "Just make sure to announce it on Voice of America—they don't listen to any other kind of radio."

WHEN I WAS eight, I saw a super cool Soviet action film called *Pirates of the 20th Century*. It was about nasty international hijackers (sponsored by the USA) and good Soviet sailors and agents. After this film, I began to dream of making a working walkie-talkie. My plan was to use two empty tooth powder tins, an antenna, and a microphone. There had to be, I thought, a way to string them all together that would leave me with a functioning means of long-distance communication.

The project never really got off the ground, but the idea itself was not an unusual one. Many people in the USSR tinkered with their radios or built their own. Like most useful things, radios were expensive and hard to find in stores. Also, they usually couldn't tune into many of the wavelengths that people wanted to listen to.

There were two distinct categories of radio in the USSR: regular Soviet broadcasting and what the government called "enemy voices."

The enemy voices were broadcast from bases around the perimeter of the Eastern Bloc and from mobile communications ships. They came from Western institutions, such as Voice of America, Radio Liberty, and the BBC Russian Service. In theory, it was possible to tune in to these wavelengths using certain models of radio receivers from almost anywhere in the Soviet Union. In practice, things were trickier. Ever diligent in its efforts to protect the populace from Western disinformation, the government set up a network of radio-signal-jamming towers, which filled the targeted broadcast wavelengths with irregular gurgling and hissing static. Every military base in the country had a unit devoted specifically to preventing people from tuning in to Western radio. At best you might, after half an hour of painstakingly fiddling with the dial, manage to hear five minutes of a broadcast before the jammer located the wavelength once more and drowned everything out again. But even those five minutes were worth it.

Enemy voices broadcast anti-Communist counterprogramming. They aired news that never got mentioned in the Soviet media, such as coverage of the Soviet invasion of Afghanistan. They organized readings of forbidden books on the air, one chapter at a time. They hosted religious discussions and political analysis. In short, they did everything that the Soviet media was not allowed to do.

Both Dad and Tolya had radios capable of tuning in to enemy voices, and I often borrowed them to try to fiddle my way through the jamming. When it worked, I was ecstatic. At first, I felt uncomfortable listening to these programs, not just because doing so was illegal, but also because of the shows' relentless criticism of the Soviet government. (To imagine this discomfort, try to picture yourself watching a movie with your parents and being ambushed by unexpected sex scenes.) But I got over it quickly. I especially relished the programs about banned Western rock and pop music and forbidden literature, like Solzhenitsyn's *The Gulag Archipelago*. They made me feel like an accomplished dissident.

* * *

Listening to foreign radio was not the sort of pastime one could engage in during the day without raising eyebrows, so I filled my day hours with other hobbies.

Like many kids in the USSR, I was keen on photography. My first camera was a present from Dad when I was seven or eight. It had no automatic metering of any kind; both the exposure and focus had to be set manually. After the roll of film was filled up, it had to be developed. Like many people, I learned to develop my own prints.

Turning a filled-up roll of film into ready photographs was time-consuming and labor-intensive. First, you needed a dark room. I used our bathroom. The roll of film had to be placed into a special "snail" case, which was then filled up twice with certain mixes of chemical solutions. It took about 30 minutes. Then the film had to be hung out to dry in the kitchen alongside our laundry. When it was dry, one could print photographs from it. At that point in the process, I would invite over Vova or Sasha Lesman. We would lock ourselves in the dark bathroom and examine the negatives through an enlarger. Then we made an exposure and soaked the photo paper in several chemical baths. The final prints were also dried on a clothesline, but instead of the kitchen, we strung them up over the bathtub. During all of this, the bathroom was completely off-limits to the rest of the family.

In the early 1980s, color film was very rare and expensive. Color photos were a big deal, only made on special occasions, such as weddings and graduations. When foreign tourists visiting our school showed me their government-issued IDs with color photographs, it was quite a shock. I considered it a gross misallocation of government resources. No doubt there were children starving in the streets of the USA as a result of this obscene waste of public money.

One kid who lived on the other side of our building's courtyard was infamous for having a black-and-white film roll with pornographic pictures. We were wary of him. He came from a "bad family," as our grandmothers and parents put it. But when he invited me and Vova over for a private viewing, it was an offer we couldn't refuse. We got to see this extraordinary footage through the enlarger only—he never made prints from it, since that could get him in trouble. The negatives were, naturally, color-reversed—black was white and white was black—but they gave one plenty of food for thought nonetheless.

Photography in general inspired quite a few sexual rumors. For instance, there was an urban legend circulating at the time about something called "the red film." This film was supposedly only available off the books to KGB operatives. Supposedly, if you loaded it into your camera, then all the people in your pictures would turn out naked. So whenever one of us got his hands on some nudie pics and passed them around, some kid would always say knowingly, "They aren't really naked for real. These were just taken with the red film."

At this point a highbrow reflector may wonder if glimpses of pornography provided Soviet boys with a mental space for asserting individual desires and otherwise defying the system that silenced all conversation about sex. Or was it just normal curiosity, with only the usual amount of rebellion against propriety and without additional ideological weight or aspirations of self-fulfillment? And I would tell this inquirer, it was the latter. We just wanted to look at boobies.

Crafting was probably the most popular hobby for boys in the USSR. It was making anything out of anything. The materials, methods, and purposes of crafting were legion. Just as DIY was the way of life for the adults, it was the same for us. The toys available in the stores were few and relatively uninspiring. It was up to us to make our own fun. In my room, I had a nook with a storage cabinet where I kept all sorts of tools: soldering irons, an array of fret saws, bags, and vials with chemicals. When I wasn't roaming outdoors with Vova or doing homework, I was usually making things. And for a while, it kept my mind off my obsession with Western stuff.

The government encouraged young crafters and tinkerers. After all, the hobbyist of today is the ballistic missile engineer of tomorrow. There was a great deal of tech magazines published regularly to feed our curiosity. I subscribed to *Junior Techie*. I made everything they threw at me. When I was in sixth grade, they published blueprints for a trendy thingamajig called "color music" or "light music." This device plugged into a tape player and flashed colored lights depending on the pitch of the notes. I spent about a month painstakingly following the instructions and putting one together. It didn't require any hard-to-find electronic parts, just regular stuff available at any retail radio parts store. In the end, it didn't work, but it also didn't blow up in my face when I plugged it into the outlet. That was nice.

But for a Soviet city boy of ten or twelve, the best tinkering involved making explosives and bombs. The first explosives one learned how to make as a kid—"Baby's First Bomb," as it were—involved matchsticks. Matchsticks were incredibly useful things for creative play. For one thing, they were plentiful. Most men and many women in the USSR smoked, cigarette lighters were very rare, and most stoves used gas. The demand for matches was huge, and unlike with most other consumer goods, the supply kept up with it. A box of fifty matches sold for a single kopeck. In theory, matchboxes were not supposed to be sold to children, but you could always ask an older friend to buy you some, or if you had no friend handy, a stranger on the street.

"Uncle!" you would exclaim, putting on your most innocent face. (Russian children address men and women as "uncle" and "auntie.") "Could you buy me some matches, please? My mom sent me to the store, but the saleslady won't sell me any!"

There were two types of easily crafted match-based explosives: land mines and grenades. To make a land mine, you first took a knife and shaved the sulfur carefully from five to seven matchstick heads. Then you took a huge nail, the biggest as you had, and pounded it into asphalt with a rock or a brick to make a deep, narrow hole. After you poured the sulfur mix into the hole, you set the nail back into the asphalt on top of it. The next part was the trickiest: you had to throw a brick directly on top of the nail while running like hell away from it. The friction from the nail striking the sulfur mix usually produced an explosion powerful enough to dislodge a small chunk of asphalt.

The grenade version was similar, but instead of making a hole in the ground, you poured the sulfur shavings into a hollow brass tube. Then you placed the nail into it and threw the device as far as you could. It sparked and exploded on impact.

A more advanced improvised hand grenade involved carbide, a special substance used in construction to make cement. Carbide came in the form of little white pebbles that stank and were hot to the touch. When thrown into water, these pebbles gave off acetylene, a gas used in welding.

A handful of carbide meant fun and games for days, if not weeks. First you poured some water into a glass bottle. Then you stuffed a layer of dry grass over it. Then you carefully sprinkled a layer of carbide pebbles onto the grass. Next, you corked the bottle, shook it so that the water and the pebbles would touch, and threw it as hard as you could immediately. The bottle would blow up in the air, sending glass shrapnel everywhere. That was fun! Of course, being responsible children from academic families, we never blew up these grenades in our own courtyards, only in the empty lots, remote park corners, or construction sites where we usually stole the carbide from in the first place.

One day, a boy from another school who lived in our building gave me a fascinating recipe. If one took some photographic fixer mix, ground it very finely, and then mixed it with a pill's worth of Hydroperite (urea nitrogen peroxide), the resulting compound would spontaneously combust. Both components were easy enough to find. I already had the photographic fixer, and Hydroperite was a popular disinfectant, readily available at any pharmacy. The next day, I brought the two components to school. After classes were over, I told Vova and a bunch of my other friends not to leave, because I had something awesome to show them. I led them over to a dead-end hallway and mixed the powders on a windowsill.

The kid didn't lie; the reaction worked beautifully. White smoke instantly filled the air around us. Suddenly, a teacher appeared from behind our backs and began to yell at us. This was unexpected. Fortunately, he wasn't one of our teachers and didn't know us by name, so instead of following him to the principal's office, we all looked at one another and ran. But the burned spot remained on the windowsill for a long time, attracting curious glances and inspiring rumors. Eventually, the sill was repainted, but the school custodian must've been out of white paint, because the whole thing got painted pale yellow. It became a point of pride for me: I had left my mark on my old school.

At age eleven, I discovered magnesium bombs. Their biggest drawback was that they required a ready supply of this metal and the only way to score a meaningful quantity of it was through scavenging. One day, Vova and I received intel from some other boys that we ought to check out the garbage dump by the airport. We thought about it for a while. The airport was so far from our familiar stomping grounds in the city center that it might as well have been in another city. We had never ventured such a distance on our own before. We considered our odds of making it there and back alive and intact.

"What sort of *gopniks** are there?" I asked Vova.

"Very nasty motherfuckers," he replied confidently. "Much worse than in the center. They all carry *zatochkas*,** and they throw them. And they hate kids from other districts."

"Shit. What about the cops?"

"Much worse, too. They would pick us up without any questions and report us straight to the principal."

"Shit, shit. There may be soldiers, too." I sighed.

But we decided to chance it. The next Sunday, Vova and I—two nerdy, relatively well-dressed mama's boys from the posh downtown—took the subway to the end of the line, then got on a bus out of town, and then walked for two or three

*Soviet hoodlums
**Sharp metal pikes

kilometers. Along the way, we still wondered what kind of security we'd find at the dump. Would there be a barbed-wire fence? Guard dogs?

At last, we arrived and saw that there were no guards or dogs, and the chain-link fence had no barbed wire. What it did have was holes—lots and lots of holes. We picked one and squeezed through without much effort. The dump was even better than we had imagined: a cemetery for old abandoned aircraft. A dozen or so civil and military airplanes stood all around us in various states of decay and mutilation. Some had clearly been placed there only recently; others, with pieces missing from their fuselages and their bodies nearly crumbling into dust, did not resemble any aircraft known to us. The smell of kerosene filled the moist air. We scanned the lot for movement, but everything was still. Only a cold wind brushed through the long grass growing between the decaying corpses of former helicopters and fighter jets.

Metal files in hand, we began to climb all over the machinery, testing various metallic surfaces that caught our eye. Aluminum and magnesium are hard to tell apart visually (both are silvery), and we had no particular use for aluminum. To test what we found, we would file off some shavings from a metal part of the aircraft carcass and set them on fire. If the shavings burst into bright white flame, then the part was made of magnesium, and we would set to harvesting it with special metal saws.

Over the next few weeks, we spent most of our leisure time after school filing down into metal dust a piece we'd recovered from one particular retired airplane at the "cemetery." Eventually, we had enough. It was time to make the actual *vzryv-paket* (explosive charge).

We took some potassium permanganate, which was a disinfectant that pharmacies sold in the form of dark violet crystals, and mixed it with some of our magnesium powder. Then we packed the mix into an empty matchbox and wrapped ten layers of sticky tape around the package. Now all we needed was a fuse. Once more, matches came to the rescue. We taped a bunch of them together, head to head, in a straight line, went outside behind the garages in the courtyard, lit the last match, and ran to safety. The matchbox finally caught fire, and *kaboom!* A fireball. It was one of the most satisfying moments of my life thus far.

If you're wondering how I kept this dangerous hobby from my family, the answer's simple: I didn't. They knew all about it and didn't care much. In fact, my mom, a chemist herself, bought me a Soviet children's chemistry set. It contained an alcohol burner, glass test tubes, special boiling tubes to put over the burner's flame, some plastic bottles containing various liquid concoctions, and a bunch of chemicals in little baggies. What it didn't have were gloves or safety goggles.

Unfortunately, my fascination with explosives came to a head one Sunday afternoon.

Vova and I had spent most of the day making a particularly potent magnesium bomb. Now we were sitting on the windowsill of my room's open window and congratulating each other on a job well done. The only question left was when and where to blow it up.

"Why not now?" I suggested.

We looked around. There were younger kids playing in the courtyard, but they weren't nearby. Since this particular bomb would produce no shrapnel, we decided to go for it.

I lit the matchbox and tossed the bomb out into the courtyard. One of the little kids, who had been watching us, saw something getting thrown out the window and dashed toward the mysterious object.

I yelled in panic, "STAY BACK! IT'S GONNA BLOW!"

The infernal device exploded into a three-meter pillar of orange flames. The boom echoed loudly throughout the whole courtyard. The kid who'd run over was unharmed but terrified; the bomb had exploded right in front of him.

Immediately, a pack of grandmothers who had been sitting on benches and watching the children play began to gather under our window.

"What is this?"

"Whose kids are you?"

"Are you out of your minds?"

"We're calling the police!"

Eventually, the racket attracted Grandma's attention. When she came out to the window and the grandmothers started yelling at her instead, I realized that I was in major trouble.

To get ourselves away from the line of grandmotherly fire, Vova and I ran out of the apartment and up to the third floor of our building. There was a small window by the staircase there from which we could eavesdrop on the argument unfolding below. For a while, it seemed that our goose was cooked, and that the horde of grandmothers was going to storm the third floor and drag us to the nearest police station.

Eventually, though, the frightened boy went home, the shouting ended, and the vengeful mob dispersed. But my passion for bomb making was soured for good.

* * *

Homemade IEDs aside, our lives were generally peaceful. There were occasional minor fights between boys at school, but overall, our neighborhood was quite safe: no murders, robberies, or anything of the sort.

I had only one memorable run-in with a *gopnik*, and it was over my bike. I was riding to visit Vova, who lived about ten minutes away. Suddenly, some big kid came out from around the corner and grabbed my bike.

"Lemme have a go," he demanded.

It was perfectly obvious that he wanted to steal it. I was short and small; fighting him was a losing proposition. So I decided to be sneaky. Down the street was a man walking, dressed in a military uniform. I watched him and made sure the other kid noticed him, too.

"Why don't we get off the street and into the courtyard?" I suggested. "You can ride it there. I don't want you riding it out on the street."

The boy agreed, now wary of having his delinquency observed by the serviceman. He turned around to head into the courtyard and let go of my bike. As soon as he had taken one step away, I took off at full speed and left him behind. For about a year after that, I took a different route to Vova's house.

Most children walked everywhere alone. Parents only walked their kids to and from school on their first couple of days so that they could remember the way. After that, they were expected to manage on their own.

I had my first solitary ramble when I was five. Grandma and I were walking home from kindergarten. On the way, we came across a line for milk sausages at a nearby store. Grandma could not pass up such an opportunity. So she spoke to the last person in the queue, asking them to remember her face, then walked me to our courtyard. Before she returned to the shop, she instructed me as follows:

"Now you go straight home, Serezha. No playing in the courtyard. Knock on the door hard. Mom is home; she'll open the door for you. Got it? Repeat everything back to me."

I repeated everything, waved to her as she went back to the store, and went home. At the door, being too short to reach the doorbell, I started knocking—politely at first, then with both hands, and finally with my feet. No one answered.

A line for sausages was a serious business. I knew it could easily be an hour or more before Grandma came back with her haul. So I ran back to find her. I didn't know how to cross streets safely yet, so I just walked with the rest of the pedestrian pack. I also had only a vague idea of where the store was located, but I figured I was bound to find it eventually. No one batted an eye at seeing a five-year-old preschooler out by himself, crossing streets as he searched for the sausage crowd. Ten minutes later, I found the queue and reunited with Grandma, who was not too surprised to see me.

No one worried that a child might get abducted off the street. However, if the same child misbehaved, for instance by laughing too loudly with friends at a bus stop, it was considered perfectly all right for an adult stranger to "make a remark" to them, like, "Young man, you are making too much noise. This is not an appropriate way to behave in public." A child on the receiving end of such a remark was expected to correct his behavior immediately. Of course, we usually did so, then stuck our tongues out at the adults as soon as their backs were turned. But still, we complied. (These days, of course, approaching an unknown child in the street in Russia for any reason, let alone in an attempt to discipline him, could have consequences ranging from a blast of pepper spray to a fist in your face.)

* * *

If topics of social designation—like whether one was a *gopnik* or from a good family, or from central Leningrad or the city outskirts—were discussed among us kids, we really did not care, and we never talked about ethnicity. In my class, we had an Armenian girl, a Georgian boy, two Ukrainians, and many Jewish kids. I never saw anyone pick on them. I remember when we were talking about our future college plans, my friend Sasha Lesman said that he would not be applying to Leningrad State University, as he was Jewish and would not get in. This was quite shocking to me, and it was the first time after years of friendship that the point of his ethnicity surfaced.

However, the topic of Jewishness had been ingrained in the Soviet adults' DNA and equally in government affairs. Jews were always among the first to be suspected of undermining the Soviet state. This was particularly absurd, as the largest part of the leading revolutionaries and officials of the young Soviet state were Jewish. In my time, pogroms and "the doctors' plot"* were long in the past, and only harassment-lite remained. Everyone knew, for instance, that securing a spot at a prestigious university, where admission was theoretically entirely based on test scores, was impossible for a Jewish kid, however talented. As for the more modest Soviet colleges, these had unofficial admission quotas. When an otherwise well-qualified Jewish student was denied admission, he was said to have "flunked the fifth article"—ethnicity was listed on line five of one's internal passport.

But on a day-to-day level, one rarely saw instances of anti-Semitism. We lived in downtown Leningrad, where many residents were Jewish and certainly weren't the odd man out.

The odd man out, weirdly enough, was myself. I looked Jewish. Grandma was always on the lookout to ensure that none of the more Semitic aspects of my appearance were

---

*In 1952, the government accused a group of prominent doctors, most of them Jewish, of plotting to poison high-ranking party officials. These allegations drove an anti-Semitic campaign in the Soviet press.

highlighted. Similarly to how she gave delicate aesthetic instructions to my circumcision surgeon, Grandma hovered nearby whenever Mom was cutting my hair in the middle of the kitchen, and made straightforward stylistic demands like, "Vera, leave enough hair to cover his ears! You don't want him to look like a little Jew, do you?"

Not that it helped much. For all of Mom's styling efforts, I still looked suspiciously ethnic. And, frankly, I always felt somewhat of a kinship with the Jewish kids, because my own national origins were murky and irregular. Neither Grandma nor Mom ever pretended to be either Russian or Soviet, except on official documents: their tastes and points of view were always very distinct from those positioned as "normal" for the Soviets. I myself never felt any connection to Russian folklore or the songs that permeated the media. Mawkish Russianness harnessed to the government propaganda machine outraged my young but already cosmopolitan and snobbish mind.

In any case, the fifth line of my own passport proclaimed me "Russian."

In my forties, I took a DNA test and discovered something interesting: evidently, quite a bit of me *is* actually Sephardic, through my French, Greek, and Italian ancestry. Good eye, Grandma!

August 19, 2011

There were no direct flights between Florence and Saint Petersburg. My connection was through Munich Airport. After takeoff, I watched the sensibly arranged German landscape recede underneath and enjoyed the first of many libations courtesy of Lufthansa's liberal business-class alcohol policy.

To a ten-year-old me, everything around me would have looked like a scene from a science-fiction film. Flying on a Boeing airplane between cities in Europe? Unimaginable. Even movies about children stepping through a magic door into the Communist future never showed their protagonists traveling to the West. At most, they might go to a planet from a faraway galaxy or another dimension. But Munich? Florence? That was too far-out.

Next to me, a fashionably unshaved guy in a green sweater started watching *Breaking Bad* on an iPad. I found myself looking over his shoulder.

I never speak to anyone on planes. Air time is me time. But this time around, it was as if some magnet inside me reversed polarity.

"That's a great show," I said. "Probably the best ever. Which season are you on?"

"Third. But I'm rewatching it. It's my favorite, too."

We got to chatting about TV, then about film, then about the financial markets and the likelihood of another correction, then about our lives. Ulrika, our curvaceous German flight attendant, did her utmost to stimulate this discourse by occasionally topping up our wineglasses.

Jonas turned out to be an asset manager from Zurich, flying to Saint Petersburg to meet with his Russian girlfriend. She had been trying to get out of the country to move in with him for two years, but her visa kept getting rejected. Western countries don't like to give visas to young unmarried Russian girls, and when you are rejected by one country, you will be rejected by others. Now Jonas commuted to Saint Petersburg to see her every other weekend.

If you had asked me the day before if I often accepted rides from strangers, I would've said never. But by then, our tender drunken feelings had practically turned Jonas and I into blood brothers. So when Jonas's girlfriend met him at the airport and they offered to give me a lift to Nevsky Prospect, I said yes.

Getting out of the car by my hotel, I was filled with an uplifting feeling of universal brotherhood—an entirely novel sense for me. Mixed as it was with my sadness over losing Grandma, I was plunged into a sort of luminous hopeful melancholy.

I never saw or got in touch with Jonas again. Our brotherhood dissipated with the alcohol fumes.

As I was falling asleep, I tried not to think about the two days ahead. I knew what awaited me: tedious Russian bureaucracy, awkward encounters with relatives, and lots of vodka. And in the midst of all that, there would be no moment for me to reflect on the meaning or the magnitude of Grandma's death.

CHAPTER 8

ON TV

One old man tells another, "I don't know why the kids are going nuts for these Beatles guys. They sound like crap."

"Where did you hear the Beatles?" asks the other.

"Boris Borisovich hummed some of their stuff for me."

AS THE YEARS passed, my love of Western culture grew. But every aspect of Soviet life seemed to conspire to keep it from me. Until I was eleven, there were only two television channels in Leningrad: Channel One, which broadcast nationwide from Moscow, and Leningrad regional television, which only started broadcasting in the midafternoon.

Color television sets were hard to get and expensive. At home, we had only a black-and-white TV. When you turned it on, it took five full minutes to start showing images, because the lamps inside it needed to warm up. So ten or so minutes before our cartoons were due to come on, Grandma would tell me and Alyosha to go switch on the TV to warm it up.

Understandably, television in the Soviet Union was commercial-free. Between shows, an announcer came on to tell the audience about the next program or read out the schedule for tomorrow. It was nice but not really necessary, because everyone subscribed to *Programma*, the weekly TV guide with a detailed schedule for the week ahead. It also said whether a show would be transmitted in black and white or in color. Every Saturday, Grandma would get out her copy and circle all the shows she planned to watch the next week.

Tolya's favorite show, which we often watched together on Saturday afternoons, was *Evident, but Incredible*, a popular science show covering cutting-edge discoveries and research. It was hosted by Sergey Kapitsa, a leading Soviet physicist and the son of a Cambridge-educated Nobel laureate. Grandma was also fond of the show *Health*, which was hosted by Dr. Yulia Belyanchikova and consistently got top ratings due to the general Russian tendency toward hypochondria. Dr. Belyanchikova was a tall blonde with a full figure and a soothing voice. Vova once told me that he had seen pictures of her naked. I knew he was lying, but even so, the seed was planted: the bosomy presenter became an object of my prepubescent erotic fantasies for quite some time.

Like everything else in Brezhnev's Russia, television programming mostly stayed the same, year in and year out. Shows that I watched as a young child were still on the air ten years later, usually with the same characters and the same actors and anchors. When anything changed about the shows people watched—a new host, a new time slot, even a new opening or closing credit sequence—it was a big deal. In a world of ultimate stability, innovations were not welcome.

On weekdays, children's programming was limited to *Good Night, Little Ones!*—an after-dinner show somewhat reminiscent of *Sesame Street*—and the occasional ten-minute cartoon.

Other kiddies' shows were aired all at once on Sunday mornings. For those who got up early, there was a morning exercise show at 8:45 a.m. Not exactly wild stuff, but it made for cheery background noise to one's morning buckwheat porridge. At 9:30, I watched the always-entertaining *Alarm Clock*, which had cartoons and funny skits. Then, for no discernible reason, the viewer was subjected to the hour-long show *Sluzhu Sovetskomu Soyuzu*, the title of which translates to "I serve the Soviet Union."* It was, as you might guess, a show for servicemen. Why it got sandwiched so awkwardly in the middle of children's Sunday matinees was a mystery. I'm guessing the authorities figured it was never too early for children to start looking forward to their mandatory stint in the army. Finally, at 11:00, it was time for *Morning Mail*, a musical revue. After that came arguably the dullest TV show on the entire planet, *Rural Hour*, which was for and about collective farmers. That was a perfect time to go work on some minor explosive device or just bugger off to the park to play.

* * *

Today, kids all over the world watch, wear, write with, and eat off the same merchandise derived from Disney's and Pixar's cartoon creations. Soviet children were raised on a very different diet of characters to their Western counterparts. Although these characters were occasionally of Western origin, the cartoons they starred in were always domestic.

The most popular cartoon in the USSR, *Nu, Pogodi!* (*Just You Wait!*) was about a wolf chasing a rabbit, with understandable intentions. Each episode was only fifteen minutes long,

---

Standard response given by soldiers being promoted or decorated in front of the troops

and there weren't that many of them. New episodes came out only once every year or two, and premiered, with great fanfare, on the TV show *Kinopanorama*.

Then there were Cheburashka and Gena, the stars of another very popular stop-motion series. Cheburashka was an odd tropical beastie that got shipped to the USSR by accident in a crate of oranges. He had huge round ears and looked somewhat like the love child of Minnie Mouse and a black-skinned Winnie the Pooh. Gena, on the other hand, was a perfectly normal, civilized crocodile. He wore a fedora and a suit with a tie, and he played the accordion. He and Cheburashka made friends with all sorts of people and critters around their town, while constantly being undermined by a mean old crone in an old-fashioned hat, and her pet rat, who lived in her purse.

Then there was Neznajka, literally "Know-Nothing Kid." He was a fidgety, academically challenged boy who always wore a bright blue hat, canary-yellow trousers, an orange shirt, and a green tie. He and his friends, known as "shorties," lived in Flower City. Although they were described as being "the size of a medium cucumber," they still got up to some big adventures. One of these was a trip to the moon, which was a crude stand-in for the capitalist West. Upon arrival, the naive shorties, spoiled by their cushy Communist lifestyle, discovered that everything on the moon cost money—which was predictably enumerated in cents rather than kopecks—and were immediately thrown in jail for not having any.

Not all cartoon characters were Russian in origin. There was also Buratino—namely Carlo Collodi's Pinocchio, whose story was "rewritten" by Aleksey Tolstoy in 1936 with somewhat different characters and adventures. The moral of the story was also updated; unlike Pinocchio, Tolstoy's Buratino never abandons his mischievous ways, nor does he become a real boy. Instead, he learns the value of staying true to his friends and himself—a new moral for a new century.

Soviet children were also lucky enough to know Kiddo and Karlsson in their cartoon incarnations. These two were created by the Swedish author Astrid Lindgren, whom Western kids know best from her Pippi Longstocking books. Karlsson was a short, stout (if not to say egg-shaped) middle-aged man with a propeller attached to his back. He lived on some unspecified roof. All the stories revolved around him regularly visiting a certain seven-year-old boy called Kiddo while he was home alone, doing all sorts of fun things together with him, and forbidding him to speak of these visitations to any adult. Truly, the world was much more innocent in the '70s.

Unlike kids, adults got no reprieve from propaganda. There was only one main evening newscast, *Vremya* (*Time*), which aired at 9 p.m. sharp. Most adults watched it for the lack of anything else to watch. (It was aired by all channels simultaneously.) It contained very little in the way of actual news and was primarily a medium for government propaganda. During my first two years at school, I was sent off to bed when the show started in the evenings. I had trouble falling asleep and usually only nodded off while listening to the weather report music. It was an instrumental rendition of André Popp's melancholy song "Manchester and Liverpool." Not that I knew that at the time, of course. I just lay there, lullabied by this downhearted melody full of existential languor. After the news, there was usually one more program or movie shown, and the channel signed off by 11 p.m.—the recommended bedtime for all good Soviet workers and peasants. After all, they had a long day of building Communism ahead of them.

But the appeal of all these shows was destroyed once I caught a glimpse of Western animation as a kid. I happened upon it while watching a TV documentary about world cinema that involved a short overview of American animation. It was presented in the spirit of investigative reporting rather than entertainment, and was conclusively negative. I did get to see a few snippets of *Snow White*, and Tom and Jerry chasing each other and smashing plates wildly. It looked bizarre, ultra chaotic, and very fun, unlike anything on Soviet TV.

This is how I recounted the short scene to Vova, who missed the documentary:

"Check it," I said, relishing his envy. "The cat had all these plates stacked on top of one another, and the pile was, like, two meters high! Then he tried to carry it, and it was wobbling back and forth, like whoa, whoa! And the mouse—BANG!—whacked the cat on the ass with a stick, and all the plates fell down on the cat's head one after another! Ha! Ha! Ha!"

"You know, in America they have cartoons where everybody's naked," Vova mused with an air of solemn confidence.

I was going to tell him about another sequence they'd shown, from *Snow White*, but suddenly realized there was no point. Besides, Vova and I were already in perfect agreement: American cartoons were the coolest, and American kids must've been the happiest buggers in the world.

CHAPTER 9

THE PRINTED WORD

A woman brings Leo Tolstoy's *War and Peace* to a typing pool and asks to get it typed.

"Why?" asks the typist, surprised. "It's not forbidden. You can buy it in a bookstore."

"I know; I just want my teenage children to want to read it!"

THE USSR LIKED to boast that the Soviet people were the most literate in the world. This was probably true. People had so few options for keeping themselves entertained that it was either read or drink.

Soviet reverence for books often crossed over into consumerist fetishism. Books as physical objects were "deficit" goods, so most family libraries had to be painstakingly assembled over the course of many years. Like all Soviet industries, publishing was planned centrally and not attuned to supply and demand. To make matters worse, bookstores had to reserve a substantial amount of shelf space for ideological and propaganda publications: the collected works of Lenin, patriotic literature, and monographs and autobiographies by Communist Party leaders.

If someone yearned to reread Brezhnev's war memoirs or browse the minutes of the latest CPSU congress, then any bookstore was at their service. But of course, no one read that crap—not even Brezhnev himself, since every single one of his literary works was ghostwritten. Yet the bookstores still had to stock them, which left less shelf space for books people actually wanted to read. Getting your hands on a Russian translation of Alexandre Dumas's *The Three Musketeers* was a quest worthy of the musketeers themselves. The same went for anything by Jules Verne or Agatha Christie, and as for Arthur Conan Doyle, Professor Moriarty was as elusive in Soviet bookstores as he was in London's underbelly.

One way to acquire books was through recycling efforts. In this area, the Soviet Union was, by necessity, way ahead of its Western rivals. Every twenty kilos of paper would get them a special coupon they could use at a bookstore to buy a book—or rather, to buy the right to buy a book, since you still had to pay full price for it. And so, voracious Soviet readers collected newspapers, cultivated friendships with people in the publishing industry, and in general did everything possible to grow their libraries. Their means were not always legal. One of my cousins was married to a man who made his living by dealing books on the black market, the same way a young man might deal drugs in the West. Eventually, he got caught by the authorities and was sentenced to four years in prison. My cousin ended up divorcing him.

Books were kept in the family for generations. My grandma still hung on to her *Brockhaus and Efron Encyclopedia*, which she got from her older sister, Tatiana Klado. Being of noble origin, Tatiana spent a large part of her adult life in labor camps and in exile in Siberia. She had left all her most treasured possessions with Grandma back in Leningrad, the encyclopedias among them. Over the years, Grandma (who luckily escaped serious prosecution by being just one year old when the Revolution happened) gradually sold off the family antiques and knickknacks, but she kept the encyclopedia as a memento of her sister. Its twenty-nine volumes, which were published in 1917, had survived the Revolution, confiscation raids on our family's property, the Civil War, and the Siege of Leningrad.

* * *

Despite the Soviet obsession with literacy, the literary curriculum in our schools was rather narrow. Mostly it focused on "the classics," namely works by Pushkin, Tolstoy, Dostoyevsky, and other literary luminaries from the nineteenth century. All texts were meticulously curated to convey total congruence with Communist ideals.

At the end of every school year, teachers would issue summer reading lists, which, like many things in the USSR, were only nominally optional. So when Grandma and I were on summer vacation in Estonia, I would visit the local library and dutifully check out all the required books, even though they bored the stuffing out of me. No thirteen-year-old has any business slogging through 1,500 pages of *War and Peace*. The brilliance of these books only dawned on me when I reread them decades later. It's hard to forge a genuine connection with a literary classic as part of a homework assignment. As for literary analysis, there was no discussion of themes or authorial intentions: we received the correct opinions prepackaged from the teachers, and regurgitated them back onto paper in our exam essays.

Reading for pleasure was a very different matter. In our spare time, my peers and I mostly read foreign literature in translation. Adventure stories by Dumas, Kipling, and Jack

London; detective stories by Arthur Conan Doyle and Agatha Christie; sci-fi by Jules Verne or Isaac Asimov—these books were the real lifeblood of our childhood. I read practically all of Dumas in bed after curfew, with a flashlight under the bed-cover to avoid Grandma noticing.

Why was I so crazy about Dumas? Sure, there were adventures, and drama, and passions of all kinds, and intrigue, but deep down I devoured his books because Dumas, while a bit dated, was still a Western writer, offering me a glimpse of a richer material world. In his books, people didn't wear shapeless Red Triangle Factory coats with no waist and lopsided shoulders; they wore cerulean doublets and gold-embroidered baldrics. They did not dine on stale mass-produced macaroni or meatballs with cockroaches, but rather on pheasants and fine cheeses. And while Soviet children's literature boasted plenty of heroic accounts of Young Pioneers or Komsomol adolescents laying down their lives for the motherland during World War II, none of said Pioneers ever ate veal cutlets or drank champagne while under musket fire in a besieged fortress.

But the real joy came from reading banned literature. I don't mean this in any vague "100 Banned Books" sense that Americans use to entice apathetic youth into libraries. These books were genuinely illegal. Possessing them was a criminal offense punishable by a prison sentence. Naturally, any book that was placed on the forbidden list became a huge underground hit.

There were two kinds of forbidden books. First, there were books that had been printed in some form in the USSR once upon a time but then subsequently banned and taken out of circulation. For example, a censored version of Mikhail Bulgakov's *The Master and Margarita* was serialized in a magazine in 1967, but was never printed as a separate book.

Aleksandr Solzhenitsyn's *One Day in the Life of Ivan Denisovich* was also first published in a literary magazine, during the Khrushchev Thaw. But after a few years, the authorities cooled on Solzhenitsyn's exposés of the Soviet labor camp world, and from that point on, his works had to be disseminated illegally. Luckily, Tolya still had both books from his youth. His *The Master and Margarita* was a photocopy, likely made at some research institute by an intrepid grad student.

The second kind of banned books were those that had never been published in the USSR at all. Authors like Voinovich and Zamyatin were branded anti-Soviet from the get-go, as was the Bohemian "parasite" poet Joseph Brodsky. In fact, any Russian writers and philosophers who criticized the USSR or Communism in any way were right out.

Although banned books could not be printed or distributed through legal channels, they were nonetheless widely read within intelligentsia circles thanks to *samizdat*, or "self-publishing." This meant borrowing a banned book from a friend, retyping it at home on a typewriter through carbon paper, and distributing the resulting copies to trusted friends for recopying and further dissemination.

People produced and acquired *samizdat* books as much to make a private statement of dissent as to read. Here and there, usually at house parties, one heard mysterious half-whispers, such as a famous innuendo, "Erika takes four." (Erika was a reliable brand of East German typewriter that could yield up to four legible carbon copies.) Typewriters were the main copying method for *samizdat*, but they were not the only way. At scientific institutes and in research centers, people would reproduce books on huge, clunky computers with continuous-feed paper. In the end, the book would come out on one long sheet with perforated edges and could then be rolled into a scroll.

In addition to *samizdat*, there was also *tamizdat*—namely, "published over there," meaning abroad (i.e., in the Russian émigré press). These books were produced in far-off and exotic locations like Paris, West Berlin, or Ann Arbor, and obtaining them required very special connections in dissident circles. *Tamizdat* books were smuggled into the USSR by foreign tourists. For instance, there was a group of brave women from France who made regular trips into the USSR, bringing in literature almost in bulk before they were eventually busted. How they kept getting past the customs inspectors for so long remains a mystery.

Because *samizdat* literature was both scarce and dangerous to own, few people kept it in the house permanently. Most of these books were in permanent circulation. The standard lending period was two days. That's how long I had to read the copy of Nabokov's *Lolita* given to me by a friend in tenth grade before I had to return it. Two hundred pages the first evening and two hundred more the next. Of course, adding a "race against the clock" aspect to what was already an act of political rebellion only made *samizdat* more alluring.

* * *

When I was thirteen, I accidentally stumbled upon a literary treasure trove. It happened while I was performing my monthly Young Pioneer duties—namely recycling paper. Every schoolchild had to collect and bring to school at least five kilograms of paper on the first of every month.

Alyosha and I filled our paper quota with newspapers. In the USSR, most people were obligated to subscribe to newspapers. Which ones and how many depended on where the person worked and whether they were members of the Communist

Party. All Young Pioneers had to subscribe to *Pioneer Pravda*, all the older kids to *Komsomol Pravda*, and all members of the Communist Party to the actual daily *Pravda*. It's no surprise that the Soviet Union consistently set and beat all kinds of world records for newspaper circulation. Tolya was a party member and had to subscribe to both *Pravda* and *Leningrad Pravda*. Both of them went straight from the postbox directly into the recycling stack. Then on the first of every month, Alyosha and I would tie them up into packs with twine and carry them to school. Besides these pro forma publications, Tolya also subscribed to the much more engaging *Soviet Sport* and *Football & Hockey*, which he actually did read.

One day during recess, as I was wandering through the piles of paper in the school courtyard to see what my schoolmates had brought this month, I came across a thin stack of old *Time* magazines. Real ones, in English. I almost fainted. It was like stumbling on a treasure chest heaped with gold. Who had thrown such prized contraband away? Whose parents even had access to *Time* magazine? Whatever possessed them to recycle them? *Time* was sold in exactly one location in Leningrad: the press kiosk at Evropejskaya, the main hotel for foreign visitors. The kiosk was for hotel guests only, and it only accepted dollars. Regular Soviet citizens were not allowed inside. Regular Soviet people were also not allowed to own dollars, under threat of severe criminal penalties. In short, regular Soviet people and *Time* magazine did not belong in the same universe.

Needless to say, I collected every single one of these magazines, took them home, and cherished them for years to come. Whenever I got bored, I would pull one of them from the stack and leaf through it, reading the titles and looking at the photographs. My English wasn't good enough to read the articles themselves, but I would look at the pictures and imagine myself against the colorful, exotic backgrounds. What would it be like to be around such luxury? Automobiles, skyscrapers, people in colorful, well-fitting clothes . . . These pictures kept the flame of my dreams alive.

CHAPTER 10

BIG SCREENS, SMALL TAPES

"Comrade Brezhnev, do you have a hobby?"

"Yes, I collect popular jokes about myself."

"And how many have you already collected?"

"About three and a half labor camps."

"OF ALL THE arts," wrote Vladimir Lenin in 1922, "the most important for us is the cinema." Sixty years later, this was definitely still the case for me and my friends. Of course, Lenin was referencing cinema's potential as a tool of propaganda. For me and my friends, it was pure escapism.

Our reality was tedious enough to warrant maximum escaping. Whenever we got together on weekends, or even on weekdays after school, the odds were good that we would swing by a movie theater and check out what was playing. There was no other easy way to find out—no phone number to call for showtimes, no publication to consult. Going to the movies was always an adventure.

There were several movie theaters in our neighborhood. A children's matinee ticket cost ten kopecks; regular tickets cost thirty. Some cinemas had cafés inside where you could buy ice cream before the show. The saleslady would weigh your waffle cup several times before giving it to you. If you paid twenty kopecks for two hundred grams of ice cream, then you were getting your regulation two hundred grams of ice cream, not an iota more or less. You had to eat it fast: food was not allowed in the screening room. As for popcorn or Coke, the nearest place to buy them was probably Miehikkälä or Kuurmanpohja two hundred kilometers away, on the other side of the Soviet-Finnish border.

The movie-rating system was simple: there were movies that admitted everyone and movies only for people aged sixteen and over. Nevertheless, even the movies rated 16+ were censored to within an inch of their lives, not just for ideological content but also for propriety. The Soviet Union enforced a strict no-nipple policy.

In the mid-'80s, however, censorship started to loosen. This did nothing to improve the overall quality of Soviet movies, but it did allow for some daring imports. One awful Polish flick called *The New Amazons* broke all Soviet box office records, because it featured several frontal glimpses of topless women. One of my school chums, Sasha, who had an entrepreneurial streak, would actually skip school to stand in hour-long lines for tickets to its showings. There was a limit of four tickets per customer, so scalping opportunities were limited. He would buy his allotted quota, then return to the end of the queue, again and again. Then Sasha resold the tickets at our school for a substantial markup, charging eighty kopecks for a ticket that had cost him thirty. I, too, was one of his customers. That movie ticket got me two memorable things: a cocked-eyebrow, *You are clearly going far in life, young man* look from Grandma; and my first erection.

To be shown in the USSR, Western movies had to be completely child-safe and either entirely apolitical or political in a way that favored the Soviet viewpoint on world affairs. *All the President's Men*, for instance, was released in Soviet theaters right along with the rest of the world, since it detailed the corruption of Richard Nixon's administration. The Italian film *Save the Concorde* was allowed because it depicted an American corporate plot to sabotage a French Concorde aircraft. There was also a very popular American movie called *Capricorn One*, about how NASA faked a Mars landing. That one starred, of all people, a future veteran of the American justice system, O. J. Simpson.

Regardless of genre or subject matter, all foreign movies were insanely popular and would run in the theaters for months on end. People went to see them over and over. Vova and I could easily see the same foreign movie three, five, ten times. One judged a movie's quality by how often one felt compelled to rewatch it.

But my love of cinema exploded when, at age thirteen, I learned about the existence of VCRs. My classmate Anton's father was the manager of a taxi company—a stratospheric job rich in connections and unwritten privileges in the Soviet economy—and he had somehow gotten his hands on one of these devices. Sometimes, when Anton's parents were out, my friends and I went to his place to watch flicks like *Emmanuelle*, *The Fruit Is Ripe*, or *Once Upon a Time in America*. Not from start to finish, of course—just the bits with boobies in them. These scenes we would watch over and over. We appreciated Anton's hospitality and the danger it put him in. These films were risky to own, but even riskier to watch with friends; having people over to view them could land one in jail for "distribution of pornography."

Even though VCR ownership was never widespread in the USSR, the devices were a significant contributing factor to the country's eventual downfall. Until VCRs came about, Soviet people knew American movies only from heavily curated imports or else from denunciations made by the Soviet media that such and such a film was nothing more than anti-Soviet propaganda. VCRs brought with them a whole new wave of cultural experiences. Suddenly, the Iron Curtain became more like a flimsy see-through shower curtain.

I accepted Western movie stars into my own panoply of celebrities without any second thoughts. Since action films were the first ones to trickle through the borders, actors like Arnold Schwarzenegger, Chuck Norris, Jean-Claude van Damme, and Bruce Lee quickly became my favorites. But the unquestionable king of the Soviet underground video scene was Sylvester Stallone. To some extent, the Soviet authorities had only themselves to blame for his stratospheric popularity. Every magazine and newspaper that touched on the subject of Hollywood sleaze made sure to take a swipe at Stallone and his awful "anti-Soviet" movies. After reading about his films so often, Soviet citizens (myself included) naturally wanted nothing more than to see them.

Mom and Tolya had friends who had worked in Iran and brought a VCR back with them to Leningrad. The news of this purchase quickly made the rounds among all their friends and acquaintances. My brother and I whined and begged to be taken along whenever my parents went to visit them. Finally, it worked. At their place I first saw *Rambo*, *Rocky*, *Lone Wolf McQuade*, *From Russia with Love*, *Police Academy*, and *Enter the Dragon*.

It was like watching the life of aliens through a telescope. Everything about the films—the stories, the characters, and the places—was so utterly different and so much cooler than what we normally watched or experienced.

Every time, Alyosha and I went home amazed that there were people out there who lived in those realities every day. It seemed so different than living in the world of *The Three Musketeers* or Sherlock Holmes.

* * *

My second-favorite escape from reality was music. As young teenagers, we were in a tough spot music-wise. The official Soviet music scene had nothing to offer us, or almost anyone, really. In 1983, the Ministry of Culture of the USSR decreed that all professional and amateur musicians, when giving concerts, had to devote 80 percent of their stage time to songs written by members of the Union of Composers of the USSR. The average age of those composers at the time was sixty, and the union had not accepted new members since 1973. Basically, pop music in the USSR was like that annoying uncle at a family reunion: old, lame, completely square, and absolutely convinced that he's still "hip" and "with it" and that all the kids look up to him.

Since official music stores sold nothing good, everyone did the same thing with records as they did with forbidden books: they copied them.

The technology for domestic *magnitizdat* (meaning "magnetic publishing")—i.e., recordings of Western rock and Soviet underground music—was not always user-friendly. Older folks used reel-to-reel recorders, with huge round metallic spools. My parents' baby boom generation favored LPs, however, making them required special equipment and materials. They were usually pressed at underground labs onto discarded plastic

X-ray images, and were consequently called LPs "on the bones." Having a Beatles or a Rolling Stones record on the bones was considered the height of countercultural chic.

The spread of cassettes and cassette players in the early '80s facilitated a *magnitizdat* breakthrough. Compared to reels and LPs, audiocassettes were very easy to both record and use. The trouble was getting ahold of them. Soviet-made blank cassettes were scarce and, at four rubles a pop, quite expensive. Also, their sound quality was fairly awful, and they could record only thirty minutes on either side. I hated Soviet tapes because whenever I copied a forty-five-minute album, I had to use both sides, and fifteen minutes of the precious tape would go to waste. This offended my thrifty sensibilities.

Around the time of the 1980 Moscow Olympics, the government started selling blank tapes from Japan. These were ninety minutes long, but they cost ten rubles, the equivalent of thirty-three cinema tickets or fifty ice creams. That year, an empty Japanese cassette tape was the most coveted New Year's present for kids like me. Denon, Maxell, TDK, JVC—these tapes were the stuff dreams were made of.

As with *samizdat*, where errors crept into each manuscript every time it was recopied, the quality of *magnitizdat* recordings degraded over time. Western albums brought into the country by some lucky kid's parents would be copied five, six, seven times—by the child's classmates, the classmates' friends, the friends' relatives, et cetera. After a certain number of copies, the actual music was practically drowned out by static.

Starting from the mid-1980s, dissemination of rock music, both domestic and foreign, was no longer prosecuted. Within a couple of years, "sound recording salons" began to pop up. These establishments charged one ruble per album to record proper high-quality music onto your blank cassettes from actual studio-grade reels. I often picked up some ABBA. They were super popular at the time, along with Boney M, a West German disco group who sang in English and looked very American: three girls and one guy, all of them black, which for the USSR was mega cool and exotic.

But the summer of 1984 saw the acquisition of my ultimate music purchase. I sold my foldable bike to a consignment shop for eighty rubles, added thirty rubles of precious birthday money, and bought myself a Walkman. Not a Sony Walkman, obviously, but some acceptable Taiwanese substitute. It came with headphones and had a fantastic sound quality. No screwdriver tempering required. (At the time, 110 rubles was my largest personal expenditure ever, and it was a significant amount by any measure: about a month's salary for a teacher or a junior engineer.)

On the day I got it, I went to bed with headphones on and decided to check out a tape I had copied recently from my classmate Max Shkud. He said it was of some black singer from America named Jackson, and the horror-music album was called "Thrilling." I had heard of the artist before and was skeptical, but decided to give it a shot.

I ended up listening to Michael Jackson's *Thriller* in one go in bed, with my eyes closed. And then, for weeks, I continued listening to it nonstop wherever I went. The singer's voice, wobbly and androgynous, resembled nothing I'd ever heard before in Soviet pop music, which was rock solid on classic gender normativity. And the songs themselves were rich, so filled with the freedom of creative experimentation. It felt like the singer really didn't care about what people thought of him. Even though I hadn't seen the music video, the title track seemed totally cinematic. I could envision the opening of coffins and the mist rolling through the graveyard.

Even today, when I hear "Human Nature" or "Billie Jean," I physically feel like I'm thirteen again, walking under a cold Leningrad drizzle with orange headphones on my ears.

CHAPTER 11

THE UNBEARABLE HEAVINESS OF SOVIET SCHOOLING

"Mom, today at school the principal asked if I had any younger brothers or sisters. I said that I'm the only child."

"And what did she say?"

"She said, 'Thank God!'"

AS ENJOYABLE AS these diversions were, they couldn't keep the Soviet bleakness at bay for long. I needed something greater in my life, something fulfilling. Since I couldn't fool myself into thinking that I was going to lend a hand to building a great Communist future, I tried to focus on my own future—namely, on academics.

In fifth grade, we began to study organic and inorganic chemistry, astronomy, physics, and ever more advanced math. These were multiyear courses, and none of them were optional. This emphasis on the STEM* subjects was no accident. As far as the Soviet authorities were concerned, the country had no need for more "lousy intelligentsia" like philologists, historians,

*Science, technology, engineering, and math

and rhetoric and composition specialists. It needed more engineers who could design superior nukes, faster warplanes, and quieter submarines.

We also kept up with our English. In general, foreign languages were studied quite diligently in the USSR, even those spoken in the capitalist West. Kids in regular schools were usually started on a foreign language in fourth grade; special-focus schools like mine did it earlier, in second grade. There were a couple of Hindi- and Chinese-intensive schools in Moscow, but otherwise the future socialist polyglots were oriented westward, toward the realm of the "probable enemy." English, French, and German dominated.

There were also a few other subjects, however, that my UK-educated children would not find familiar at all.

Nachalnaya voyennaya podgotovka, or NVP, translates to "basic military training"; however, it bore no resemblance to the grueling weeks of boot camp in the army. NVP was taught in a classroom setting, and it was compulsory for all boys and girls throughout the USSR, even though only boys were subjected to the draft.

Our NVP teacher was a very well-mannered World War II veteran. In his class, he taught us simple and useful life skills, such as how to assemble and disassemble a Kalashnikov, an AK-47 assault rifle, in less than thirty seconds. For those who've never tried it, give it a shot. The "Kalash," as it is known in Russia, is a beautiful and elegant machine of twelve easily assembled pieces. Pulling it apart and putting it back together is quite satisfying. Let no one tell you that schoolboys in Texas or Chicago grew up more privileged with respect to firearms than kids in the USSR. We would have been very surprised to hear that boys and girls in other parts of the world were not taught such an essential—and sexy—skill. One of the best weapons handlers at our school was a well-proportioned girl named Marina Anohina, two years younger than us. She could take apart and reassemble an AK-47 in eighteen seconds. I had a huge crush on her.

We also took part in those infamous drills of climbing under one's desk in the event of a nuclear attack. But we went a step further. Our instructor would yell out, "Flash to your left!" or "Flash to your right!" and we had to fall accordingly. Did you know there's a proper way to fall in case you see a nuclear explosion nearby? According to our instructor, you had to fall with your feet facing the blast, no matter how much you might want to look at it. As for what to do with your hands, there were two popular sayings among students on that: "Hold on to your head, to keep it from flying off," and "Hold your AK-47 away from your body so that the molten metal doesn't drip on your boots; the army will reuse them."

In NVP, we spent an inordinate amount of time discussing and preparing for nuclear war. It was the height of the Cold War, after all. Our classroom was festooned with war-readiness posters. Despite all that, none of us took this threat seriously. After the horrors of the struggle against Nazi Germany, who could ever wish for such a conflict again? So even when Soviet propaganda told us that America was promoting an arms race, and that its leaders were prepared to risk global annihilation, no one really bought it.

By the 1980s, even children had become immune to government propaganda. If the state media claimed that Americans wanted war, then the opposite had to be true. So, the nuclear drills and the gas-mask hallway crawl were just like any other exercise you had to master in order to pass, like rope climbing in PE. Our NVP teacher mostly shared our viewpoint. For him, all these lessons were just being done "for the check mark," as it was said. Lesson on the principles of civil defense—check. Learning what a nuclear mushroom cloud looks like—check. Identifying the impending attack warning siren—check. Disassembling and cleaning an AK-47—check. All of it bored me beyond belief. As far as I was concerned, there would never be a nuclear war with America, and we were all wasting our time.

Another subject that my kids have missed out on was *trud*, "labor." Americans of my generation will remember it as either "shop" or "home economics," depending on their gender. Starting from fourth grade or so, we had a double period of *trud* twice a week.

For boys, this took place in a separate building across the schoolyard. There was one room with workbenches for metalworking and one devoted to carpentry. We made decorative wooden spoons, metal hooks for hanging up gym clothes, and various wooden and mechanical toys. We even learned how to cut metallic bolts. Unlike math or chemistry, *trud* never felt like actual labor. There were no formulae or homework, and no one rushed us. It was as good as school ever got. Looking back on it, the facilities and equipment we had were quite impressive. The authorities must've known full well that the country wouldn't be transitioning to a service economy anytime soon, and that it was in everyone's best interests to train the kiddies to do for themselves.

The girls' curriculum was different. It mostly centered on clothes repair and cooking. Gendering in the Soviet Union started early and persisted to the grave. Officially, everyone was addressed as an asexual "comrade," rather than a "miss" or a "mister." But there was no doubt that women's role in society was fundamentally distinct from—and inferior to—the men's. For all its pretense to being a harbinger of the glorious Communist tomorrow, the Soviet state was much more conservative in matters of gender and sexuality than the capitalist societies it considered outdated. This is still the case in today's

Russia. For instance, Putin's government actively fights against "gay propaganda," by which they mean any mention of homosexuality in the media, and refuses to introduce any sort of sexual education in schools. (Unsurprisingly, Russia today has the highest level of abortions per capita and one of the fastest HIV growth rates in the world.)

* * *

In sixth grade, we started a new subject: *politinformatziya* (political information). In Western terms, it was a current events elective, except that it was actually not elective but entirely mandatory. Many things were "elective" in this way in the USSR: going to the November 7 parade, subscribing to *Pravda*, attending trade union assemblies, et cetera. They were not technically things you *had* to do until you actually failed to do them, at which point the authorities would express their displeasure with your lack of comradely spirit.

These sessions took place once a week in the morning, before the first class. That alone already made them hateful to everyone. In the first week of my group's classes, it was decided that the person responsible for keeping everyone abreast of current events would be . . . me. From that point on, from grade six to eight, every Thursday I had to deliver a brief news bulletin to my classmates about global political happenings.

The night before, I would read newspapers, clip interesting articles, and underline relevant passages. Pure domestic events in the USSR tended to fall under headlines such as, "Plowing/sowing/harvesting continues apace on the fertile fields of the Ukraine despite challenging weather conditions," and "The Lenin Factory on Lenin Street in Leningrad was decorated with the Order of Lenin in commemoration of Lenin's anniversary."

So, usually I reported on local events that had some connection with Western Europe or the United States and seemed more interesting.

For instance, I had the pride and privilege of informing my classmates that for the first time, a Soviet factory would soon be producing licensed Adidas sneakers. I also covered the election of Helmut Kohl in West Germany, and the triumphant ascent of eleven Soviet alpinists to the top of Mount Everest, even as the Anglo-American expedition tackling a different slope of the mountain at the same time failed. . .

But a year into my new duty, I hit a snag. On September 2, the Telegraph Agency of the Soviet Union published a brief notice that an unidentified aircraft flying without lights had strayed into Soviet airspace but was escorted out of it by brave Soviet interceptors and was last seen flying off toward the Sea of Japan. However, people partial to listening to "enemy voices" on the radio were whispering to their friends that something else had happened altogether: the interceptors had shot down a Korean Airlines Boeing over the Soviet island of Sakhalin, killing all 269 people on board, including 62 Americans.

By September 4, the authorities published a second notice, where they condemned the "propagandist hoopla" raised by the West over a so-called passenger airplane "supposedly" shot down by the Soviet air force, and asserted that in all likelihood, it was a spy plane. Finally, four more days later, a third notice was published, this time with condolences over the tremendous loss of life—and also a complete abdication of all responsibility. In short: nothing happened, and even if it did, it was nothing important, and even if it was, America was to blame.

What the Soviet authorities didn't know was that Japanese air traffic controllers had recorded all Soviet communications during the pilot's pursuit of Korean Airlines flight 007. It was quickly discovered that the pilot had reported seeing the plane's blinking lights, which indicated that it was a civilian passenger aircraft, but that his commanding officer on the ground either didn't hear or chose not to hear him and gave repeated orders to open fire. The government's lies were blown wide open.

What was I supposed to say? As much as I would have liked to blow the lid off the government hypocrisy, not one word of this story made it into any of my *politinformatziya* sessions. I learned early on what was and what wasn't proper to talk about outside of one's own kitchen. Anything involving the enemy voices was definitely the latter.

Even so, I tried to make my *politinformatziya* as entertaining and lively as I could for my sleepy, grumpy classmates. I did this mostly by adding in bits from popular scientific publications about cool new inventions being researched and developed in the West. This was permitted, even if the invention in question was American, as long as a Soviet paper or magazine had covered it.

On balance, my briefings probably did the Communist Party more ideological harm than good. Sure, we were all proud of our country's achievements in space, but even with the limited information we had, it was clear we were seriously lagging behind the West in all earthbound technology: cars, computers, music players, and all other everyday gadgets and appliances.

I didn't intend it, but this was a pretty subversive idea. The official position of the government was that the Soviet Union was superior to the decaying capitalist West in every respect, including inventiveness. Moreover, the government insisted this had been the case even back in tsarist Russia, which may have been the Dark Ages politically but still boasted a great number of *samorodki*, naturally gifted people.

According to Soviet historiography, Russians invented just about everything. The printing press? That wasn't Johannes

Gutenberg. It was Ivan Fedorov, a Russian cannon maker. So what if he did it 120 years after Gutenberg? You get a 2 in history, Gutenberg-loving comrade.

Now, who invented the airplane? What? The Wright brothers? Incorrect. It was Alexander Mozhaysky. Sure, his wing design never generated enough lift to get off the ground, but he did the best he could with what he had, like all Russians ever, and at the end of the day, isn't that what counts?

The first steam locomotive was invented not by the Brit Richard Trevithick but by two Russian brothers by the name Cherepanov. Penicillin was discovered not by Alexander Fleming but by a Russian woman, Zinaida Ermolyeva. Okay, here's an easy one: What about radio? Am I hearing Guglielmo Marconi? Wrong again! It was Alexander Popov!

Interestingly enough, we were never told that Russians invented the television or the first helicopter, even though those two were actually closer to the truth. Vladimir Zworykin was the first to file for a patent for the television. And the first single-rotor helicopter was designed by Igor Sikorsky. The reason neither of them merited a mention in our textbooks was that both had immigrated to the United States shortly after the Revolution. Soviet authorities had no kudos to give to those freaking émigré traitors.

One theme that my teachers required me to address in my political information sessions was the USSR's role in "fighting for peace" around the world. There was no one set way to fight for peace. Olympic athletes fought for peace as well as for gold in their venues. Diplomats fought for peace in the political arena. And of course, wherever the Red Army invaded—be it Hungary, Czechoslovakia, or Afghanistan—it was always there to fight for peace.

But it wasn't just athletes, diplomats, and soldiers. Young Pioneers, Komsomol, the Communist Party, and in fact all

Soviet citizens were said to be "fighting for peace" in some way. What that fight entailed was uncertain, but one thing was clear: we were fighting for said peace against evil American imperialists and their capitalist lapdog allies.

Every year we held a Day of Fighting for Peace at school. On that day, our homework was to make anti-war banners and posters. Vova and I had little time to spare for this nonsense. One year, inspired by our own hands-on explosive pursuits, we decided to simply draw a nuclear mushroom cloud, boldly crossed out in red. It was quick, easy, and satisfied the political demands of the occasion. However, when we brought it to school, it turned out that about two-thirds of the class had had the same bright time-saving idea. For a long while afterwards, our homeroom walls were overgrown with crossed-out atomic mushrooms in various shades of cheery orange.

When we were not busy celebrating the Soviets Union's extensive contributions to world peace, we were celebrating its glorious triumphs in World War II. All of the USSR celebrated Victory Day on May 9, the day when the USSR ratified Nazi Germany's unconditional surrender. When I was growing up, everyone over the age of forty or so had lived through the war. May 9 was a day for the survivors to mourn those they'd lost, to remember what they had fought for, and to pass on to the youngsters whatever wisdom they could about those years. (Sadly, in today's Russia, May 9 has become an empty bacchanalia of drunk bluster about how "we kicked everyone's ass before, and we can do it again!")

Leningrad also commemorated Siege Day on January 27, when the Nazi blockade of the city was finally lifted in 1944. Every year around that time we had classes called *uroki muzhestva*, "lessons in courage." In these class periods, World War II veterans came to speak to us about their experiences in the war. These accounts were never quite in line with Soviet propaganda. Sure, they were as rich in violence as any book or movie about the war, but the grand narrative of a nation liberating itself and the rest of Europe from the ultimate evil was missing.

I always found these visits very entertaining, because the veterans were rarely vetted for child-appropriate language. The men would often slide into heartfelt military banter so heavily seasoned with swearing that the thread of their accounts became difficult to follow. The women veterans, usually front-line medics, didn't swear, but they made up for their PG-13 language with NC-17 gore. One lady, for instance, described in juicy detail how a close explosion from behind would make soldiers' brains shoot out of their eye sockets. Needless to say, such "lessons of courage" made for great conversation over snack break.

* * *

Soon, it became clear that good grades were not going to quiet my restlessness. I decided to focus on my social circle.

At school, boys mostly socialized through competition and posturing. Getting excused from class was one such competition, and we often played to see who could get out of class with the most bogus excuse possible:

"I have to go get vaccinated."

"I have a headache. I need to wait outside for the aspirin to start working."

"I must prepare for the district Olympiad in math/ geography/English."

Sasha B., one of the boys in my homeroom, earned his spot in the annals of school history when, during a test, he asked to be excused to the restroom at the beginning of the class and came back only a minute before the bell. When the teacher demanded to know, quite reasonably, what he was doing in the restroom for forty minutes, he just shrugged and said laconically, "Shitting."

Of course, he got into trouble for cursing, but his immortality in school lore was assured.

The most foolproof excuses were political ones. Teachers were reluctant to question our political engagements, lest someone question their mindfulness. And there were so many wonderful ways to blow off class in the name of building Communism!

"I have to go to an inter-school Young Pioneers meeting."

"I have an interview with the district Komsomol committee."

"I have to help set up for the upcoming election day."

That last one might sound curious: after all, how could there be elections in a totalitarian one-party government? Well, a little totalitarianism is no impediment to democracy. There were no real elections in the USSR, of course, but there were simulacra of sorts. Sure, people couldn't vote for the general secretary of the Communist Party of the Soviet Union (i.e., the head of state). However, every few years, they could vote for their local representative to the Leningrad Soviet or the Supreme Soviet.

One would think an election ought to involve options, at least from a purely linguistic standpoint. But in the USSR, matters were simplified: one candidate was offered, and people could vote either "Yes" or "No." If you were voting "Yes," you simply dropped the ballot into a voting urn. If you were voting "No," you'd cross out the name of the candidate first, then drop it in. It was like a vote of no confidence. Or rather, a vote of extreme confidence: the typical outcome was 99.9 percent in favor. Of course, nobody bothered to count the ballots.

* * *

Another aspect of my school's social structure was the booming market for plagiarism. Recess was prime time for finishing your homework for the upcoming class. Or rather, for hastily copying it off someone more diligent than yourself. Many people did this. The principal copying resource were *otlichnitsi*, "excellencies," overachieving girls who got only 5, or "Excellent," on everything they did. Everyone knew who among them permitted having their homework copied and who refused. Predictably, the girls who allowed ne'er-do-well boys to cheat off them were much more popular. I was on friendly terms with a group of such girls and occasionally copied off them as well. When I brought homework to school, I always let others copy off me. For a boy, it was considered dishonorable to refuse, because it'd mean denying help to a comrade in need.

But that was just boring, everyday cheating. The real deal started during term finals. Cheating during tests was practically a competitive sport. A cheater wasn't just matching wits with the teachers; they were also trying to outdo their classmates. Everyone except the "excellencies" was always on the lookout for some clever new way to swindle.

From a disciplinary standpoint, cheating was not considered a big deal. No one busted for cheating ever got suspended, much less expelled. Perhaps this was another manifestation of the Soviet mindset in action. Adults, including those in positions of authority, understood very well that everything around them was either an outright lie or a partial concealment of the truth. So it probably made no sense to them to punish schoolchildren for cheating, given that they were doomed to live in a world of lies anyway.

I also suspect that our teachers knew that the most popular method of cheating, namely making crib sheets, actually did more to encourage learning than to distract from it. Think about it. Suppose you want to make a tiny crib sheet to sneak into the classroom on a test day. To make it, you would first need to go over the relevant material, break it down, and figure out the best way to summarize it as concisely as possible. Then you had to copy it onto a tiny sheet of paper. If you miscalculated the amount of room available, or if the ink smudged, you had to toss that draft and start over. By the time the crib sheet was finally ready, there was often no longer any need for it.

I am proud to say that at one point in my school career, I became the acknowledged class champion of cheating. My pièce de résistance was a crib sheet I made for a geography test. I inserted it between two pieces of sticking clear plastic and pressed the pieces together with a hot iron. Then I made a hole in the now-laminated crib sheet, threaded a string through it, and let the card hang inside my uniform's left sleeve. The other end of the string I passed through the inside of my jacket and tied to a button on the right sleeve. Now I could hold this crib sheet in my left hand for reference. If I saw the teacher approach my desk, I'd just straighten my right arm, and the incriminating artifact would retreat back into my sleeve.

Crib sheets were not limited to tiny pieces of paper. They could also be written on the pencils themselves, using three of their hexagonal sides. Some people wrote notes on their linen handkerchiefs. Girls were considered to have an advantage when it came to competitive cheating, because the knee-length skirts of their uniforms allowed them to write test answers on their bare legs. When they were seated, they simply moved the skirt out of the way and copied to their hearts' content.

The most hard-core type of crib sheet was called a "bomb." It was only used for exams in subjects like literature or history, which had a defined list of thirty or so written questions assigned to students by lottery. How do you cheat on an essay question? You prewrite the essay. A bomb could be written on either A4 sheets or plain notebook paper. However, one had to be careful: in rare cases, a teacher would give students stamped sheets of paper to write on. This made such a test "unbomb-able," because now you couldn't switch sheets.

The first step was to prepare all thirty potential essays at home. Then you had to find a way to smuggle the essays into the classroom, to effect the switch at the end of the exam period. The easiest way was to hide them all in the restroom and ask to be let out during the exam. However, there was always a risk that the teacher would not let you go. The second option, which most people went with, was to hide them on your person.

Our homeroom's acknowledged virtuoso of bombing was the class Amazon, Olya Bezverhova. Her surname literally meant "no top part." People often looked up at her and said, "Just imagine if there was a top part as well!" With legs that long, there was a *lot* of room in her socks for essay sheets.

* * *

Finally, I attempted to occupy myself with after-school activities. The Soviet Union did not afford its people many opportunities to gamble. If you were a betting man, there were only two ways to indulge—one entirely illegal and one absolutely legit. The illegal way meant visiting an underground billiards room, poker basement, or, believe it or not, chess or checkers club where people played games for money.

The legal way was buying a government lottery ticket. There were not many of these to choose from: a keno-type game called Sportloto or the DOSAAF lottery. The acronym stood for Volunteer Society for Assistance to the Army, Navy, and Air Force. The grand prize was a car, a brand-new Volga, and winning it rivaled winning the Powerball, in terms of both a player's odds and the emotional impact on the winner. But there were other very desirable prizes: motorcycles, cassette players, cameras, and other hard-to-find electronics. A lottery ticket cost fifty kopecks—not exactly chicken feed. (Actually, the USSR imported a lot of grain from the USA and Canada, so Soviet chicken feed must have been quite pricey.) Numbers were drawn once a quarter and published in the newspapers. Since fresh issues of the main Soviet newspapers were pasted daily onto the sides of many bus shelters, one always knew when the numbers went out because all the passersby would congregate around them.

Just before the Moscow Olympics, the government introduced a new form of instant lottery. They were not scratch-offs but little sealed paper packets, with another piece of paper inside with the result on it: "No win," "One more ticket," "Fifty kopeks," et cetera. This new form of petty gambling was an instant hit. I spent quite a bit of pocket money on these tickets myself, with not much to show for it.

Vova, who was an entrepreneur at heart, took note of this new racket. He made a bunch of similar-looking paper packets and filled them with handwritten tickets of his own that said, "No win," "One more ticket," "Five kopecks," or even "Ten kopecks." Then he brought a little baggie of them to school and started selling them for five kopecks each. After a day of brisk business, he cleared about a ruble. The next day, he decided to tilt the math a bit more in favor of the house by not adding any more winning tickets to the mix. As a result, not one of the tickets he sold yielded a monetary prize, and Vova walked away with three rubles and twenty kopecks in pure profit—about sixteen quality ice creams' worth! But then one of the younger kids complained to our homeroom teacher, and Vova's number was up. The next day, his parents were called to school and informed that they were raising a capitalist piglet.

* * *

When the Friendship Club ended in grade eight, I tried to fill the void in my afternoons by going to various other clubs.

After a certain age, organized extracurriculars slowly but surely displaced outdoor playtime from the lives of intelligentsia children. Afternoons became filled with music school, or art school, or some sports academy, or, as in my case, a society of hobbyists, like photography or radio club.

Starting from age eight, after doing my homework at home, every other day I would take the number fifteen trolleybus to the Young Pioneer Palace where Nevsky Prospect crossed the Fontanka River. Club activities ran from about five to seven. All clubs were free, but the popular ones always had more people wanting to join than there were spaces available. Membership in them was merit-based, not first come, first served. To be admitted, you had to demonstrate genuine interest, commitment to the hobby, and sometimes a preexisting degree of proficiency in whatever the club was about. Of course, there were also boring clubs, which were usually half-empty. Few people were eager to get into a balalaika club, or a stuffed-toy-making club, or the Artistic Word Studio elocution club.

My family put no pressure on me, and I was free to try out any club or society that struck my fancy. I attended a fencing club, a judo club, and the electromechanical toy club. A couple of years later, Vova and I decided to try the math club. Our math teacher thought I showed promise, and regularly sent me to represent the school at academic competitions, so I assumed I could hold my own among the junior math elite of Leningrad. It didn't take me long to realize how mistaken I was. The Leningrad Children's Math Club was filled with genuine prodigies, many of them already on their way to being world-class mathematicians.

After breaking free from the math club, I found something else to try: the Archaeological Society. We got together for an hour and a half every week at the Young Pioneer Palace and listened to a lecture given by the club leader or an invited speaker. We learned a fair bit about archaeological digs being done in Egypt, Iraq, China, and other places. We also got homework assignments, for instance to find and read a book about a famous archaeologist or some ancient culture, and then write an essay about it. The assigned books were often old and out of print, so looking for them in the library was a bit of a treasure hunt in and of itself.

Sometimes we were visited by researchers from the Oriental department of Leningrad State University or the Oriental Studies Institute, which was its own separate thing. At the time, under the heavy influence of reading a book that Vova had given me about Schliemann's discovery of Troy, I was seriously considering a future career as an archaeologist. I liked ancient history; I enjoyed doing academic research on it; and I loved the idea of digging up old artifacts and analyzing them.

In eighth grade, I decided to try to get into the Hermitage Museum club. Truth be told, I had already tried out for it once, back in fifth grade. Belonging to the Hermitage club was considered *le bon ton* for children from "good families," so there were a lot of contenders and rather few spots. To get in, one had to pass a rigorous art-appreciation exam. Vova and I tried out for a spot together. At the interview, I was shown various works of art and asked to offer my opinion of them. I had no idea what the evaluators expected to hear, so I just told them my honest opinion. One was an Impressionist painting. I was not a fan of the Impressionists, and I let the interviewers know this. It did not make a good impression. I did not get in.

Grandma was quite appalled by this. It wasn't so much that she expected better of me—she didn't. However, a friend of my dad's worked at the museum, and she was sure he would vouch for me and sneak me in. It took her a while to get over this and stop being mad at Dad for not overseeing my admission process more diligently. Meanwhile, Vova, who had no personal connections at the museum but also no misconceptions about what the authorities wanted to hear, passed the exam with flying colors and spent a great deal of his free time from fifth to seventh grade at the club, studying Western art.

But that was then; this was now. Or rather, that was Zen, this was Tao. In eighth grade, the club began accepting applications to study Oriental art. The new goals were rather ambitious. Club members would get an overview of the history and ethnography of every culture that had ever been known as "the Orient," from Japan all the way to Egypt, through art. The Hermitage Museum, a repository of cultural treasures purchased or commissioned by generations of Russian tsars, had in its possession a tremendous amount of Asian art treasures and artifacts, and it was going to let the club kiddies study them.

This time, I was determined not to fail. Both Oriental studies and the Hermitage were practically in my blood. One of my ancestors, Marie Brosset, was an Orientalist scholar, a member of the Imperial Russian Archaeological Society, and the director of the numismatic collections of the Hermitage from 1851 to 1879. Perhaps competition had lessened now that Western art was no longer on the menu, or perhaps I had grown wiser and more circumspect in my opinions since fifth grade. Be that as it may, this time I got in.

A typical club meeting went as follows. On Saturdays at 3 p.m., after school and lunch, we would gather in the foyer of the Hermitage Museum. The instructor would give us a short breakdown of what we'd be looking at that day, and then we were off to look at art and artifacts. We started with Egypt, then moved on to Mesopotamia, then Arabia and Persia, and so on eastward, through India, Tibet, China, and finally Japan.

The Hermitage is a gigantic museum. At any given moment, only a few rooms are open to visitors, because it's too cost prohibitive to staff and maintain all the expositions at once. In those days, practically all Tibetan, Chinese, and Japanese collections were closed to the public. So we club members were the only people admitted to see them, besides seasoned academics and specialists. And sometimes, these specialists would be our guides for the day, taking us though specific styles or regions or eras. My favorite weeks were the ones we spent studying Oriental influences on Western art. Ironically, that meant by and large the Impressionists, whose works were plentiful at the Hermitage.

I made some new friends in the club. For instance, there was an older boy named Daniil, who everyone called Dan, in the Western fashion. He seemed like a progressive, cutting-edge type of guy. Once, I invited him over to my house to hang out, to show him my handcrafted mechanical toys. The playdate did not go well. At some point, he had to call his father and tell him he was going to be at my place for a while. As luck would have it, his dad had just come from a PTA meeting, where he'd been publicly shamed for his son's behavior. Apparently, Dan had stolen something from someone at school. I didn't intend to eavesdrop, but it was frankly impossible to tune out their conversation, because Dan was screaming into the phone that it was all bogus and he was innocent. Yet when he left, Alyosha and I discovered that our prized stash of Donald chewing gum, which we kept on our shelves and used to trade rather than chewed, was gone. Needless to say, that potential friendship died on the vine.

* * *

It is a truth universally acknowledged that the best thing about school is the field trips.

Our school had a tradition. In late May, just before the end of the school year, all the upperclassmen (in this case, sixth grade and up) were taken on a day trip to Zelenogorsk, a small town on the Karelian Isthmus, about thirty miles northwest of Leningrad.

We passed our day in the Zelenogorsk woods doing typical outdoorsy group activities, such as orienteering, building bon-fires, crossing small streams over a tightrope, and seeing who could put up their tent the fastest. Everyone loved it. So we were all rather dismayed when the trips came to an abrupt end in 1985. This happened after an incident involving two boys from the seventh grade.

One of them, Egor Druzhinin, was not just a boy. He was a massive child celebrity and screen actor famous for the hit movie *Vacation of Petrov and Vasechkin, Usual and Incredible*. During the Zelenogorsk trip, "Vasechkin" was practicing knife throwing, aiming for a tree, while another boy sat nearby. One badly aimed throw, and the knife was lodged two inches deep in the other boy's back.

Luckily, the knife didn't nick anything important. Still, the boy ended up spending two weeks in the hospital. I can only imagine what sort of "talks" our principal was summoned to in a variety of supervisory institutions. After this incident, the Zelenogorsk trips ended for good.

To console us, the next year, one of our particularly cool teachers took my class on a three-day camping trip in the woods, on her own initiative. Our destination was a bit farther away, about an hour from Leningrad by train. We pitched our tents on the edge of a lake and stayed up late sitting around the campfire, playing guitar, singing, and telling jokes. It was right around the time when the boys and girls in my class were starting to socialize again, after many years of mutual avoidance.

For dinner, we caught a few fish, cleaned them, and made fish soup, working together and feeling very adult as we did so. I shared a tent with Vova. We read together from an illegal *samizdat* copy of Bulgakov's *The Master and Margarita* that I had daringly brought with me. It was a fitting end to the day. I had a vivid feeling that momentous things were underway. I was finally growing like a weed and squawking in a breaking adolescent voice. Vova and I were reading a cool forbidden book, risking all sorts of trouble thereby. And there were two nice-smelling girls sleeping in another tent just a meter away!

On that trip, I finished my first cigarette. Granny had given me a ruble for emergencies, and I spent fifty kopecks of it at the train station on a pack of Bulgarian Rodopi.

Most Russian men smoked. They started in high school and didn't stop until someone pried the last cigarette from their cold dead hands. There was just a handful of public places where one wasn't allowed to smoke. Everywhere else, people lit up. My friends and I started smoking around age fourteen.

Later on, I shared the pack with the guys, and most of them smoked one or two cigarettes by the campfire. Our teacher decided to ignore our misconduct. I found tobacco unexpectedly nasty; after just one puff, my head started to spin and I grew nauseous. Disappointed and upset at having spent Grandma's hard-earned cash on this vice, I threw away the rest of the pack. But my narcotic misadventures didn't stop there. Before leaving for the trip, I had also nicked one of my mother's sleeping pills, figuring that I might need it with all the inevitable singing by the campfire and Vova snoring next to me. The pill turned out to be much stronger than I'd anticipated. The next morning, I stumbled around like a zombie, tripping over every tree root as we hiked through the forest.

All these experiences, however memorable and fun they were, were nothing but a set of tiny sparks of color on the endless canvas of the bleak Soviet reality.

CHAPTER 12

THE MOST WONDERFUL DAY OF THE YEAR

Late on December 31, a couple is rushing home with bags full of groceries. They come across a drunk man vomiting in the gutter.

"See?" says the man. "We are still shopping, and the normal people are already having fun. . ."

WHEN YOUR DAILY routine is fairly bleak and dull, holidays shine all the brighter. Russia's most important holiday was and remains New Year's Eve. Regardless of who rules the country, it remains devoid of ideology, hurrah patriotism, and other potential mood spoilers. Contrary to what one might expect, New Year's Eve in the USSR did not revolve *entirely* around getting roaring drunk. Rather, it was more of a family holiday, kind of like Thanksgiving or Christmas in the West, except far more boisterous and with no Jesus.

Christmas itself ceased to be an official holiday in the atheist Soviet Union in 1929, only becoming one again in 1990. Since religious sentiment was liable to get people in trouble, those who continued to celebrate it did so very quietly behind closed doors. Meanwhile, all the festivities and traditions associated with Christmas shifted to New Year's Eve. Santa Claus (in Russia, Father Frost) was still there, and he still delivered presents, but he wore a long blue robe rather than a short red coat, rode in a sleigh pulled by a troika instead of reindeer, and was accompanied by a hot blonde female assistant, Snegurochka (Snow Girl). Christmas trees, after being permitted again in 1935, were renamed "New Year's trees" and topped with a red five-pointed star.

Each year, tree bazaars would pop up in Leningrad in the last half of December. Of course, they usually ran out of trees way ahead of schedule, even the misshapen, crooked, or balding ones. Getting your hands on a nice tree was quite a challenge. Those unable to harness the magic powers of *pol-litra* (the staple half-liter bottle of vodka, a universal inducement) or other bribes often had to settle for a tree that was more naked branches than needles, and cover its shame with extra tinsel and garlands.

On a Saturday afternoon before the New Year of 1986, Tolya came home saying that he'd looked for a tree at every one of the local outlets and they were all sold out. However, one manager had whispered to him that new festive plants would be delivered around eleven o'clock that night. So I was allowed to stay up late and accompany Tolya back to the bazaar. Sure enough, around midnight we saw beautiful new trees getting trucked in. The hour was late, and the weather was poor, so most of the bazaar employees had gone home. Tolya and I climbed up on one of the trucks and for the next couple of hours helped the manager unload the trees. When we were done, we picked the best tree of the lot, bought it, and brought it home. But our late-night escapade had a consequence. The next morning I woke up with a crazy fever and spent most of the New Year festivities and half of the winter holiday trapped in bed with a terrible cold.

Gifts-wise, when I was little, I got toy animals, board games, or construction blocks, just like any Western kid. As I got older, I started getting cash presents instead. Perhaps due to my well-conditioned Soviet affinity for delayed gratification—the result of standing in all those lines—I was rather good at saving up.

As for our parents, Alyosha and I usually gave them stuff we had made ourselves. My membership in the electromechanical toy club was invaluable in this respect, as I was able to make any number of small yet nifty gadgets for my folks.

But that year, I decided to get my mom a real grown-up sort of gift and bought her a bottle of shampoo from one of the new cooperative shops that were starting to pop up in Leningrad. Most of the stuff sold by the co-ops was crap. But by the standards of the day, it was a solid gift, since consumer goods of any quality were hard to find. I was quite pleased with myself. She said, "Oh, thank you! You shouldn't have! It must've been very expensive!" and put it aside.

New Year's Eve always unfolded the same way. The first half of the day was pretty much business as usual. Unless it fell on a Sunday, everyone went to school on December 31 with a smile on their lips and a song in their heart, anticipating a night of great food, great TV, staying up late, and presents, and most importantly, the start of a ten-day winter break.

New Year's Eve meant setting the best table of the year. Unlike the American Thanksgiving or British Christmas, which are also late-in-the-year celebrations of gluttony, the key to a Soviet New Year's Eve table was not hot dishes but appetizers: cold cuts, pickles, mushrooms, smoked fish, and salads—lots and lots of salads. The centerpiece and sine qua non of most Soviet New Year's tables was a large bowl of a salad called Olivier. It originated at the turn of the century, supposedly courtesy of some French chef employed by a Moscow nobleman. After seventy years of ever-improving socialism, none of the fancy ingredients in Olivier's original salad—grouse, veal tongue, capers, smoked duck—were available anymore. So people swapped them out for cheaper items with similar textures: boiled chicken or beef, potatoes, cubed sausages, and the key ingredient, canned green peas, which were also surprisingly hard to find.

Another must-have New Year's Eve delicacy was *seledka pod shuboj*—literally, a "herring under a fur coat." This was a traditional layered salad made of chopped pickled herring, eggs, beets, carrots, potatoes, and some type of mayonnaise-based dressing. Admittedly, I have never tried it in my life—the fishy smell of this yucky mess puts me off.

Of course, the feast did not end with appetizers. There were also all kind of pies and turnovers, and sides like fried eggplant. On very rare occasions, there might be a small jar of red caviar, or an even smaller jar of black caviar. Caviar was expensive, very hard to get, and considered to be good for the blood. I've still never eaten it. Apparently, when I was a toddler, Grandma got her hands on some black caviar and spread some on a piece of buttered bread for me. I scrutinized the offering and rejected it, saying, "Grandma, why did you put this stinky dirt on my bread?"

On regular days, we all ate in the kitchen. For New Year's Eve, a proper table was always set in the living-room-slash-master-bedroom, with cloth napkins, our best china, the silver tea service, and extra chairs for guests. Champagne was an absolute must. The only type available was domestic swill by the predictably generic name *Sovetskoe shampanskoe* (Soviet champagne). Most people kept bottles of it stored away for holidays, for months. Like all scarce goods, it was bought up right away whenever and wherever it went on sale, even if it was February and the next New Year's Eve was ages away.

The TV was usually left on the entire night so that everyone could watch the nonstop New Year's Eve entertainment programs, which were interrupted only by the irritating congratulatory address made by the general secretary. When the Kremlin clock on the TV screen struck midnight—the Soviet version of the ball drop—the champagne was opened and everyone toasted the New Year.

Then we continued stuffing ourselves and watching what was always the best television of the year. Firstly, there was *Goluboi Ogonek* (*The Blue Light*), on which many of the popular Soviet musicians, singers, and comedians delivered three continuous hours of songs and sketches.

Since 1977, Soviet censors had occasionally treated the people to a show called *The Melodies and Rhythms of Foreign Pop*. It featured performances by the biggest music stars from Bulgaria, East Germany, Czechoslovakia, and other Eastern Bloc countries. However, sometimes it even showed Italian pop stars, Boney M, or clips from Eurovision. Of course, they never showed any real American or British pop stars, but even that little glimpse of the Western music scene was awesome.

On New Year's Eve, Mom and Tolya usually stayed at home with Grandma and us kids until midnight, to ring in the New Year together, and then they went off to party with their friends the Mikhailovs. It was like a switch flipped in them. The year I gifted Mom the co-op shampoo, I saw, just as she and Tolya were leaving for one of these parties, her pick up my gift and, without even worrying that I could see her do it, put it in her purse to give to her hostess. Yes, regifting was normal, too.

CHAPTER 13

THE BEGINNING OF THE END

"What would happen if a crocodile swallowed Brezhnev?"

"It would shit medals for a week."

IT'S SAFE TO say that Soviet Police Day, celebrated on November 10, was no one's favorite holiday. The only good thing about it was the annual televised variety show, which always featured a fantastic lineup of the most popular comedians and pop stars of the day.

On November 10, 1982, viewers all over the USSR tuned in to Channel One to listen to superstars like Alla Pugacheva, Sofia Rotaru, Valery Leontiev, and Mikhail Boyarsky, who had recently played d'Artagnan in a massively popular TV adaptation of *The Three Musketeers* and would have probably been voted Sexiest Man Alive had the USSR condoned such awards.

However, at the scheduled hour, instead of singing, the viewers were treated to dancing, namely a prerecorded broadcast of the ballet *Swan Lake*. No explanation for the change followed. Something was very wrong. Soviet TV schedules were ironclad; even the tiniest changes had to be approved from the very top. Moreover, the concert was a greatly anticipated television event. What could have happened?

The next day, we were wrestling with our first $y = ax^2$ functions in third-period math class, when the door creaked open and our homeroom teacher walked in. Ignoring our curious eyes, she whispered something to the math teacher. The math teacher nodded, and the homeroom teacher left again. The lesson went on. Thirty minutes later, the bell rang. As we began packing up our stuff, the math teacher said something inconceivable:

"Children, I have something to tell you. Brezhnev has died."

Numb, we descended to the lunchroom for our daily snack time. Brezhnev was dead? How could this be? Just four days ago, we all watched him salute the Revolution Day parade on TV. Some of our parents even remarked on how good he looked, not like his usual sickly self.

We couldn't quite grasp the situation. For our whole lives, Brezhnev had always been there, an immutable part of our world. Sure, on some level we all knew he was old, but even his old age seemed permanent. Deep down, we all expected to grow up, marry, have children of our own, and still see Brezhnev on TV every so often, drawling his way through yet another three-hour speech. (For those inclined to laugh at this idea, I have one word: Castro.)

Through all fifteen minutes of recess, we stood around with solemn faces and asked ourselves and one another, *Now what?* Most of us were in agreement: there would be an atomic war. Why? With whom? We had no idea. All we knew was that war was an earth-shattering cataclysm, and so was the death of a head of state. And, as the Russian proverb has it, "When a calamity comes, throw open the gates" (i.e., when it rains, it pours). One disaster was sure to lead to others.

At our school, a guard of honor made up of two Young Pioneers was posted by a large portrait of Brezhnev, all jowls and huge eyebrows. Their job was to stand in continuous salute until they were relieved. Upperclassmen walked around with the somber, preoccupied air of junior ministers and debated which member of the politburo was going to succeed Brezhnev in office: Gromyko? Andropov? Tikhonov? As for us, we kept sneaking glances out the window after returning to class, half expecting any minute to see a bright flash and a mushroom cloud on the horizon.

* * *

The period of Brezhnev's rule is now referred to as the era of *zastoy*, or "stagnation." He had no grand plans, either malevolent or benevolent. He was just there. People did not particularly like or dislike him. Some considered him a "fighter for peace" and a deterrent force to American imperialism. But most people either pitied or mocked him. In the last years of his tenure, Brezhnev was a decrepit old man. He had severe speech defects, which stretched out every public address he made to multiple hours. His tremendous bushy eyebrows looked like two fluffy black caterpillars perched on his forehead. He loved Kiev cake. He adored military awards. (Every year, he would award himself a new medal or order to wear proudly on his chest. The rows multiplied to the point where one couldn't help but be impressed that a man so old and frail could lug around all that metal and not topple over. By the last count, he had over a hundred decorations.) He liked to embrace and kiss his party comrades and foreign dignitaries on the mouth.

When they heard the news of Brezhnev's death, a lot of people cried from sheer shock and panic. The eighteen years under

Brezhnev's rule had been, for all their drawbacks, stable: no famines; no political upheavals; no mass arrests; no war (other than the one brewing in Afghanistan, which most people still didn't know about). More and more often, political dissidents were committed to short spells in insane asylums rather than sentenced to decades in the Gulag labor camps. The arts were not flourishing, stifled under censorship, but no one besides the dissident intelligentsia cared much about that. In short, things could be much worse.

Here's another way of putting it. Living in the USSR was a lot like being born into a cult. Lenin was the Soviet equivalent of the messiah, a being of pure genius and the pathway to mankind's salvation. Karl Marx and Friedrich Engels were akin to Old Testament prophets who had supposedly foretold Lenin's coming—they even had the big, bushy beards. But a living church requires a living leader and interpreter of the holy writ, a pope. From 1964 to 1982, our Communist pope was the general secretary of the Communist Party of the Soviet Union, Leonid Ilyich Brezhnev. By the time he died in office, he had been Lenin's representative on earth for eighteen years. His death left a terrifying sucking vacuum at the helm of the Soviet ship. For all his faults, "dear Leonid Ilyich" was considered, in his heart of hearts, a kind man. There was no guarantee that his successor would be one, too.

* * *

Brezhnev's funeral took place four days later, on Monday.

Adults went to work as usual, but all schools were closed. Some teachers told their kids that they were obligated to watch the funeral on TV, and they had to do it standing, as a sign of respect. My teacher told us no such thing. As far as we were concerned, it was just an extra day off, albeit one where we had to be careful not to play or laugh outside.

Entertainment-wise, the three preceding days had been dreary. In their zeal to turn up the mourning mood to the max, the authorities canceled all children's shows and cartoons, as well as all sports programming. The only thing broadcast on TV was either ponderously depressing orchestral music or endless reruns of *Swan Lake*, which by now was making people physically ill.

By the morning of the funeral, Vova and I were more than ready for a distraction. So we went to our favorite movie theater (simply called Leningrad) to watch *The Mirror Crack'd*, a 1980 imported Agatha Christie mystery with Elizabeth Taylor and Tony Curtis. Predictably, there were just a handful of cinemagoers apart from us. How this thrilling foreign matinee didn't get canceled on a day such as this was a mystery of government miscommunication. The mirror of Soviet reality was, indeed, starting to crack. . .

The movie finished later than I had expected. Walking home under a persistent, miserable snow drizzle, I was surprised by a sudden hellish noise. It was the combined howl of every factory whistle, every car horn, and every boat horn in the Leningrad area. When I finally got home, hounded by all the sirens, the funeral was already halfway over.

I was greeted at the door by Alyosha. He was boiling over with some kind of news.

"They dropped him!" he exclaimed.

"What?"

"The coffin! They dropped the coffin!"

What had happened was this. Brezhnev's grave under the Kremlin wall was not a simple hole in the ground but a rectangular burial chamber under the paving stones. The coffin with the deceased general secretary was supposed to have been lowered, slowly and somberly, into this chamber on planks supported by wide swathes of white linen held by two men, one at the head and one at the foot. But as soon as the coffin was out of sight, there was a loud bang; the white linen bands were pulled halfway into the grave, and one of the men accidentally let them go.

Grandma shook her head at the TV, where top Soviet statesmen were now receiving condolences from a long line of foreign dignitaries from Africa and Latin America in the opulent St. Georgij reception hall.

"A bad omen," she said. "To drop the coffin at a funeral, that means three more years of deaths in the family."

Grandma's words turned out to be eerily prescient.

* * *

The man who ended up succeeding Brezhnev as general secretary of the Communist Party was Yuri Andropov, a former head of the KGB. Portraits of Brezhnev were carried out of various institutions, including our school, and replaced with those of Andropov. The new head of the Soviet state had a huge, shiny bald forehead and unfriendly eyes. And that was that. Life went on as before. The only other thing changed by Brezhnev's death was that it was no longer necessary to write essays on his multivolume memoirs, *The Small Land*, *Rebirth*, and *Virgin Lands*. Heaps of these works, once required reading and now suddenly garbage, ended up under the school stairs, where they moldered for a while until they were finally relegated to recycling.

Andropov worried people. This was the man who, as the Soviet ambassador to Hungary, ordered Soviet tanks to roll into Budapest and crush the Hungarian uprising in 1956, killing over 2,500 protesters in the course of a week. What if this bloodthirsty Chekist suddenly decided to do something similar in Russia and turn the clock from 1983 to 1938?

Indeed, Andropov soon began a massive anti-corruption purge of the party ranks. Criminal prosecutions were being launched left and right. Since corruption was rife in just about every Soviet institution, Andropov had plenty to work with. Gastronoms, fisheries, cotton plantations—no industry was safe from his audit. The KGB had files on everyone going back decades.

As for the little people, Andropov had plans for them as well. He believed that over the course of the two decades under the bumbling, benevolent Brezhnev, Soviet citizens had grown lazy and complacent. Instead of putting their backs into building Communism, they wasted away great chunks of their workdays lollygagging in lines for food and clothing. And so, in his new-broomish eagerness to sweep clean, Andropov began a massive campaign against absenteeism. What this meant was that in the middle of the day, cops would swoop down on some public location—bathhouse, hair salon, café, store, or even a public park—block off all exits, and demand to see everyone's passports. Then they would ask every customer caught inside to explain why they were there during work hours. Those who couldn't come up with a good enough reason got reports sent to their place of employment notifying the management that so-and-so had been busted for absenteeism.

This initiative also covered schoolchildren playing hooky. On the last day of the spring quarter, Vova and I decided to blow off classes and go to the movies. We were meandering along Nevsky Prospect toward the Coliseum movie theater, on the way to see for the fourth time a hilarious French spy comedy called *The Umbrella Coup*, when we got stopped by two policemen.

"What are you doing out here?" they asked.

We decided honesty was the best policy. "We're off to the movies."

They asked to see our tickets. Thankfully, we had already bought them ahead of time.

"Why aren't you in school?" they asked.

"School's already out for the quarter today," said Vova. Technically, it wasn't a lie. School really was out today, just not until the day's classes were over.

Our faces must've been insufficiently earnest. The cops led both of us to a *voronok* (a paddy wagon, literally "little raven" from back when they were painted black).

Besides us, the cops' only haul that day was a few stray alcoholics. For a while, Vova and I sat in the car and tried not to breathe through our noses. The smell coming off the other offenders was unbearable: stale booze, dirty clothes, piss, and unwashed bodies ripened with sickly sweat by the springtime sunshine.

About half an hour later, we were finally driven to a police station. Once there, we explained as calmly as we could to the officer on duty that we had been wrongfully detained. He had us write explanatory notes. We wrote that as it was the last day of the term, our school had canceled classes. Fortunately, they did not bother to phone the school. They did, however, call our parents. It's a miracle that this phone call didn't give both of our grandmas simultaneous heart attacks.

* * *

When Yuri Andropov died after only fifteen months in office, no one was surprised. Everyone knew he had been sick. Moreover, unlike Brezhnev, he was not missed at all.

Andropov's prematurely ended term left behind only one positive memorable innovation: a new, cheap kind of vodka made with low-quality spirits, competitively priced at four rubles and seventy kopecks for a half-liter bottle. The public wholeheartedly approved it and nicknamed it "Andropovka."

When it was announced that schools would be closed on the day of his funeral, boys in our class looked at each other and said, "Well? Same time, same place?"

Just over a year before, when school was out on the day of Brezhnev's funeral, some boys from my homeroom decided to go play soccer in the morning. Afterwards they went to a coffee shop on Zhelyabova Street for coffee and *pyshki*—doughnut-like pastries, except fluffier and fattier. In the noble tradition of street food everywhere, *pyshki* were baked in disgustingly overused oil and dusted with confectioner's sugar. Eating several at once could put you in a food coma. The coffee—or rather the dubious, milky pre-mixed and pre-sweetened coffee substitute—was ladled out of a giant vat. In short, these two things together made the perfect treat to mark a monumental event in the life of our nation.

Now that Andropov was gone, another fun day of soccer and artery-clogging *pyshki* pastries beckoned.

* * *

The trouble with staying in power for almost two decades is that your cronies, confidantes, and trusted comrades age right along with you. By the 1980s, time had whittled the top echelons of the Soviet government to a handful of old men who, despite the efforts of the best physicians in the country, were ready to ascend to the great big commune in the sky.

Andropov's funeral committee and procession was headed by Konstantin Chernenko, who was soon named as his successor. Physically, Chernenko was a wreck on day one. A lifelong smoker, he had suffered from every lung complaint known to man. To make matters worse, in August 1983, he got severe food poisoning, which sent him into a tailspin from which he never recovered. Most of his eleven months in office were spent in the hospital.

The people, long over their terror of what a leaderless tomorrow might bring, laughed themselves to pieces at the geriatric heads of the Communist Party.

"What is the world's most luxurious retirement home?"
"The Kremlin"

"What's the difference between a monarchy and socialism?"
"Under a monarchy, power is transferred from father to son. Under socialism, it's transferred from grandpa to grandpa."

An anchor reports a Telegraph Agency of the Soviet Union announcement on the evening news: "Dear comrades: you're going to laugh, but the Communist Party, and the entire Soviet nation, has once again suffered a great loss. . ."

"Did you hear? You won't need an invitation anymore to attend the funeral of a general secretary; now you can get a season's pass!"

The only thing Chernenko had time to do during his brief stint at the helm was to exact revenge on the US for boycotting the 1980 Olympics by mounting a ban of the 1984 Games in Los Angeles in return. He made out the decision to be a matter of security. According to the politburo, given the atmosphere of hatred toward the USSR and all things Soviet in America, it would be unwise to send our athletes to a place where their safety could not be guaranteed. TV and newspapers were flooded with government propaganda about how LA was full of gangsters and violent crime. Like most Soviet kids—and indeed adults—at the time, I didn't much question this. Even though I listened to Western radio, and even though I was in obsessive love with everything foreign, I was still a Soviet kid and, deep in my heart of hearts, a patriot. Even though the West clearly had superior food, clothes, and toys, I still considered the USSR to be the best place on earth and my countrymen the best people.

When Chernenko kicked the bucket on March 10, 1985, my classmates and I didn't even bother coordinating anything; everyone just showed up at the soccer field on the day of his funeral, ready to commemorate yet another departed general secretary with a day of soccer and *pyshki* doughnuts.

It was to be our last such outing. The next general secretary was to leave his office in a wholly different and entirely unpredictable manner. Little did we know that with his ascent to power, our entire stale universe would begin to implode.

CHAPTER 14

SICK

"Doctor, I have sharp pains in my behind!"

"All right, let's take a look . . . Oh my! You've got a rose up there!"

"It's for you, Doctor!"

JEALOUS ADULTS LIKE to say that childhood passes quickly, that it's over in the blink of an eye. I can't agree. When you become an adult, that's when life starts roaring by, like the Tupolev Tu-144 jet plane pictured on packs of imported Bulgarian cigarettes. When I was a kid, time crawled like a snail. And during some parts of the year, like the start of the winter quarter after the New Year holidays, it crawled like a snail through chilled molasses. Coming back to school after the New Year break, with three months of uninterrupted six-day school weeks ahead, I felt like a cosmonaut on a journey to Cassiopeia through the endless void. (During the last-period Russian class on Saturdays, time seemed to grind to a halt altogether or even go in reverse.)

Any day—nay, any hour—spent outside school was precious.

Sometimes, the weather provided a welcome reprieve. Russia is a country with many climatic zones, ranging from cold to damn cold. To avoid having kids freeze off their vital organs in the winter, there were strict rules for every region, setting the precise temperature at which school would be cancelled for the day. For Leningrad, snow days started at −30 degrees Celsius.** When that happened, we all just put on an extra layer or a bigger hat and played outside anyway.

My other way out of school was through a teacher's illness. When regular teachers were absent, there weren't any substitutes covering for them—we just got a free period. One of the most cherished phrases of my childhood was *"ko vtoromu uroku"* (second-period start). It meant that the teacher of the first scheduled lesson was ill. This meant we'd have no homework due for that subject and we could sleep in for an extra hour in the morning. Plus, there was always hope that the teacher was down with something nontrivial that might require extensive bed rest or even hospitalization, and that there might be more "second-period starts" ahead. When I was in sixth grade, this happened with our Russian language teacher, Oktyabrina Ilyinichna. She was out for three weeks with gout or sciatica or some such. For three blissful weeks, we all slept in until second period.

In any case, the surest way to get out of school was to get sick yourself.

Notably, Soviet attitudes toward children's health were, to put it mildly, inconsistent. On the one hand, no one cared when kids did dangerous and stupid things that could easily get them killed. My mom and Grandma didn't care much that I was walking rooftops, making bombs, or sticking self-crafted metal objects into electric sockets. They did, however, insist

*22 Fahrenheit

that I wear a hat and scarf from October till May, regardless of the actual weather; that I never drink from public soda glasses; and that I never, ever touch the rubber handrail of the subway escalator: "Those rails are notorious hotbeds of germs!"

Every upper respiratory infection was treated as though it were a whole order of magnitude more impactful than it really was. A typical Soviet childhood was an endless parade of injections, checkups, quarantines, and hospitalizations. If a Western child wakes up feeling under the weather in the morning, they are given something for their sore throat and sent off to school. When I was little, a cold was grounds for forced bed rest. Anytime my temperature popped above 37 degrees Celsius,* Grandma immediately ordered me to bed and called the clinic to request a home visit. The USSR was set up pretty well in this respect. When you got sick, instead of schlepping to the doctor, you got a house call. The doctor would arrive within a few hours, examine you, write the necessary prescriptions, and even do a follow-up visit several days later.

* * *

Unlike other kinds of shops, where shelves were often empty, pharmacies were usually reliably stocked with the basics. They sold only medicine and vitamins. (No moisturizers, skin-care products, diapers, tampons, or diet pills—because they did not exist in the USSR.) Almost everything in the pharmacies, including strong antibiotics, was available without prescription. To compensate for the shortfalls of Big Pharma, Soviet citizens made heavy use of things that would be considered alternative medicine in the West.

*98.6 Fahrenheit

For instance, most people in the USSR were big believers in homeopathy. Grandma was one of them. She kept a ton of tiny round sugar pellets with supposed homeopathic properties in her medicine cabinet. So did Mom. (Following our family's schismatic tradition, we had two medicine cabinets, one Mom's and one Grandma's.)

External boo-boos were treated with marigold ointment, which got slathered on everything from burns to hemorrhoids. To treat the "nerves"—a concept encompassing everything from mild anxiety to clinical depression—there was herbal Validol, Korvalol, and valerian root extract drops. Most quarrels between Grandma and Mom about whether Alyosha or myself got the biggest chicken drumstick at lunch ended with the two participants "calming down the nerves" with valerian drops.

And then there were mustard plasters: pieces of paper covered with a layer of mustard paste. These were moistened and stuck to your back or chest, where they would adhere and work their stinging, burning magic. We used them to treat bronchitis, pneumonia, arthritis, and other illnesses for which heat was considered salubrious.

One could also improve blood flow with the millennia-old Chinese cupping treatment, which for some inexplicable reason became a commonplace remedy in the USSR. This required several little glass jars, which were held upside down one at a time, passed over a flame of burning cloth soaked in spirit to burn off the oxygen, and placed immediately onto the patient's back, where they suction-sealed themselves to the skin. They were usually left in place for half an hour or so. When they came off, they left behind round purple welts.

In the '80s, after Vietnam started pulling itself together economically, a new product appeared in Soviet pharmacies that became known as "the Vietnamese salve." Its other colloquial name was "starlet" because the tiny red-and-green tin it came in was branded with the yellow star of Vietnam in the center. It was the Vietnamese version of Tiger Balm. This "starlet" was intended to soothe aching muscles, but like many medicines in the USSR, it was self-administered for a great number of other ailments as well—from headaches and the flu, to stinky toes.

Finally, there were the two pillars of Soviet home remedies: *margantsovka*, or potassium permanganate; and *zelenka*, "green stuff." *Zelenka* is a Russian artifact invented during World War I that, to my knowledge, has never been used anywhere else in the world. It is an alcohol solution made from a triarylmethane dye called "brilliant green." *Zelenka* is fairly effective against gram-positive bacteria, and unlike iodine, it doesn't irritate mucous membranes. As one would expect, it turns your skin a magnificent (and I mean spectacular) shade of emerald.

Potassium permanganate, which we've already met as a component of my homemade magnesium bomb, was also a disinfectant. It was used to treat irritation in sensitive areas, like the genitals. One washed the part in question with a weak solution of these crystals. If one suspected food poisoning, one drank a full glass of an even weaker solution of this stuff. If cleaning one's tiny willy with it was marginally tolerable, drinking it was truly revolting.

Medical specialists were some of the most revered of all professionals (of course, barring meat shop salesmen and butchers). Though they were all state employees and received state-regulated salaries, they didn't see just anyone. Some of them only saw patients they were introduced to personally, via recommendations. Being friends with a good doctor was invaluable.

Although all medical services in the USSR were free, it was customary to give presents to the specialists one consulted. The most popular presents were hard-to-find delicacies like a box of chocolates or a can of instant coffee, and for a female doctor, some hard-to-find perfume or a pair of pantyhose. And yes, giving the latter was absolutely normal and carried no erotic connotations whatsoever. If your malady was especially time-consuming or difficult, a Kiev cake might have to be deployed.

* * *

A simple cold usually meant I would be forced to stay in bed for a week. If I had even a low-grade fever, Grandma didn't allow me to walk. As soon as it became apparent that I was getting sick, Grandma would carry me into her own room and air out the bedroom I shared with my brother. Once I was resettled in my own room, I would not be allowed to leave it again for a good while. For the next few days, my life would revolve around pills, hot milk, and endless gargling. Since I wasn't allowed out of bed, instead of having me gargle in the bathroom, Grandma would bring me a basin and a glass with the gargling solution right to my bedside. It was usually some heavily salted and herbal liquid, with a hint of iodine. Despite its horrible taste, it actually did make my throat feel better. The same logic applied to peeing: a variety of portable vessels were repurposed as bedpans, depending on how severely bedridden I was.

The second half of any illness was basically extra vacation days. I would laze around in my bed reading my stash of *Time* magazines, listening to foreign records, and daydreaming. Even though I went a little stir-crazy, it was better than school. After a week of bed rest, I had to go to the clinic for a full array of blood and urine tests. Only after being given an unequivocal bill of health was I permitted to return to school, with the option of remaining excused from PE for at least another week.

Despite all these positives, lying trapped in bed for days, with or without a fever, brought on tedium, and eventually anxiety attacks. Being bedridden distilled and magnified all the worst aspects of existence. The food, though it seemed scarcely possible, got even blander. The entertainment got even scarcer, and if Grandma decided I was too sick to "strain the eyes" reading, it disappeared altogether. So did freedom of movement, especially if I wasn't even allowed to go to the bathroom and had to use the bedpan. If it starts to seem like I'm describing solitary confinement, it was not far off. The Soviet system of care for its wards, whether criminal, psychotic, free-thinking, or merely feverish, replicated itself faithfully throughout all institutions and households.

* * *

Sometimes when I was sick in bed and staring at a tiny square of sky through the window, it would occur to me that if I could get sick, then so could Grandma. And from there, I would arrive at the inescapable fact that she was old and eventually—possibly quite soon—would die.

This thought did not occur to me altogether spontaneously. Grandma stoked my fears of her demise at every opportunity, both fitting and not. Whenever we went to visit the cemetery where Grandpa was buried, she would always sigh and say, "This is where I will be when I die—right here." But she could also answer a simple inquiry about whether she'd like a new blouse by saying she didn't need any more new clothes, period. "I won't even have time to wear out the things I already have before I die," she'd assert.

When I ran a fever, the unavoidable fact of Grandma's permanent disappearance would almost become a physical sensation. Once, when I was about ten years old, in bed with real bad flu, I broke into tears under my thick blanket thinking about it. I had a high fever and felt awful, and I was just so tired of the never-ending winter, its total monotony and the darkness that fell on the city at three o'clock in the afternoon. To top it all off, the day before, someone at school had stolen my favorite 3-D cowboy soldier, the really rare and hard-to-get one, with a lasso, that could stand on its own and be put on a horse!

I started to cry loudly and purposefully enough for Grandma to hear me from wherever she was, the kitchen or her room, and come to console me. A minute later, she appeared on the doorstep.

"What's wrong?" she asked.

"Nothing . . ." I mumbled, looking at my matte reflection in the door of the lacquered cabinet next to my bed. I could see the tears roll down my reflected cheeks.

"*Nu*, it's all right. I'm here," she said, thinking it was just my temperature talking. "Are you thirsty? I'll bring you some water with lemon."

She left again. I promised myself that when she came back, I would buck up and tell her. When she returned with a glass of sugared water with lemon juice, I blurted out, "Granny, I'm scared that you'll die!" I began to sob.

She smiled and kissed me.

"Don't worry," she said. "I'll be with you for a long, long time. I'll make sure that you grow up and finish school first. And then we'll see. . . Here, take a sip. I promise, by the time you're done drinking it, you'll feel right as rain."

I believed her, and I drank. And I fell asleep.

Grandma did not lie to me. She lived for three more decades, dying at the age of ninety-five.

August 20, 2011

When I entered Grandma's empty apartment the next morning, all the mirrors had already been veiled by her aide, following an old tradition that this helps the deceased get to the next world smoothly. Her body had been removed the day before.

Burials in Russia have always been a bureaucratic maze. Custom dictates that there is only one appropriate time to bury anyone, and that is on the third day after the death. (This one is a Christian tradition linked to the concept of the Trinity and the belief that only on the third day after death will the link between the body and the soul be finally broken.)

It was now day two, and the clock was ticking.

I spent the day running around various offices and frantically filling out paperwork. I had to register Grandma's death, cancel her internal passport, inform the registration office of this fact, and get approved for a refusal of the postmortem. This being done, I headed to the cemetery to secure her burial plot. Grandma had always wanted to be interred next to her husband, my grandpa Roman. There could be no one else laying claim to that spot, so I hoped this part would be easy.

My hopes were in vain. The cemetery manager—an oily man with small, beady eyes and a gold tooth, dressed in soiled gray overalls but sporting a substantial Swiss IWC watch—sat me down on a bench in the cemetery office corridor.

"We've got a problem, Mr. Grechishkin," he said with a smile that promised nothing good. "A birch tree."

"A birch tree?" I asked.

"Yes. It grew, you see. On the plot. And sadly, we're not allowed"—he smiled even wider—"to dig a grave within a meter and a half of a tree trunk."

"Why?" I asked.

The question stumped him, but not for long.

"Ecological regulations. It might disturb the ecosystem and start root rot. And then the tree might die and fall over. What if a mourner is at the grave at that very moment? It would be tragic."

"So cut it down," I said.

"Unfortunately, it will take about two weeks to secure the permission for that. Maybe even three weeks, since it is August, you know, dacha season . . ."

I knew exactly where this conversation was heading.

"We have to bury my grandmother tomorrow," I said, resigned. "Maybe you could think of some . . . alternative solution?"

This question always leads to a real burst of creativity among Russian officials. And so our real conversation started. First, he asked for 250,000 rubles cash (about 5,000 USD) for a brand-new plot at this cemetery, which officially stopped allocating new plots in the 1950s. I had a brief vision of some poor, forgotten fellow being dug up out of his resting place in the middle of the night to make room for Grandma, and declined. Then he asked for 100,000 rubles to close the administration's eyes to the issue of the birch tree on Grandma's plot. It was not a terribly big birch yet, after all. Had Grandma lived another five years, the price might have been double. Arming myself with my entire arsenal of investment banking negotiation skills, I went to battle. When all was said and done, I was out just 30,000 rubles, and Grandma would sleep in peace next to a birch.

I left the graveyard in the evening under pouring rain, thinking that modern Russian cemetery administrators might just be the most corrupt people in Russia, and therefore on earth, making their cynical living off mourners in no condition to negotiate.

Also, I thought, why did it have to be a birch, of all things? Grandma hated Russian birches.

Tomorrow was going to be a hard day.

CHAPTER 15

CHANGING BODIES, CHANGING LIVES

A boy goes in the morning to his parents' bedroom, but the door is locked.

He looks through the keyhole for a while, then, shocked, goes back to his room, mumbling to himself:

"And these people have the nerve to lecture me about picking my nose. . ."

IN 1982, THE United States and the Soviet Union held a teleconference. This "tele-bridge," as we called it, was a sort of proto-Skype session connecting Moscow and Los Angeles. Its purpose was to bridge ideological differences as vast as the oceans. An auditorium filled with people sat in front of a huge screen in Moscow, connected via satellite to another auditorium on the other side of the world. The two groups would trade questions through interpreters. The event was a huge success, so the authorities started organizing them every year or so, switching between Moscow and Leningrad. People all over Russia tuned in, curious to catch a glimpse of life inside the United States and hear actual Americans talk about themselves. Over the course of five years, 180 million Soviet citizens watched these telecasts. I never missed one.

In July 1986, the tele-bridge connected Leningrad and Boston. Its theme was "Women Speaking to Women." Actually, a few of our school's teachers took part in it. This event was hosted by Vladimir Pozner on the Soviet side and Phil Donahue on the American side. The two of them would later spend five years cohosting a show on CNBC, *Pozner & Donahue*. Vladimir Pozner, who was born in France and grew up in Manhattan, spoke English like a native, so he was a natural fit.

The tone of the show was somewhat passive-aggressive. Each side would ask the other pointed questions about unemployment, militarism, freedom of speech, and race relations, while trying to explain, not very subtly, how much better life was on their side of the Iron Curtain. The Soviets asked about the difficulties of childcare and health care in America without the social safety net. Americans brought up the downed Korean Airlines plane. The Soviets sideswiped with the *Challenger*. Americans asked how things were going in Afghanistan. The Soviets parried with Vietnam.

But the iconic moment of the show came toward the end of "Women Speaking to Women," when one American participant asked a question about advertising.

"Our advertising revolves around sex," she said. "Do you have TV ads like that?"

Her Soviet counterpart, a hotel administrator, answered very earnestly, "We don't have any sex, and we are absolutely against it."

She meant that there was no sex in TV advertising, first and foremost because the USSR had no TV advertising at all. But audiences on both sides burst into uproarious laughter and applause. A meme was born: "There is no sex in the Soviet Union."

Indeed, there was no sex in the USSR. Sex was a taboo subject. No sexual revolution ever happened in the USSR. Even the word *sex* itself was considered practically unspeakable. The only two kinds of words describing sexual congress between two humans were either medical terms or obscenities.

It wasn't always this way. There was a brief period of euphoria in the 1920s, at the dawn of the young Soviet state, when there was much talk about the emancipation of women and sexual freedom. But when Stalin came to power soon after, he took a hard reactionary stance on everything pertaining to the personal affairs of his citizens. Abortions were outlawed, homosexuality was criminalized, and divorce became much more difficult to obtain.

The Soviet world was absurdly prudish. Female nudity was not allowed in any publications or films and was censored in foreign movies, along with any indication of lust beyond a regulation-length on-screen kiss. Naturally, this led to a vibrant black market for pornography. On commuter trains, peddlers would walk up and down the cars selling homemade black-and-white erotic photographs or decks of playing cards with naked women on them. For some reason, these people were usually deaf, or at least presented themselves as such, perhaps as an effort to discourage police attention.

Prostitution existed but was carefully concealed from the public eye. At our school, rumors circulated about loose girls who hung around railway stations wearing rings made of three- or five-ruble banknotes, depending on what they charged. Everyone also knew there were higher-class ladies of the evening who worked in foreigners-only Intourist hotels. Naturally, these women were curated by the KGB.

Sex education was completely absent from the school curriculum. A visiting alien might well have thought that Soviet citizens reproduced through budding. The government had many momentous things to impart to us: how and why the Revolution happened, who were the good and the bad guys in the world of geopolitics, why Western capitalism was doomed in the long term. But with respect to sex, it offered only two things: nineteenth-century literary romances and a brief breakdown of mammalian sexual reproduction in biology class. It was assumed that young people would just figure things out on their own.

My parents and my grandma didn't talk to me about sex, either. When I was about seven, a family friend got married and had a baby shortly after.

"Why do babies only happen after people marry?" I asked Mom.

"I don't know," she replied without looking at me. "Ask Dad." (She meant Tolya, who was sitting right there with a cigarette and a newspaper.)

I redirected my inquiry to him. Tolya said that he didn't know, either, and went back to his sports page.

And that was it. Not even an "I'll tell you when you're older." I remember being very surprised at their answers—how could they not know? It was clear that they were intentionally concealing something from me.

Later that year, while Grandma and I were on holiday at a cross-country skiing retreat, I became friends with an eight-year-old boy who was more than willing to explain to me where babies come from, in graphic detail. It all sounded deeply bizarre. It couldn't possibly be true, I thought. But when I got back to school after the break, it turned out that Vova had the same account of things. After discussing it for a while, we came to the mutual conclusion that there must be a variety of ways children come about, because no way would our parents ever do anything gross like that. Just NO way.

Naturally, we were taught nothing about contraception or STDs, either at home or at school. In my late teenage years, I learned from the girls that there was some sort of "Hungarian pill," but that it supposedly wasn't good for you, and very few girls were taking it. The most common form of contraception in the USSR was the pull-out method, combined with douching with a weak solution of *margantsovka* (potassium permanganate). Women would jump out of bed and run to the bathroom, where they had a rubber douche filled with that pink liquid ready to go. The same was sometimes also done with lemon juice, but that was much harder to find and very expensive. Both substances were supposed to kill the little swimmers, or at least make them less mobile through acidity.

In some pharmacies, one could acquire a domestically manufactured *prezervativ* (condom). They were probably five times as thick as condoms today. The word *prezervativ* itself was practically a swear word, and *gandon*, a corruption of "condom," was one of the very worst things you could call somebody. Pharmacy shoppers usually referred to it as "product number 4" and even that was said in a whisper. And as if that wasn't humiliating enough, you also had to tell the already reproachful saleswoman your size, since there were three to choose from. The condoms themselves were each packaged in foil with a stamp across it that read "Tested by Electronics." Which would be fine, except that in 1979, a children's movie had come out where the main character was an adolescent android named Electronik. Vova and I used to joke that the kid from the movie must've gotten himself a sweet gig.

* * *

To say puberty was unkind to me is to say that Russia has somewhat chilly winters.

I was the youngest and the smallest boy in my class. Grandma was proud that her grandson was smart enough to start school almost a year early, but I hated it. Still, it was relatively easy to deal with when we were all kids together. But then puberty hit, and it hit everyone but me.

During a medical checkup in grade eight, the doctor dealt me a severe psychological blow: I saw him write "Delay in sexual development" on my chart. I tried to tell myself that he probably just didn't check my birth date and simply went by general pubescent benchmarks set for all boys of my class year. But in my heart, I knew it was the truth. In seventh grade, my friends started to tower over me. In eighth grade, they were already growing whiskers. Meanwhile, I remained stubbornly short, button-nosed, and hairless. To add insult to injury, I still chirped in a boy's soprano. Whenever my friends called me on the phone and I answered, they often thought I was my mom.

No one in my family understood the extent to which this bothered me. Mom made all the usual noises about how big I was getting and how I would have underarm hair soon, but to me it just sounded like mockery. And as for armpit hair, I agonized over its lack endlessly, wishing and hoping that I might finally get some. Every few days, I would shave my hairless armpits with Tolya's electric razor, hoping that it would somehow stimulate the hair follicles to finally cough up the goods. But over a year into the general pubertal bacchanalia, I was still as smooth as a dolphin. When my friends and I were in communal showers, some of them would ask me, in all earnestness, why I shaved *everywhere*. It was mortifying.

Negotiating first relationships was tricky. At school, boys mostly socialized with other boys, and girls with other girls. The genders only mixed in the first grade or two, and then in the last ones, when mutual wariness finally gave way to romantic stirrings. But for most of the school years, they stayed apart. Approaching your crush to ask them out was tremendously awkward.

We were helped somewhat by two holidays. The USSR didn't celebrate Valentine's Day, so there were no state-sanctioned days of open flirtation and overtures, but it did celebrate Red Army and Navy Day on February 23 and International Women's Day on March 8. On Red Army and Navy Day, women gave gifts to all the menfolk in their family. (In the USSR, all men were considered to be in the armed services, whether their enrollment was in the past, present, or future.)

The gifts were as predictable as any Father's Day haul in the West: ties and colognes for men, school supplies for boys. At school, girls would also give gifts to us boys. For the most part, it was done rather unsentimentally: the class representative bought every boy the same thing so that nobody would feel slighted. But some of the girls would slip their personal crushes a little something extra—a note, or a piece of candy, or a small toy.

Two weeks later, the boys got a chance to reciprocate. Unlike February 23, March 8, International Women's Day, was a national holiday. On March 8, the courtship roles of Red Army and Navy Day were reversed, and now the boys lavished attention and gifts on the girls. Now the boy who had received an extra token from some girl could choose whether or not to give her something special in return.

March 8 was a much grander holiday than February 23. Its scope extended beyond immediate family or one's classroom.

On that day, men were supposed to offer compliments, flowers, and gifts to *all* the women in their lives—not just family members and classmates or coworkers but every woman and girl around, down to doctors and saleswomen. So we dutifully brought gifts for our female classmates and flowers for our female teachers, usually bouquets of fluffy yellow acacia flowers colloquially called *mimoza*. We also wrote endless cards for our female relatives and made tons of kitchen utensils in shop class for our mothers and grandmothers. And of course, we wished every woman we met that day a happy March 8.

Unlike mythological King Midas, who turned everything he touched into gold, the Soviet Union turned everything it touched into shit. International Women's Day was a good example. The original purpose of March 8, when it was established by the suffragette movement in 1909 in America, was to promote women's struggle for gender equality and the right to vote. In the Soviet Union, it had become something like the Western Mother's Day and Valentine's Day rolled into one—a festival of sexism and celebratory acknowledgment of women being the *slabyj pol*, "the weaker sex." I've always felt there was something odd about congratulating half of humanity indiscriminately simply for being born with ovaries. It's a sort of pathetic, pseudo-chivalrous overcompensation for the systematic misogyny in place the rest of the year.

Meanwhile, our teachers had no need of shy courtship rituals. Our school was a veritable hotbed of teacher-on-teacher action. The students followed their torrid affairs as closely as they would a Brazilian soap opera.*

---

*Not that we had ever seen any. The first mega-popular Brazilian telenovela to be broadcast in the USSR, Escrava Isaura, was still four years away.

The teachers' affairs were as tawdry as they were torrid. The gossipy upperclassmen's favorite pair was our geography teacher and our physics teacher. Everyone constantly compared notes on who'd seen them together and where. Every day, it seemed, they were spotted coming out of a closed physics lab, red-faced and with shirts buttoned up all wrong. Both of them were married to other people. But they were not the only adulterous pair. Our married art teacher was also having an affair, with our married shop teacher. It ended in two divorces, one new marriage, and an eventual emigration to the US.

When I was fourteen, a cute Armenian girl from my class named Karina, who played the violin, called me at home and asked me out to a classical music concert at the Conservatory. When I heard her speak, I almost fell over, I was so stunned.

"Sergey, my music teacher gave me two tickets for Tchaikovsky's Violin Concerto on Friday evening. I was going to go with Vika, but she can't come. It's her dad's birthday. Would you like to go with me?"

I desperately wanted to say yes, but I was terrified. I had no idea how to behave at a concert with a girl. What were the rules? When Vova and I went to a concert, we spent half the time shoving each other awake with our elbows and the other half making plans for what we were going to eat at the café during intermission. Presumably, this was not the thing to do with a young lady. But what was? And what would happen if news of my naïveté got out? I would be the class laughing stock! Crippled by awkwardness, I declined Karina's invitation.

"That sounds great," I finally said, hating myself for being a coward, "but I have a lot of homework for Saturday. . . and I also already promised my stepdad that I would help him with a thing on Friday. . . I wish I could. Sorry. . ."

And I hung up on her, like the loser I was.

* * *

In eighth grade, two momentous things happened.

The first thing was that our whole class had to undergo a series of medical checkups. One of the tests involved getting a fluorography, a type of chest X-ray made against a fluorescent screen. It was used to check one's lungs for tuberculosis, which was still a big public health issue in the USSR. The boys went first, then the girls. There was only one female teacher with us, so when the girls went in for their turn, we were left to wait outside.

The room where everyone was being "fluorographed" was on the raised ground floor. Its windows were not very high up, and there were no curtains or blinds on them. Needless to say, the second someone saw the first girl getting undressed for her procedure, all of us started jumping up and down to get a glimpse of her boobies. We were dismayed to discover that the girls were being screened in their bras. But we continued jumping nonetheless. Since there were no actual breasts to be seen, we contented ourselves with discussing the color of everyone's bras and the level of their transparency.

The second, and more lasting thing, was that a new girl transferred to our homeroom.

This was a big deal. In all our years of school, only three or four people in total either joined or left our class. The new girl, Olya Moskvina, was a disruption to our well-established dynamic. She was also very easy on the eyes. In fact, she looked a bit like the American singer Madonna, whom I'd seen on a cover of a smuggled audio cassette, with everything in the right place, as far as we guys were concerned. And if that weren't enough, she was the daughter of two very well-known figure skating coaches. They had been world champions in their own right in the 1950s and '60s, before going on to make equally successful careers coaching many of the top Soviet Olympic figure skaters. The USSR was obsessed with figure skating, so the Moskvins were genuine celebrities; everyone knew who they were. Because her parents often traveled abroad, Olya also had a lot of foreign stuff that normal Soviet children could never dream of and didn't even know existed. This gave her an air of quasi-Western glamour. Every boy in our class fell in love with her, including still-squeaky, still-little me.

In the evenings, before the snow season started, Vova and I would get together to jog around our district. Our route took us around the Tauride Gardens. On the way back, when it was already dark, we would often swing by Olya's house and hang out in her courtyard looking up at her window.

Olya was not my first crush. The first one was Yana Poplavskaya, the star of the film musical *About Little Red Riding Hood*. Mom and Tolya thought it was totally hilarious and teased me about being in love. My next crush, some years later, was on Natasha Guseva, the actress who played Alisa, the protagonist of the sci-fi miniseries *Guest from the Future*. Alisa was very pretty, amazingly athletic, highly empathetic, and a polyglot. However, she hailed from the bright Communist future, where she was just a regular person. I could watch her do somersaults over a fence all day. (I mean, I couldn't, of course: there was no way to rewind live TV, and almost no one in the USSR had a VCR yet.) It wasn't just her looks or acting talent. Something about her appearing on TV at the precise moment when everything in the country was poised for massive changes created for me a sense of congruence between the fictional world on TV and the real world outside. For once, the regular world marching toward a brilliant tomorrow on TV looked exactly like the world all around me. I had been told for years that the future was going to be amazing; that year,

I sensed tension and anticipation in the air and, for the first time, felt like I was not being lied to. Something big and exciting was coming.

But eventually, the hormone fairy arrived on my doorstep as well. One day I was still tiny and squeaky, and then, seemingly overnight, I shot up fifteen centimeters. By the end of tenth grade, I was second tallest in the class—1.9 meters, which is about six foot three.

Around age fifteen or so, my friends and I had finally gotten over our collective fear of girls, and we began to hang out with them. Everything we did together fell under the umbrella term of "strolling" or "promenading" (the Russian equivalent of "going out," with a more insouciant twist). In the evenings, after all the homework was done, I would call one of my pals, and we would go to one of our courtyards or boulevards.

Kalyaeva Street, like many in Leningrad, used to have rails. Before the Revolution, horse-powered streetcars ran on them. Afterwards, the city took out the rails and made the center of the street where they lay a pedestrian walkway complete with benches and shrubbery, from Liteyny Avenue to the Tauride Gardens. When I was in my last years of school, this was where we hung out almost every warm evening. We earmarked a few benches as "our" benches and we'd sit there for hours chatting with girls. My friend Vasya Bazanov, who lived across the street, would sometimes bring his dog, Jack, a scruffy, slobbery, monstrously huge mutt whose looks seemed to hint at wolfhound and Newfoundland ancestry. Jack was a big aficionado of everything female: passing dogs of every size and breed, our girlfriends, even stuffed toys. He expressed this admiration by constantly humping the air in the direction of the object of his attention, which we all found hysterical.

There wasn't much we could do as a group. We couldn't get together at anyone's place; all of us lived in tiny apartments or even single rooms, and we shared them with parents, grandparents, siblings, and other unwelcoming occupants. Sure, I could visit Vova or Sasha or Vasya at home, but I could hardly bring five or six people with me. So whenever we were more than three, our options were courtyards, boulevards, or possibly a café on Tchaikovsky Street that we all called "Roaches." (Three guesses as to why.) Roaches was a good place to blow a few kopecks on some awful coffee and slightly less awful ice cream.

My fondest memory of Roaches is from when we were in eighth grade. Our school had volunteered us to do some community service raking fallen leaves in Letny Park. Afterwards, a bunch of us went over to Roaches, pooled our pocket change, and bought ourselves a bottle of Soviet champagne to celebrate our heroic labors. Technically, at fourteen we were not allowed to buy alcohol, but the saleswoman—bespectacled, permed, and remarkably curvaceous like most Soviet saleswomen at cafés, grocery stores, and other sites of improved nutritional access—knew us and considered us well-behaved children. Besides, one bottle of champagne split ten ways or so left everyone with just a few drops. Be that as it may, those drops were rich with ceremonial significance. Buying and consuming one's first bottle of alcohol in public felt like a huge milestone on our way toward Soviet adulthood. The sense of impending adventure was overwhelming, and we all stumbled home in high spirits, intoxicated in a way that could not be measured by any breathalyzer.

When the season permitted it, many of us went skateboarding in the evenings. Skateboards were all the rage in the mid-'80s in the USSR, largely because they were so very Western. Sometimes we boarded on my street, since the asphalt there was nice and even; other times, we'd head to the Engineers' Castle, an eighteenth-century palace on the beautiful Fontanka River quay. There were so few cars back then that we basically had the entire run of the street to ourselves. (Statistically speaking, even in the relatively wealthy Leningrad, there were only 70 vehicles for every 1,000 people in 1985, as opposed to 570 in the United States. When I finished my well-off city-center school in 1987, out of my class of twenty-eight people, only four families had cars.)

*   *   *

In ninth grade, the two homerooms of our grade level were merged into one. Some kids had left school to enroll in specialized schools, various technical or trade colleges, for which entry required only eight years of schooling. It was an exciting time. For eight years, our two classes had passed each other like ships in the night, only coming briefly into contact at recess and at lunch, and now we were all going to have lessons together! It was a time for new friendships and new crushes.

It was also time to say goodbye to Vova. His parents decided that he should apply to a renowned Leningrad school, Number 239, with extra hours of math and physics. The school took in kids for their last two years before college, and it was considered to be an incubator of genuine eggheads who would have no trouble getting into the university of their choice upon graduation. Vova got in, and that was all she wrote.

Nothing would change, we thought. And it didn't—at least not at first. School 239 was not far away from our old 185, and also not far from both our houses. The gravitational pull of central Leningrad remained as strong as ever. We hung out after school as before, then, as time went on, less and less often, until about six months later we both got so busy with our schoolwork, clubs, and new friends that we were only ever talking to each other on the phone, and even those calls petered out to nothing after a few months. It was a very common story. Thus I found myself approaching my last years of school all alone: no girlfriend and now no best friend, either.

Later, I would hear from mutual friends that Vova's parents and his little half sister immigrated to the US, but Vova remained in Leningrad to look after his grandma, in a reversal of their earlier roles. By then, I was getting ready to leave the country myself.

Three years ago, I finally saw him again, after a twenty-five-year break. To our mutual joy, we shot the breeze as if no time had passed, though this might be due in part to the extraordinary amount and variety of beverages we consumed that evening. I wonder sometimes what would have happened if Vova hadn't gotten me interested in archaeology in the first place. My entire life rolled out of that book about Schliemann's search for Troy.

Vova Nadezhdin, wherever you are today: thanks, man!

CHAPTER 16

EVERYTHING WAS FOREVER, UNTIL IT WAS NO MORE

Brezhnev, Andropov, and Chernenko chat in heaven:

"So, who supports Gorbachev these days?"

"Nobody, it seems. I'm as surprised as you. He seems to be able to walk entirely on his own."

MIKHAIL SERGEYEVICH GORBACHEV, elected by the politburo to be the general secretary three hours after Chernenko's death in March 1985, was a very different breed of general secretary.

"Mihalsergeich," as he was usually called, was a southerner and spoke with a thick accent, which carries the same connotations in Russia as it does in the US. To our refined northern intelligentsia ears, he sounded like a country bumpkin, constantly emphasizing the wrong syllables and even making grammatical errors. This was not unusual. Soviet leaders often came from far-off regions, and they were not an eloquent bunch. Stalin was a literate man, but he came from Georgia and spoke with a strong Georgian accent. Khrushchev was Ukrainian and was charismatic but poorly educated and crude. Brezhnev's bouquet of speech defects had made him sound as though he were chewing a boiled rag. And as for his two short-lived successors, they weren't around long enough to make a lasting aural impression on the populace.

My grandma always listened to political speeches on the radio or on TV with a sneer. She was brought up to speak "properly," and the inarticulateness of her rulers distressed her on a profound level. But Gorbachev softened her aging heart. His country-boy accent just made him sound more genuine and sincere.

And then there was his age. At fifty-four, the new general secretary of the Communist Party of the Soviet Union was a stripling. He belonged to a completely different generation than the three gerontocrats who had shuffled off their mortal coils before him. He was the first Soviet leader to have been born well after the October Revolution. One look at his glowing, youthful mug with its huge, oddly decorative port-wine birthmark on the forehead, and it was instantly obvious that our tradition of football and *pyshki* doughnuts in commemoration of dead general secretaries would have to be put on ice.

But his uniqueness was more than just a matter of a new generation ascending to power. When Gorbachev visited Leningrad shortly after his appointment in May, his motorcade rolled down Nevsky Prospect. But something strange happened: his car stopped. And then we watched, completely agog, as our new, energetic leader got out and went to shake hands with people in the crowd! This was unprecedented. No previous general secretary had ever glad-handed with the masses. Gorbachev's predecessors had belonged to a loftier realm, one insulated from the hoi polloi by concentric circles of advisers, aides, staff medics, and security personnel. And here was this new guy, acting all normal!

And he went and delivered a speech unlike any we've ever heard before. He said things we'd never heard from any Soviet leader. He openly admitted that the Soviet economy was stagnating, that the domestic industrial machinery was in poor condition and out of date, that the Soviet standard of living was unacceptably low. He also said that the party could no longer be focused exclusively on the needs of the working class at a time when the number of college-educated white-collar workers was skyrocketing.

The censors didn't know what to make of it. Statements this critical of the USSR had never appeared in the official Soviet press. Had anyone but the general secretary said the same words out loud in a Leningrad public square, they might have been detained by the police for anti-Soviet propaganda. At the end of the day, the censors decided to err on the side of caution and snipped out all the ideologically iffy bits. When the speech appeared in the papers, it was blue-penciled down to only a few paragraphs. Television censors were also flummoxed. Unlike the newspapermen, they had to deal with video footage, which wasn't so easy to cut up at will. In the end, it would take them four days to get it in the right shape to be aired.

"I'm here to listen to the people of Leningrad," Gorbachev said to the rubbernecking crowd around him and the men in suits accompanying him. It was unusually warm that May in Leningrad. The sun was shining and the fresh spring winds were gently wafting from the Baltic Sea. And everyone could feel that something was happening.

"What would you like to tell me? I'm listening," he continued.

"Carry on the way you started!" shouted a man from the back of the crowd.

"Thank you," said Gorbachev. "I will."

And oh boy, did he ever. . .

* * *

Convention had it that Communist Party congresses, which in my lifetime took place every five years, were written in Roman numerals. The twenty-seventh session, which took place in February and March 1986, was therefore rendered as XXVII. If you squint, and you're an adolescent boy, from a distance that looks like the Russian word ХУЙ, namely, "cock." This word was always rich in meaning and connotations and a big favorite with fledgling graffiti artists. It could be found on stairway walls in apartment buildings, school windowsills, and just about every fence.

But this "cock" was only the second-most interesting thing about this particular congress. The most fascinating thing about it was that the Communist Party of the Soviet Union changed its final objectives. It no longer officially set its sights on "building Communism." Now, it aimed for "perfecting socialism." It also made plans for doubling the economic potential of the USSR and providing each household with a separate apartment by the year 2000. (But by now no one believed the party's fairy tales anymore.)

Gorbachev's plan for perfecting Soviet socialism lay in *uskorenie*, "acceleration." The economy was stagnant, and he wanted to give it a boost. To do this, Gorbachev wanted to accelerate the pace of industrial development in the USSR, primarily through advancing heavy industry. This meant increased funding, improved labor discipline, and a review of management. In the Marxist view of economics, heavy industry would then pull up the rest of the economy with it.

Gorby made mention of other things in his opening speech at the party congress: *perestroika* (restructuring), *glasnost* (openness), and *demokratizatziya* (this one's pretty obvious). But for now, they were just the side dishes. The entrée was acceleration.

Infusing heavy industry with money was easy enough. But tackling labor discipline was a whole different matter. Broadly speaking, it was a shambles. The two biggest reasons for this were alcohol and theft.

Alcohol permeated every aspect of Soviet society. To put it bluntly, getting drunk was the primary pastime for tens of millions of Soviet citizens. It's also something for which the Russian language has many dozens of handy synonyms and euphemisms:

- *poddavat*—to drink regularly, but only a little each time;
- *kiryat*—to drink with your closest buddies;
- *obmyvat*—to "wash" a large purchase (like a car or a fridge) with the ceremonial consumption of alcohol;
- *propit*—to lose something (an inheritance, or even that same car or fridge you were "washing" just a short while ago) by drinking it away;
- and, my favorite, *nedoperepit*—to drink more than you should have, but less than you could have.

Before the Revolution, Russians drank no more than people in other northern countries where the long winter months left peasants with little to do while their fields lay dormant under snow except to drink and to make more peasants.

After 1917, the new Soviet government at first launched numerous campaigns to reduce alcohol consumption. After all, it wouldn't do for the workers—i.e., the builders of a bright and glorious Communist tomorrow—to be stumbling drunks. But these benign intentions were scrapped by World War II.

Out on the front lines, soldiers were encouraged to surge into battle with a vodka toast to the motherland and Stalin, and those who returned from combat were rewarded with more of the same. After the war, with the country devastated, the male population decimated, and the Soviet economy in ruins, it turned out that, once again, alcohol, while not exactly a solution to the country's woes, helped the otherwise despondent find the strength to live and work through another day. Like any drug, it hooked the consumer and thereby yielded growing sales, continuously boosting the GDP and government revenues alike; vodka production was, after all, a state monopoly. From that point on, vodka became the government's go-to budget fix. Every time the state ran a budget shortfall, the obvious answer was to produce and sell more vodka, since one could be absolutely sure that it would all be bought up.

My childhood coincided with what was probably the peak alcohol intake of the USSR. Statistics say that the annual alcohol consumption averaged out to about fourteen liters (almost thirty pints) of pure alcohol per capita (i.e., for every man, woman, and baby) per year.

Everyone in the USSR over the age of eighteen knew the prices for different vodka volumes by heart. There was "vodka at 4.12," and "vodka at 3.62." Vodka was sold in quarter-liter, half-liter, and three-quarter-liter containers. If any member of the Soviet public were asked to continue the sequence "0.25, 0.50, 0.75, ___," they would have filled in the blank space with "one liter." The handy quarter-liter bottle was known to be just a touch excessive for one person and not enough for two. However, it had the benefit of fitting into the inner pocket of a suit jacket. The ubiquitous half-liter bottle, or *pol-litra*, was the classic staple of Soviet society. It was drunk *"na troih,"* which is to say split three ways. It even had its own phrase: "to figure it out for three."

Vodka was also a universally preferred currency for transactions with any male laborer. Your toilet is blocked and resident services say that the plumber is booked till next week? *Pol-litra* will make him forget about all his other jobs, first figuratively and then literally! Your dacha garden plot needs to be dug up for potato planting? Offer a *pol-litra* to almost any local passerby and it will happen in no time!

Pol-litra also carried some subtle class attributes. Vodka was a working-class beverage. Once, Mom had nothing else suitable at home and resorted to giving a bottle of vodka to her gynecologist after an appointment as a requisite token of appreciation. When Grandma learned about it, her social barometer went off the scale.

"Vera, how could your hands even dare to shove a bottle of vodka at Boris Moiseevich? Vodka! As if he were a janitor, or a peasant from a collective farm!"

People often "figured it out for three" in semi-public places, like alleys, courtyards, or parks. It was not uncommon to see someone stumbling dead drunk at a bus stop or on the subway, or even lying in the middle of the sidewalk. If enough passersby took exception to this intemperance, a government vehicle would pull up and haul the offender to a *vytrezvitel*, a sobering-up station. These were dorms of a sort where the detained could sleep off their intoxication, drink some water, take some headache pills, wash up, and be on their merry way. The catch was that the sobering-up service would always notify the person's employer of their detention, which led to disciplinary strikes. For career-oriented people, a visit to the *vytrezvitel* could seriously damage one's standing with the party or Komsomol. These recreational services were also not cheap: as payment, and also as a deterrent to future use, twenty rubles was withheld from each client's salary at the end of the month.

No one ever drank for pleasure or taste, only to get drunk as quickly and as thoroughly as possible. The classic *zakuska* (post-vodka-shot nibble) was usually bread, pickled cucumber, or a bite of a processed cheese called Druzhba, which translates to "Friendship." Whatever process was used in creating this Friendship, it left behind a gluey, cloyingly sweet mass only vaguely reminiscent of cheese.

If none of these options were available, there was always the peculiarly intimate option of throwing back the vodka, then sniffing your drinking buddy's unwashed oily hair. Resourcefulness was the second name of the Soviet people.

Alcohol was a universal social lubricant. A person who didn't drink could not really be a proper part of any social gathering, dinner party, bonding session with colleagues, or even kitchen table discussion in certain households. He might even be regarded as a *seksot*, a "secret colleague" of the KGB; what if he didn't drink because he wanted to stay sober while everyone else became intoxicated so that he could write down everything the others said and report it?

Drinking was not just the scourge of the working classes. The intelligentsia drank, too, and drank *hard*. At the end of the day, all of them were stuck in the same dreary gray world, with no way of escaping it. A typical get-together of my dad's bohemian circle of poets, writers, and painters often started with everyone having a full glass of Cognac. Then they would sit down at the table and eat, debating philosophy and literature and drinking more all the while. And then it was anyone's guess what would happen. Usually it would be something idiotic and dangerous. One time in the middle of winter, when it was −20 degrees Celsius* outside, my dad and his friends went for a swim in an ice hole in the Neva River for a bet on

*4 Fahrenheit

who would chicken out first. Another time, Dad spent several months on crutches after falling out of the second-floor window while supposedly washing it. As if anyone believed that for a second. My father, an infamous self-indulgent slob, washing a window? Yeah, right.

Gorbachev decided to tackle the country's crippling alcoholism anew. Alcohol was not banned, as in 1920 in the United States, but access to it was curtailed severely. Many liquor stores were closed permanently, and the remaining ones were put on reduced working hours, only opening in the afternoons, from 2 to 7 p.m. Lines to buy alcohol grew to preposterous lengths.

Andropovka disappeared from the stores entirely. All liquor prices were hiked. Starting from August 1986, the cheapest vodka was priced at a whopping 9.10 rubles! The campaign hit wine producers as well as hard liquor distillers. In the Crimea, Moldova, and Georgia, whole wineries, some of them hundreds of years old, were shut, and vines were chopped down.

The government began to promote the idea of weddings without alcohol, especially for the apparatchiks and their families. For all except the most conscientious party members, this simply meant that no liquor bottles were displayed on the tables; instead, all the booze was covertly dispensed from teakettles. Scenes with people drinking alcohol were censored out of movies. At factories, special committees were created to monitor the sobriety of the workforce, and were empowered to dispense fines for workplace drunkenness and recommend repeat offenders for expulsion from the party.

Needless to say, Gorbachev's popularity with the drinking classes—i.e., the vast majority of the population—plummeted, never to recover.

* * *

A popular, though perhaps apocryphal, story tells us that about two hundred years ago, the Russian writer and historian Nikolay Karamzin visited France. Russian emigrants living there asked him, "Tell us, in a few words, how things are back in the motherland?"

Karamzin only needed one word: *"Voruyut!"* (They steal!)

One could write an extensive psychological case study on the prevalence of theft in the Soviet Union. The general agreement is that it's a fairly fundamental trait of the Russian national character. The Russian language has as many synonyms for petty theft as it has for imbibing alcohol. Some of them are pretty telling. For instance, someone who steals everything that isn't nailed down is said "to pick up everything that lies poorly," a turn of phrase that deftly shifts the responsibility for the theft onto the item's original owner.

Nor was the Soviet Union as a country particularly averse to stealing. Leaving the question of international copyright to academics, the USSR nicked American schematics for the atomic bomb, West German blueprints for radios, and anything else its industrial spies could get their mitts on. Foreign electronics were constantly pulled apart, analyzed, and meticulously copied. A great number of Soviet products were calques of Western prototypes reassembled with domestic parts.

The Soviet mindset vis-a-vis state-owned property is best captured by this lyric from a popular song:

Everything around belongs to the collective farm,
Everything around belongs to me!

This sort of propaganda was meant to develop a sense of ownership among the peasants being forced to toil on industrial-scale government farms without ever seeing any tangible fruits of their labor. But no sentiment, however lofty and noble, can counteract reality for very long. Desperate to improve their living conditions—and sometimes merely survive—peasants and workers robbed their places of employment blind, carrying off everything that the government "lay poorly." Even though the Soviet criminal code punished theft from the government more harshly than theft from private citizens, most people didn't even consider it theft at all, but rather a minor redistribution of the communal goods. After all, if everything that belongs to the collective farm belongs to me, then what's the harm?

People who pilfered from their workplace were called *nesuny* (literally, "carriers-off"). By the 1980s, their effect on the economy was reaching catastrophic, if not to say absurd, proportions. There was no element of Soviet society that was immune to the "embezzlement of socialist property," as it was termed in the criminal code. Taxi drivers stole from the government by driving people without turning on their meters and pocketing the fare. Zookeepers stole meat from the tigers in their charge, which made for slightly leaner tigers and slightly fatter zookeepers. On collective farms, farmers stole feed and seed from the communal storage bins to fatten up their own animals. In factories, the staff colluded to steal as a collective and form barter agreements with other factories, trading under the table, say, stolen chocolates for stolen salami.

News and rumors of the exploits perpetrated by *nesuny* abounded, many of them mundane but some downright inspiring. One woman would pilfer sausage links from the meat-processing factory where she worked by wrapping them around her waist under her clothes. A man who worked at a car plant wanted some paint to decorate his house. Since he couldn't just waltz out of the facility with a large can of paint, he put on special high-visibility clothes, took the paint, and walked out of the factory along the train track that ran all the way out the back. Every three meters, he'd stop and make a tiny white mark on the rails. The security at the door naturally had nothing to say to this employee, who was clearly out on important logistical business.

* * *

Unlike government property, private possessions were guarded zealously. People went to extraordinary lengths to protect their own stuff. Our apartment door, like many others, was outfitted with two locks and a latch that must've weighed five pounds. In the late '80s, it became possible to acquire and install metal safe doors at home, and millions of people did so, just to feel safer.

One of the high-water marks of the late Soviet lifestyle was owning a car. When I was fifteen, Tolya borrowed tons of money from friends (lending banks did not exist, since no one needed such things), and after two years on the automobile waiting list of Leningrad State University, he acquired our first car, a dinky Lada Zhiguli. This was a big deal of cosmic proportions.

Since the layout of Leningrad was established in large part in the eighteenth century, the city did not anticipate automobiles and had no designated private parking and very few garages. So Tolya would park our "bolt bucket" right under our window so that we could keep an eye on it. He also outfitted it with the following security features:

- an electric car alarm that responded to the car being rocked in any way;
- the car's unique engine number engraved on all the windows and mirrors;
- a massive cast-iron padlock fitted around the pedals, immobilizing them in the owner's absence;
- anti-theft bolts on all the wheels, designed to prevent said wheels from getting removed by standard wrenches.

Before leaving the car anywhere, even for two minutes, Tolya would lock the pedals, turn on the alarm, and then remove the final temptations for the sticky-fingered: side mirrors and windshield wipers. All of this was pretty much standard procedure for any private car owner in the USSR.

The same mentality of constant vigilance extended to everything else in life. Once, around fifth grade, I invited a number of my classmates, including Misha P., a stocky fellow with a permanent expression of idiotic bliss on his round face, to my birthday party. As was her custom on such occasions, Grandma set the table with the good silver so that we could all enjoy our tea and cake in a manner befitting "boys from good families." But when she collected the silver at the end of the party, one of the spoons was missing. Grandma's suspicious eye fell upon Misha, whose family did not quite measure up to her standards of gentility. Without thinking much of it, Grandma picked up the phone and phoned Misha's father with her suspicions. Say what you want about prejudices, but her profiling skills did not fail her: the spoon was quickly found and reunited with its siblings.

Three years later, Misha's sticky fingers went a-plundering once more. The father of one of our classmates, a shy, nerdy kid called Kostya, went on a business trip to the actual, honest-to-goodness capitalist Austria and bought Kostya a pair of Nike sneakers, which were then considered the apex of coolness and fashion. Kostya wore them to school the very next day. When it was time for PE, he changed out of them and into his regular gym shoes. Changing rooms had no lockers and, predictably, when he returned after class, the shiny new sneakers were gone.

Suspicions fell once more on Misha P., who on that day had a note from the doctor and was not in PE with everyone else. Misha denied everything. However, a couple of weeks later, Ilona, a girl in our neighborhood, had a birthday party, and Misha showed up to it wearing—you guessed it—Kostya's Nike sneakers. It was hard to credit his desperate insistence that he bought them from a black market dealer. Misha could've liquidated his parents' entire estate and not scraped together enough for a pair of black market Nikes. Also, Kostya might well have had the only pair of that design in the entire country. Vova and I were very angry with Misha for taking advantage of a nice kid like Kostya. So the next day, we broke one of the cardinal rules of Soviet boyhood: we went to our homeroom teacher and turned Misha in. She said that she understood the delicacy of the situation and that she would deal with it. We never learned what went on between her, Misha, and his parents, but two days later, Kostya found his Nikes in the same place he had left them before PE class.

CHAPTER 17

GOING POTATOES

In the Soviet Union, there is freedom of speech.
But it's not written anywhere that one should be
free after his speech.

GRANDMA REFUSED TO send me to Young Pioneers
summer camps. As far as she was concerned, they were for the
children of proletarians who didn't have the skills or the means
to organize their children a proper summer. Grandma preferred
to do things her way. After many summers in Pärnu, on the
coast of Estonia, she then started to take me to the Lithuanian
town of Trakai, which stood surrounded by forests next to a
huge lake.

These idylls accounted for my summers until eighth grade,
when I finally went to a summer camp. However, it wasn't the
kind of camp younger kids went to, with sports and swimming
and hiking and arts and crafts. This was a "labor and recreation
camp," and attendance was mandatory to help the local collective farms with the harvest.

The vast majority of the young people of the nation, from
schoolchildren to graduate students, did this every year. This

was called by a generic term, *ehat' na kartoshku*—"to go potatoes." It didn't have to be potatoes; some lucky people had to
pick berries, for instance.

It must be said that although Grandma looked down on
Young Pioneers camps, she supported wholeheartedly my
participation in communal labor with my classmates. As the
daughter of a tsarist officer, she had always had to hide her aristocratic past, lest she bring down the wrath of the proletariat
on her head. Over the years, she became convinced that it was
best to be like everyone else, that one was the safest in a faceless
crowd, marching in lockstep. She supported everything that
helped me blend in. Some other people tried to keep their kids
out of these potato trips, forging doctor's notes or faking family
emergencies. Not Grandma.

Our school's camp was located in a village called Shushary,
just twenty minutes by bus from the last metro station out of
Leningrad. All the schools from our district shipped their kids
to that camp, which meant we could make new friends. But it
also afforded us a chance to finally get to know properly the
kids from our school's other homerooms, whom we had no
classes with. Labor laws in the USSR prohibited children under
sixteen from working more than four and a half hours a day
for six days a week. So we would spend Monday to Saturday
mornings in the fields, then return home on Saturday afternoons to scrub off a week's worth of grime and eat everything
our parents had saved up to feed their little peasants.

The camp itself consisted of several flimsy barracks segre-
gated by schools and genders. The boys' barracks had about
twenty beds and a small room where our supervisor lived.
Outside of sleeping hours, the sexes mingled freely. We often
visited the girls' quarters, gaining tantalizing glimpses into
their feminine world: female undergarments strewn about

beds, lipstick tubes, and various cosmetic lotions and potions. The forbidden excitement of it was spine-tingling.

In the mornings, we woke up around 7 a.m. and lined up outside for a roll call. The USSR never let you forget that, whether you were in a prison camp or a summer camp, it was still a camp. The head administrator, who was some regional Komsomol apparatchik, would make a brief speech along the lines of "Up and at 'em, people! Time to labor for the glory of the motherland!" Then he'd make some mundane announcements about the scheduled events of the day. On special occasions, he added a few words about how the vile Americans were once again undermining the interests of people all over the world. Then we got on a bus and rode off to weed the potato fields. Exactly four and a half hours later, another bus took us back to our barracks, where we were fed lunch and left to ourselves for the rest of the day. Occasionally there was some organized fun in the afternoon: contests, get-togethers between schools, or a film screening. Once in a blue moon, there might be an assembly to discuss some Komsomol crap. But mostly we just hung out all afternoon.

Camp life was, of course, rife with pranks. A perennial favorite was smearing each other with toothpaste at night. We would sneak into the girls' barracks while they were asleep and draw little toothpaste crosses and flowers on their cheeks and foreheads. They smeared us back in return.

This camp was where I had my first half bottle of beer, which got me so drunk that I thought I was going to topple over. We procured this contraband through our class Amazon, Olya Bezverhova, who at the age of fifteen looked twenty-five and was our designated envoy to the store for beer and cigarettes.

In June 1986, while we were at the camp, the Leningrad Palace of Youth was getting ready to host some young, Soviet-friendly dudes from the United States. Since my classmates and I came from "reliable" families, some of us were given the task of preparing a variety show to entertain these foreign bores. Vasya Bazanov was in because he sang well; some other guys were in because they spoke English well; and naturally the group included a few cute girls like Olya Moskvina and Olya Bezverhova, to show Americans that we had those, too. So for a week or so, after putting in our time in the potato fields, we worked on our acts.

On the day of the event, we were taken to the Palace of Youth to set up. The show was, predictably, about fighting for peace. I mean, what else could it have been about? The plot, if one could really call it that, was given to us by the authorities and ideologically approved; all we had to do was "embody it," as the Soviet phraseology went. It was total drivel.

We had no costumes or props. It was mostly people playing guitars, dancing, and singing. For some reason, we sang the song of the Italian Communists, which was called "Bandiera Rossa"—"the red banner." *"Avanti o popolo, alla riscossa, bandiera rossa, bandiera rossa . . ."* What did it mean? Who knows. Why did we sing it? No freaking clue. I'm guessing our authorities thought that since America and Italy were both a part of the capitalist West, Americans would dig some singing in Italian.

A guy and a girl from the neighboring School Number 191, who also took part in the performance, danced a tango to "Michelle" by the Beatles. Halfway through the song, the tape was stopped, interrupting the dance, and another tape was cued, this time with the sounds of explosions. This was meant to signify the intrusion of war upon everyone's peaceful lives. But our appreciation of this high concept was somewhat derailed by the fact that the two of them were dancing awfully close to each other, and the boy's hands kept roaming freely to all sorts of places. This caused a lot of talk. We—the pupils of School Number 185—were a prudish bunch.

And finally, yours truly made a closing speech, wherein I expounded upon, in my sophisticated, fluent English, the goodness of the Soviet people, the fragility of peace, and how we weren't going to stand for its being threatened by aggressors. In retrospect, I probably came across a bit like a bank robber telling the negotiating cops outside that he's a nice guy, a real mensch in fact, and if they don't start treating him like one, he'll start shooting hostages. But as a Soviet citizen, I was taking it easy—hypocrisy was very normal, too.

Of course, the most exciting part was the after-party, where we got to hang out with the lefty Americans and talk about our hopes for the future. These mostly revolved around us and the enlightened Americans fighting against nuclear proliferation, which we of course jointly blamed entirely on Washington. We even toasted our friendship with Soviet champagne: the cafeteria in the Palace of Youth had been thoroughly Potemkinized,* spruced up and stocked to impress, like a preview of its future self under Communism. No one batted an eye at champagne being provided to adolescents.

As I was chatting about music and movies with two pretty, slightly older American girls (though I must admit, all foreign girls looked pretty to me), one of them asked, "So, Sergey, would you like to visit the United States? To come to study or maybe even to move there?"

"No," I replied immediately and firmly. This was a blatant lie; I wanted to visit the US more than anything—but these girls were still visitors from "the country of the probable enemy." Who knew who they really were, or who they really

---

*Derived from the expression Potemkin village: a fake construction built to deceive others into thinking that a situation is better than it really is.

reported to, or whether the KGB kept tabs on all their conversations? I proceeded to shore up my denial with explanations of how great it was to live in the Soviet Union, and how I didn't need or want to go anywhere outside of it. Ever. For any reason.

My passionate refusal left the girls puzzled, but they were benevolent enough not to probe me any further. All three of us knew I was shamelessly lying. But we also knew that we were in the Soviet Union. And most of the time in the Soviet Union, telling the truth was not an option.

* * *

While we did not get paid for helping heroic Soviet farmers, there were a few jobs in the USSR by which adolescents could earn a bit of dosh. My working career started in show business.

Our school was located in central Leningrad, an area rich with history. It was very close to the Smolny Institute, the place that Lenin had chosen as the Bolshevik headquarters during the October Revolution. It was the hub of all the key events of 1917. So whenever any kind of Revolution-themed film was being shot, the filming would take place close to my school. And since Revolution-themed movies were the ultimate linchpin of Soviet cinema—supposedly one could never have enough of this shit—it sometimes seemed like the same movie was being shot year in and year out, endlessly.

When I was in sixth grade, yet another film crew was hard at work in the area. One day, on a lark, I went to them and asked if they needed extras. To my amazement, the person in charge of the crowd scenes looked me over and gave me a time and a place to show up.

For two days, I skipped school to seek fame and fortune on the big screen.

I was in a scene with about twenty kids of various ages, all outfitted in street urchin rags. We ran after fancy carriages driving through the street and pretended to be terribly excited to see them. This went on for hours, and eventually got somewhat tedious, but even so, it was still great for bragging rights, to say nothing of money. For my two half days of work, I got paid eight rubles fifty, which was just shy of the price of one highly prized blank Japanese cassette tape. It was the first money I'd earned myself, and I was ecstatic.

The film appeared in a few theaters a couple of years later under a generic name, which now escapes me, like *The Way* or *The Rise of the Fall*. It was pretty awful and made no splash. Besides, by that time the clouds of perestroika were gathering over that entire film genre. No one wanted movies about the Revolution anymore. I still went to see it, of course, but I couldn't pick myself out from the crowd of urchins. I chose to believe my scenes were censored. My take on the character of Boy Who Runs after Carriages must have been too avant-garde for the censors to handle.

My second job a couple years later was in showbiz again, this time behind the scenes. I was hired to be an in-theater English interpreter at the Barrikada movie theater.

At that time, films were starting to arrive from the West, but they were neither dubbed nor subtitled in Russian; the demand for seeing Western movies immediately was huge, and the technology for preparing them for the Soviet viewer was absent. So movie theaters would hire people like myself to sit in the back of the screening room and voice the translation of the dialogue in real time. We had typed script translations to work from, but they were often incomplete and inaccurate, and I frequently had to improvise the lines.

The first time this happened, I was dubbing *Romancing the Stone*. As Michael Douglas and Kathleen Turner lay in bed after doing their dirty deed, I realized that the pages containing their post-coital dialogue were missing. Terrified, I started making up stuff on the spot:

"How was your day today? Did you have a good day today or a bad day today? Well, what kind of day was it?"

"Well, I don't know. How about you? How was your day?"

And so on and so forth, until the events on the screen caught up with the pages in my hand.

At the next screening, I came prepared. This time around, the characters expounded on the therapeutic benefits of afternoon naps. The next showing had them discuss treatments for premature baldness. There was no end to this joy. I did not feel the least bit bad about it. The way I saw it, someone dropped the ball on those missing pages, and so it fell to me to fill in the dead air. I did sometimes wonder if anyone saw the movie more than once, and if so, what they made of the ever-changing dialogue. In any case, no one ever raised any objections.

When I was bored and feeling particularly witty, I would also dub animal sounds. Russian animal sounds are quite different from English ones—for example, dogs don't go "woof," they go "gav," and pigs don't "oink" but say "hryu." I felt that this was as worthy of translation as anything else on the screen. Again, the audience did not object. Soviet people watching Western films for the first time made for a grateful audience.

Dubbing paid about as well as my first job did: I got two rubles and twenty kopecks per film, and I could do up to four or five screenings a day for weeks. It was not bad for the wallet. Also, now I had the dubious distinction of knowing the entire script of *Robocop* in Russian by heart. "Excuse me, I have to go. Somewhere there is a crime happening." "Dead or alive, you're coming with me!"

Eat your heart out, William H. Shakespeare!

CHAPTER 18

YOU'RE IN THE ARMY NOW
[WELL, NOT YET, BUT SOON]

"Why did the Soviet Union invade Afghanistan?"
"It decided to start in alphabetical order."

AS THRILLING AS it was watching the American army in action on the big screen, the prospect of serving in the Soviet army promised little in the way of gladiatorial glamour. All Soviet men were subjected to the draft. It was as inevitable as death or taxes; more so, in fact, since taxes did not exist in the USSR. One could do either two years with the army or three years with the navy.

I found the idea of serving in the forces off-putting, even though Grandma's family had a proud tradition of military service and my grandfather had been an army doctor. I was always repulsed by all things soldierly: the culture of military mediocrity, the sheer waste of individual time and effort, the lack of any finesse or self-irony. I hated it all, and when thoughts of the looming draft came, I pushed them away.

From the age of fifteen, if we moved addresses, the first thing we were all supposed to do was to go to the enlistment office in our new district and reregister there. At this age, boys were also summoned to the enlistment office to get a basic medical exam to determine draft eligibility, and to receive a future service assignment.

In 1986, it was my turn. At the office, I was measured and weighed, and had my chest tapped and my vision tested. Some guys from a year above us boasted that their checkups were done by hot young nurses who asked them to cough while cradling their testicles. I was not inclined to believe them. Neither myself nor the other guys in my class saw any nurses, neither hot nor cold. Instead, we were stripped to the underpants and asked to do push-ups and squats in front of a group of somber, overweight middle-aged men in full uniform.

Then each of us had a one-to-one interview with a tall, dark, grizzled officer who looked like Dracula on a low-carb diet. He mainly asked us what academic subjects we excelled at. My classmate Vasya Bazanov had none and must've admitted it, because he ended up assigned to the navy for three years and later had to serve it out. On the other hand, the interviewer must've thought that I was a valuable bighead: I got assigned to the Strategic Missile Forces—i.e., the lads who sit in deep underground wells and guard the legendary red button that would unleash a hail of ICBMs on America.

Running ahead, I must say that, luckily, this honorable duty was to pass me by. By the time I turned eighteen, Gorbachev had exempted university students from the draft. Had I been born just six months earlier, I would have had to get my head shaved.

* * *

As for the Soviet foreign policy of the '70s and '80s, it may have been stagnant, but it was not particularly aggressive.

The horrors of the Second World War had drained the Soviet population and most of its leadership of serious aggression, discounting the minor periodic suppression of Czechs or Hungarians "stirring up trouble" in the Soviet backyard.

And sure, there was a new war in Afghanistan. But in all fairness, who hasn't gone to war in Afghanistan?

Every boy of my generation was afraid of being sent to fight in Afghanistan. Everyone knew about that war, but no one discussed it out loud. On television, it was talked about as a "limited contingent" of Soviet troops doing their "international duty." By the end of 1982, more and more stories were circulating about families of draftees receiving zinc coffins with their dead sons inside. (They were zinc because Afghanistan was hot and refrigerating the remains was impossible, so the coffins had to be welded shut. Parents buried their children sight unseen.)

It was all coming too close to home. I knew that a few boys from our school who were only four years older than us had already been drafted and sent to Afghanistan. One of my mom's colleagues at her institute got her son mailed to her in a zinc casket. My peers and I lived in perpetual dread.

The "enemy voices" of Western radio were forthright, talking endlessly of the horrors and carnage taking place on the ground. For us teenage boys, all these reports and rumors formed a constant background radiation of dread. Mothers all over the country warned their wayward sons, "You better study hard, or you'll fail your university entrance exams and they'll send you straight to Afghanistan."

By 1986, numbers were starting to trickle in. Word spread that the USSR had already suffered ten thousand casualties, then fifteen thousand casualties, and so on. Naturally, the scant TV reports addressing the Afghanistan issue continued to gloss over the losses entirely. Soviet authorities were not in a habit of admitting defeat or losses of any kind.

When I was in tenth grade, one of our teachers got sick around mid-May, close to Victory Day, and we ended up with a scheduled free period the next morning. Before we had a chance to get properly excited about it, we were warned that instead we'd be having a "lesson in courage." Many people, either half-drunk on springtime or already thinking ahead to exams, decided to skip it, since it wasn't an actual real class, anyway. So the next morning, only about half the class showed up.

Imagine our surprise when instead of an old WWII veteran, we were greeted by a very young guy named Misha Chirikov. He was tall and had curly blond hair. I recognized him right away, even though I couldn't recall his name at the time. Misha was one of our own alumni, only four grades ahead of us. But he looked much more grown-up now, though he must've been only nineteen or twenty. He was wearing jeans, sneakers, and a husky army jacket, as was fashionable at the time.

It was easy to see that Misha didn't really want to be there. He didn't want to talk to us. He'd probably just stopped by the school for sentimental reasons, to see the place he had only recently left and where he'd spent ten years of his childhood and youth, and the principal must have press-ganged him into giving a lesson. He didn't try to be likeable, didn't engage with the audience, didn't show off, as one might expect a young man to do when speaking in front of a bunch of students including young ladies. He was just there to tell us about Afghanistan. He spoke at length, keeping a neutral tone and not voicing any judgments.

Misha had been drafted and sent off to a six-month boot camp somewhere in Uzbekistan. In the USSR, it was standard procedure to send all draftees someplace far from their native region. Most soldiers who served near Leningrad came from central Asia and vice versa: boys drafted from Leningrad were sent to other republics. The logic was that in case of an uprising, an army ethnically foreign to the region would have no moral qualms about shooting the locals.

Then he was shipped across the border to one of the many bases that the Soviet Union had established in Afghanistan. He was assigned to intelligence. Those guys suffered some of the heaviest losses, since they operated behind enemy lines, making secret reconnaissance tours. He talked calmly and rather emotionlessly about losing several friends on these tours. Some were blown up by mines; others were picked off by snipers. The lack of inflection in Misha's voice made his stories especially chilling. He had grown used to it all. But the thing that stunned me the most about his entire talk was his scuffed sneakers. The soldiers in Afghanistan all went to battle wearing sneakers, we learned. Back then, the entire Soviet army still wore regulation knee-high tarpaulin boots, to be worn not with socks but with foot wraps—a time-tested design that had hardly changed over the last few centuries.

Misha made quite an impression. Before him, all the veterans we'd met were grandpas and grandmas, who either proudly jangled all their military honors and medals or swore like they were still mid-battle. But here was a young guy we knew from before, and he had actually looked death in the face. When the lesson was over, we all left the classroom and went outside into the teacher-free corner of the courtyard to smoke. The guys talked among themselves about the upcoming university exams and how diligently they were going to study for them, to matriculate and avoid the draft.

Only one thought was on my mind: anything but Afghanistan.

* * *

When it became apparent to Gorbachev that "acceleration" alone would not solve the USSR's economic woes, he doubled down on his reforms. Democratization was to revitalize the Communist Party by making it a bit more competitive. Gorbachev was not suggesting a multiparty system, just the idea of multiple candidates within the party. This was already a break with the past, where only one candidate was offered per elected position.

But a more democratic approach required an engaged demos. And how could one engage a people that had been afraid to speak their mind about politics in public for the past seventy years? A new approach to politics as a whole was needed.

In May 1986, around the time I was getting poked and probed at the military enlistment office, Gorbachev revisited one of his concepts from the XXVII party congress: glasnost. He used it to mean "transparency." From now on, he said, the government's policy was no longer to silence its critics but to allow itself and its workings to be examined in full by the press, in order that the "flaws, weaknesses, and oversights" in it might be addressed.

Gorbachev was no iconoclast. He had no intentions of bringing down Communism. All he wanted was to inject energy into the gloomy and stagnant system. These liberalizations were supposed to be a way back to the true path leading to Communism. Perestroika did not mean rebuilding Soviet life from scratch, Gorbachev assured us; it was simply a correction of the course, to set things back on the proper track intended by Lenin.

However, it soon became obvious that without real free enterprise and competition, the state-owned and state-managed economy was heading off a cliff. And that's when reforms began to snowball.

Legislation was passed permitting the creation of cooperatives and mutually owned business enterprises, the so-called individual labor initiatives. Suddenly, it was possible for a privately owned firm to establish itself in the USSR! Soviet citizens could start their own companies and be their own bosses. They could own their apartments and houses. Previously, the mere ownership of a dollar bill could send a man on a lengthy all-inclusive voyage to "places not so remote." And now, we could actually buy and sell foreign currency. It even became conceivably possible to establish a firm in the Soviet Union with the aid of foreign investors.

The very idea of a Soviet enterprise doing any kind of legitimate business with foreigners—any foreigners, even capitalist Americans—was mind-blowing. It would be sort of like President Trump announcing that he was building an even bigger and better wall than previously planned, except through South Dakota and in partnership with some very friendly, hugely wonderful, just tremendous, you'll love them, folks, shape-shifting aliens from planet HD37605b of the Orion Nebula.

CHAPTER 19

DAD

A question on a Soviet job application form:
"Have you ever been arrested? If not, why?"

WHEN I WAS little, Saturday afternoons were for my regularly scheduled meet-ups with Dad, which always took place at my grandparents' place. Grandpa Sergey and Baba Valya lived on Dzerzhinskaya Street, opposite the erstwhile home of the infamous Grigori Rasputin, the eccentric peasant faith healer who supposedly held the royal family in thrall until he was gruesomely murdered by a bunch of noblemen in 1916.

Their building was neoclassical and exceptionally grand. Like many upper-middle-class houses built in nineteenth-century Saint Petersburg, it boasted a tall arch at the entrance, held up by two Atlas caryatids, and a paved courtyard, once stately but now cluttered with artifacts of Soviet life: garbage bins, wooden boxes for storing sand to sprinkle on icy patches in the winter, and broken bicycles and toboggans. Stray cats and dogs skulked through the garbage, fighting over scraps and sending fur flying through the courtyard.

My grandparents' apartment was on the fifth floor, at the top. The Soviet government rarely retrofitted nineteenth-century buildings with elevators, so it remained a walk-up. And since these old edifices usually had very high ceilings, it was quite a climb. Grandpa used to say that all the stair climbing prolonged his lifespan.

The apartment itself was practically opulent, at least by Soviet standards. It had two bedrooms and a living room where no one slept, a highly unusual luxury. One of the bedrooms was my grandfather's; the other one was used by my father whenever he stayed over. My grandmother slept in a sectioned-off part of the hallway, behind a large antique screen.

Baba Valya and Grandpa Sergey met and married in the early 1930s. When World War II broke out, Grandpa, a military doctor, was immediately deployed and served until peace was declared. As the chief radiologist for the Red Army, he was paid well, and he sent his salary to Baba Valya from the front lines.

Baba Valya's elder sister, Olga, was severely wounded in one of the first Nazi bombings of Leningrad and could not be evacuated out of the city. Baba Valya stayed behind to take care of her, working as an assistant to a midlevel party apparatchik on the city committee. When German troops laid full siege to Leningrad, cutting off practically all food supplies, this job saved Valya's and Olga's lives: food rations for government employees were a bit larger than the standard 125 grams of bread per person per day.

Like all survivors, Baba Valya was profoundly marked by her years under "the blockade," as it was known in Leningrad. No one who lived through it was ever the same. She often told my brother and me terrifying stories of that time. How all the stray dogs and cats and pigeons in the city were eaten up first, and then the house pets followed. How all the trees had been cut down for firewood, and then people started burning their own furniture, just to survive the winter cold. How people traded family heirlooms for morsels of bread. How at first those who starved or froze to death were buried promptly, but then there were simply too many dead and not enough strong people left to bury them, and corpses began to litter the streets like garbage sacks. People stepped over them on their way to work. Eventually, when there was nothing left to eat at all, they stopped avoiding them and began seeking them out. At the market, bread was expensive, but meatballs were cheap, and everyone knew why.

Hardly any of this was ever brought up publicly. Soviet authorities thought these facts "besmirched" the good name of Soviet citizens. The official story was that people scraped by and made do on pure grit. But everyone who was there remembered the cold hard truth: you can't eat grit.

Grandpa followed the Soviet army all the way to Germany and remained stationed there after the war. After the Siege of Leningrad was lifted, Baba Valya went to join him. She'd taught German for a living before the war, so there was work for her instructing the troops. They stayed in Germany until 1953.

My dad was born in Berlin, and his passport reflected this fact. Later, after the family's return to the USSR, this aroused a lot of curiosity. Trapped as they were behind the Iron Curtain, Soviet citizens were naturally intrigued by anyone born abroad. When the family returned from Berlin, they hauled an entire train car of junk with them: several sets of mass-produced German furniture, oil paintings acquired by chance, curtains that fit no window, slightly provocative gypsum statuettes of bathing beauties, and an uncountable number of porcelain dog figurines.

All this clutter was now moldering, unused and unattended, choking the dusty air and light out of the apartment.

But my grandparents did have one useful thing: a color television set. This item, rare in the USSR, was perched on a huge half-broken antique writing desk with drawers filled with stuff I loved to play with: tools, nails and bolts, stationery, German tchotchkes, et cetera.

Large as the place was, it had no piped hot water and no proper bathroom with a tub or a shower. There was only a tiny closet with a toilet in it. Water for washing hands, faces, and dishes was heated on the gas stove in a massive copper pot with a tap. Actual baths had to be taken outside the home, at a public *banya*, a bathhouse. This used to be quite common in Russia back when many buildings lacked piped hot water. Generally, people went to the *banya* once a week, paid twenty kopecks, and stayed for two to three hours.

Baba Valya was not big on housekeeping, but she was a very generous hostess. The gigantic dining room table was always set with tea things and various snacks—tiny cabbage pies, crunchy butter cookies, pieces of taffy, salted pretzel sticks. Each weekly visit was an endless tea party, not unlike the one in *Alice in Wonderland*.

* * *

Truth be told, Dad and I didn't spend much time interacting during our Saturday visitations. The day always revolved around Dad visiting his parents, not *me* visiting him. The golden boy of the family, Dad grew up epically spoiled. Like most young Soviet people, he lived with his parents well into his twenties. Even as a grown man, if he had to pee in the middle of the night, he would do so into a chamber pot, finding the walk to the toilet too incommodious. Baba Valya would then empty the pot for him in the morning. As a student at university, he would often do research at the central public library, where in wintertime there were long lines for the cloakroom. Baba Valya would take the bus to the library with him, take his coat so that he wouldn't have to lug it around, go home with it, then ride back to the library several hours later with the coat so that he could wear it on the way home.

To some extent, Dad was typical of his generation, at least among the intelligentsia. Post-war children were horribly spoiled by their parents, who treated them like fine china while simultaneously controlling their every sneeze.

When I was two, my parents divorced after Dad met another woman. Her name was Jenna (short for Genevra, a remarkably unusual name in Russia), and she was a law professor at Leningrad State University. Tall, with striking long, curly hair and a bohemian vibe, she was older than my father by eight years. My grandparents didn't like her, and she never joined Dad and me on our days together. Before my early teens, I rarely met her.

Dad and Jenna lived in a miniature communal apartment on the outskirts of the city. They shared their small two-room suite, wallpapered with art and stacked floor to ceiling with books, with an unfriendly old crone. All she ever seemed to do was cook smelly food in the tiny communal kitchen, sit on the toilet without closing the door, and complain about Jenna and Dad. Everything they did rubbed her up the wrong way.

This surly geriatric roommate, and the fact that Jenna and Dad owned a dog and two cats and couldn't have anyone over for lack of space, finally convinced Dad to start looking for a new place to live. A house in the middle of nowhere, he thought, was just the ticket after years in a communal shoe box.

* * *

When I was eight, Dad bought a house in an abandoned village called Korovkino—literally, "little cow place."

The village of Korovkino—or rather, what's left of it—sits at the southern shore of the enormous Lake Ladoga, about sixty miles east of Leningrad. The shore is hugged by two canals, colloquially known as "Peter's canal" and "Catherine's canal," on account of being dug in the time of Peter the Great and Catherine the Great, respectively. Ladoga, the largest lake in Europe, is known for its unpredictable and often stormy conditions. The artificial waterways make navigating around it less risky. Between the two canals, there is about three hundred meters of space, which forms a narrow island over thirty miles long. Korovkino sprung up at the western end of this island.

Despite its constrained layout, it used to be a lively little village, with forty households and lots of cattle. In the early 1930s, the Soviet regime launched a massive national campaign of "dekulakization," in which they robbed, arrested, and deported or executed all well-off peasants in Russia. This was done as a prelude to instituting collective agriculture, which brought almost all farming across the country under state control. Many villages fell to ruin or were abandoned, and Korovkino, being relatively wealthy, was one of them. In 1980, only three people still lived there permanently: two old men and one old lady, Baba Nastya, and even she wanted out of there.

Luckily, one of Jenna's old students, Uncle Pavel, who was now the chief of police in a nearby town called Syas'stroj (almost as awkward to pronounce for Russians as for English speakers), knew that Dad was looking for a secluded rural home. He put Dad in touch with that Baba Nastya. She owned her house outright (freestanding rural and suburban homes could actually be held in private ownership). Soon they came up with a trade: Dad would give her eight hundred rubles, and she would move out, leaving the house to Dad in her will.

* * *

My first visit to Korovkino happened on a school holiday when I was a young teenager. Dad and I took a ride from Leningrad's central bus station to Syas'stroj. It was three hours of boring industrial rust-belt landscape interspersed with poorly cultivated agricultural plots. I spent most of it reading a book I had brought, which was almost as tedious as the landscape: a thick, politically correct Soviet science fiction tome titled *Humans as Gods*. Dad tried to nap on the seat next to me. At one point he opened his eyes and started to read over my shoulder.

"Why do you waste your time on such crap?" he asked several minutes later, and closed his eyes again.

The bus was late. By the time we got into town, Uncle Pavel had already gone home from the bus stop where he was supposed to pick us up. The only public telephone nearby had been burned all over with cigarette butts and was missing the receiver. Dad consulted a piece of paper with the address, and we began to wander around the poorly lit maze of identical rectangular five-story concrete walk-ups. There were hardly any people around, just packs of dogs scavenging among the garbage bins. Luckily, we soon came across a drunk old man who was sitting with a contemplative air on a wooden bench nearby. He pointed us to the home of "whassisname Pavel, the cop."

Pavel was home. "C'mon in," he whispered, opening the door. "Sorry I missed you at the stop. Sasha is sleeping, so keep it down, okay?"

Our host turned out to be a plain, friendly man with blond hair and a strong affection for Adidas sports apparel. Fashionable three-stripe outfits aside, he lived modestly. Unlike people of that profession today, Soviet cops were by and large not corrupt.

He led us to a small bedroom. "I set up the beds in this room," he said. "Good night, sleep tight. We're all getting up at eight tomorrow."

Dad and I made ourselves as comfortable as we could on the fold-out camp beds. We didn't try to find a hotel, of course. Hotels in the Soviet Union were for artists on tour and party bigwigs on business trips. Besides, there were no hotels in the town of Syas'stroj. It was not, shall we say, a destination.

The next morning, the four of us—Dad, myself, Uncle Pavel, and his son, Sasha, who was my age—took a motorboat along one of the canals to Dad's new place six miles away.

My first impression of the house was unfavorable. Its previous owner had just moved out, and it stood empty and grimy, looking like an abandoned home in the town of Chernobyl after the nuclear accident, only dirtier, messier, and darker. A typical late nineteenth-century Russian village hut, this *izba* was made of large logs set atop one another, now cracked and discolored. Its windows were small, and some of the glass panes in them had been replaced with pieces of plywood. Inside, the house was wet, dark, and dank. Grandma would have had a fit had she seen what an "unhygienic" environment her grandson had been brought into.

Sasha and I rifled through the rags and scraps and dust on the floor in search of anything interesting. Then the adults took us out on the boat again, this time to the actual lake. It was a fine day, and the fishermen were out in force, both commercial ones and hobbyists. Since Uncle Pavel was the head of the local police, everybody knew him. Soon we had a bucket filled with fish, courtesy of the fishermen.

The sight of a bucket full of live, wriggling fish filled me with unease, as I was going through a Zen Buddhist phase at the time. Grandpa Sergey, who was into Eastern philosophy and even named one of his dogs Zen, had introduced me to some Buddhist concepts, such as never taking a life, not even that of a fish or an insect. So I'd stopped fishing, on philosophical grounds. Now I found the sight of fish struggling and dying in the boat downright depressing. Unlike me, Sasha wasn't a budding Buddhist, so he helped the fish with hammer blows to the head, which was how the fishermen did it. Later that night, Dad and Uncle Pavel boiled up a pot of fish soup. But I didn't eat any of it.

The new old house had no electricity, no heat, no telephone, no gas, and no plumbing. We did all our cooking on a large old-fashioned wood-burning stove, like the peasants of old, or American pioneers in a log cabin. In fact, the whole village remained untouched by modern civilization, as if stuck in the nineteenth century. It was hard to believe that only sixty or so miles away, a bona fide quasi-European metropolis hustled and bustled. Beyond the village and its cluster of abandoned huts, there was nothing but wilderness.

I spent many weeks every summer in Korovkino. Sometimes I brought Vova, and later my new friends and girlfriends. The lack of any amenities restricted our indoor entertainment to reading and conversation, but it was no great hardship. My father was a fantastic conversationalist, witty and remarkably erudite. Good chat was much more valuable out in an isolated village than in the city. Dad's affable banter also earned him a constant stream of local visitors: old-timers, mushroom pickers, fishermen. Even local hunters came by, to complain of their poor luck, or the low prices the government was paying for beaver pelts, or to warn Dad whenever there were wolves rambling around; Dad had two dogs and two cats, so wolves were always a worry. His house came to be known in the neighboring villages as "the writer's house."

One of the regular visitors, old but spry Uncle Lesha, soon proved himself indispensable. It is unlikely that Dad would have made it out there for so long without his help. In the years to come, when Jenna would spend half the week working in Leningrad, it was Uncle Lesha who helped Dad to chop firewood, haul water, and take care of other things around the house. He also had a flat in Syas'stroj and would often bring back from town all sorts of needed items: matches, candles, kerosene, batteries for the flashlight, as well as Dad's mail. (Korovkino did not get mail delivery.)

Life with Dad in Korovkino was very different from my life with Grandma, Mom, and Tolya in Leningrad. For one thing, Grandma kept me on a relatively rigid schedule. On Sunday mornings, I was allowed to sleep in, but my meals were still tightly regimented, and my weekday bedtime was non-negotiable. Dad didn't care about any of that. In his house, everyone was free to do as they pleased. Just like at his parents' place, the table was always set for teatime. All food items that didn't require cooking, brought to Korovkino by Uncle Lesha, Uncle Pavel, or any other visitor, went straight to the huge table in the middle of the main room, to be consumed at will. So the table was always crowded with saucers heaped with slices of bread; jam; cans of pâté, fish, and Spam; plates with cheese; open candy boxes; bags of dried berries; bowls of pickled mushrooms; et cetera, et cetera. It was a veritable Soviet cornucopia. Mealtimes became blurred; tea and coffee were consumed constantly throughout the day.

On the one hand, this anarchy was exciting. On the other, I was not accustomed to the rough life. Not having running water or electricity was an unpleasant novelty. The lack of creature comforts was further exacerbated by Dad's constant drinking with his visiting buddies. One evening, after he got drunk, he forgot that he'd already fed the stove and threw another huge log on the fire. The house quickly became a sauna. The main windows in the house did not open, for reasons of heat conservation, and the two tiny ventilation outlets, each just ten by twenty centimeters, didn't let nearly enough heat out or fresh air in.

But the straw that broke the camel's back was Dad himself. Once when he had visitors over, he got drunk and chewed me out in front of them for not being well read enough. Coming from him, it was a massive indictment. I ran off in tears. When I got back into town, I told on him to Grandma. I told her everything: that the adults at Korovkino stayed up until well past midnight, smoking, drinking, and talking bad about the Soviet government and keeping us awake with foreign radio; that we had no set mealtimes; that my father would often not get up until the afternoon to make us breakfast; and that the bedsheets we used were filthy. I even tattled on Dad's dogs, who always jumped into my bed to sleep in it. In short, I reported everything that I knew would fall short of Grandma's standards of childcare.

A phone conference was held immediately between the two grandmas. Eager to relish in my vengeance, I picked up the second receiver to eavesdrop. Grandma told Baba Valya that little Sergey would not be visiting Korovkino anymore, for a variety of reasons. Baba Valya countered that I must be exaggerating the hardships of rural life, and that I just wanted her to worry.

"Now I won't be able to sleep tonight," she complained. "Not for one second."

After the call was over, the tragedy continued in the kitchen, now spearheaded by Mom.

"I told you not to let Little Serezha spend so much time with Big Serezha!" she screamed at Grandma. "Do you get it now, finally? I told you, he's crazy and a hopeless alcoholic!"

And then she added, mysteriously, "He is already a big boy. He should know everything! I will tell him everything!"

But she never did.

Eventually, the drama died down. However, the Korovkino visits and Saturdays with Dad came to an end. At first I thought that it was because he was getting ready for his permanent move to the countryside and didn't have the time anymore. Then I thought it was because he was busy writing something. It wasn't until months later that I began to suspect something different.

Sometimes, Mom and Grandma would talk about "Big Serezha" in the kitchen in loud whispers. I would overhear words like "madhouse," "suicide," and "blood all over the floor." Eventually, I began to ask questions. At first, Mom and Grandma told me not to worry, and that Dad was just not feeling well this week. Or next week. Or the week after that. Finally, I was told Dad was at the hospital, getting treatment for his insomnia. However, I wasn't told which hospital, and no one suggested that I visit him. In fact, all talk about him was suddenly discouraged.

For almost a year, it was as though Dad ceased to exist.

Soviet parents weren't big on letting children into what they considered their private lives. Major illnesses, job troubles, divorces, and remarriages—none of these topics were considered child-appropriate. With a subject as sensitive as mental illness, the taboo was even stronger. If one had asked me what crazy looked like, I would've pointed to Uncle Vitya, a man who lived opposite our house. He often walked down our street telling every woman he saw that he wanted to marry her, and then masturbated behind the garbage cans in the courtyard. Crazy was someone who acted wildly and inappropriately in public and was reported to the police. No one wanted to face having a family member with a mental illness.

* * *

One late December day when he was still living in the city, Dad received an alarming phone call. Dmitry Likhachev, an acclaimed researcher and Dad's good friend, was calling to warn him that two of their colleagues from the Research Institute of Russian Literature had just been arrested by the KGB and taken to the Big House on Kalyaeva Street for possessing books by Aleksandr Solzhenitsyn. Another phone call from another former colleague, Konstantin Azadovsky, followed, with the same warning. Three years prior, the police had ransacked Azadovsky's place. When they found no illegal literature, they planted a baggie of cannabis in his house and arrested him on drug charges instead. He spent two years in prison.

The phone calls were not exactly out of the blue. Dad was a dyed-in-the-wool dissident. So were most of his friends and colleagues. His situation was made somewhat more curious by the fact that his wife, Jenna, taught law at Leningrad State University to future police and KGB officers (including a certain Vladimir Putin). Her former pupils were constantly arresting Dad's friends. Now, it seemed they were getting ready for him.

After he hung up the phone, Dad immediately packed and took all his illegal literature to a reliable friend. There was no reason to make the KGB's job easy, after all. Then he began to pack his prison bag in preparation for the arrival of the authorities. In those days, most people who engaged in acts of disagreement with the Soviet government, no matter how seemingly minor, had a well-thought-out plan for what to take with them when the KGB came for them. There was a whole science to packing for prison. One set aside several changes of underwear; some high-calorie food, like chocolate or nuts; pencils and paper, the thinner the better; and items of personal hygiene, like soap and a comb. Most importantly, one packed warm woolen socks. They were of paramount importance. Russian prisons, wherever they happen to be located, are cold.

The next day, a police car pulled up to Dad's house and two cops got out. Dad closed his prison bag and put on his sunglasses. A few minutes later, the doorbell rang. Dad took one last look around the apartment and opened the door.

"How may I be of service, my good sirs?" he said to the two smiling cops. Exaggerated politeness with the authorities was fashionable among dissidents.

"Hi there, Sergey Sergeevich!" said one of the cops cheerfully. "We're Jenna Igorevna's evening department students. We brought you guys a tree for New Year's Eve!"

Still, Dad expected to be arrested any day. He began to work ever more irregular hours, writing his research essays in prolonged bursts of effort that could last days. He also started drinking even more. No one around him really noticed. For one thing, he was already a heavy drinker, and most of his friends were also on their way to being alcoholics. The Soviet intelligentsia in the '70s and '80s were a boozy bunch. In the USSR, it was nearly impossible for creative people to realize their artistic freedoms. With no power of decision-making and almost no permissible creative outlets, the existential boredom became soul-crushing, and there were very few distractions available besides liquor. In this way, many brilliantly creative people drank themselves to death.

Eventually, the combination of overwork, alcohol abuse, and stress gave Dad severe insomnia. After that, it was all downhill. He stopped going to work. Soon, at drinking parties, he started hitting random doorbells and flashing strangers. Then he started hallucinating. For a long time, he refused medical attention. Attempts to help only made him lash out. He made three attempts to kill himself, by cutting his wrist veins, but each time someone found him before it was too late. Eventually, Jenna persuaded him to see a doctor she found through some personal contacts. Knowing all too well how things worked in Soviet medicolegal institutions, she firmly instructed Dad not to tell the doctor about his suicide attempts, just about the insomnia and the alcoholism. But Dad answered all the questions honestly and was hospitalized on the spot. They placed him in the "first ward," which housed the most intensely psychotic suicidal patients.

The scariest thing, Jenna said much later, was that Dad liked it there. Dissidents who were put away into mental hospitals often came back with harrowing tales of punitive injections of drugs whose entire purpose was to cause pain, of spending days in restraints, of being starved or physically abused. But Dad found the hospital entirely agreeable. He loved the intellectual discussions he had with his doctors, and he found the other crazies around him fascinating. He even became the chairman of the hospital's patients' committee. The only thing he lacked there, he would say to her, was Jenna herself. Everything else was apparently great!

He spent almost a year in the cuckoo's nest. The only people who visited him there were Baba Valya and Jenna. Grandpa, his own father, never went to see him once. Perhaps he was embarrassed, or perhaps it was something else. Apparently, when Dad was a baby, Grandpa, then one of the foremost Soviet radiology specialists, intentionally irradiated his head. (Back in the 1950s, many infants were subjected to then-popular X-ray therapy for everything from a purportedly enlarged thymus to ear infections.) Maybe Grandpa felt partially responsible for Dad's illness.

With their usual Soviet bluntness, Dad's doctors suggested that Jenna divorce him. His condition made it unlikely that he would ever be gainfully employed again. She would be better off cutting her losses. Stressed-out and depressed, she checked into an out-of-town resort to spend a few weeks away from Dad's doctors, the hospital visits, and the emotional strain. She told no one except one colleague at work where she went.

But when she stopped visiting him, Dad began to worry. After not seeing her for a few days, he somehow finagled leave from his doctors and went to visit all their friends one after another, until the right person finally told him where she was. Then Dad showed up at Jenna's resort to plead with her to stay with him.

It was all romantic and tragic. They stayed together till he passed away in 2009.

* * *

One day, I found myself at the Theater of the Young Spectator with Grandma and Baba Valya.

This was highly unusual. I mostly went to this theater with Vova or other friends. Our grandmothers, eager to mold us into "cultured" young men and keep us out of trouble, regularly dispatched us to various institutions of aesthetic enrichment, like the theater, the opera, or the Conservatory. However, today I was at the theater for reasons beyond cultural enrichment. Several days before, Grandma had said we'd be going, and added, "Your dad might be there."

It wasn't a hard promise, more of a chance. Dad had finally been released from the hospital, but no one was sure what to expect from him. So Grandma and Baba Valya arranged a meeting for him and me—in a public place, as one might do for strangers. Grandma would take me, and Baba Valya would accompany Dad. Just in case.

I saw him the second we walked into the lobby, but I hardly recognized him. The dad I knew was a tall, slim, vivacious brunet. The man I saw now was entirely gray haired and enormously overweight. He seemed to have tripled in size since I had last seen him.

I ran up to him and blurted out the first thing that came to mind: "Dad, you got so fat!"

He said nothing in return. This threw me for a loop. The dad I had grown up knowing was an easygoing jokester. He would've had a comeback ready for my faux pas, perhaps something along the lines of, "More room for cake!" This somber and quiet man I didn't know at all.

We were all seated together for the performance. During the intermission, the grandmothers beat a tactful retreat while Dad and I went to the theater café to get ice cream together. I don't recall what we talked about. Dad didn't seem happy to see me. He barely reacted to anything around him.

I was at sea. I had no idea how to feel about any of this. Should I be happy to see Dad return from the hospital? Should I be sad that he seemed so strange? Could I be making fun of him suddenly becoming so fat?

As always, I did not ask and nobody offered me any explanations.

It took many months, but eventually Dad recovered a great deal of his old cheer. Still, the illness and its year-long treatment left him disabled and in poor health. Soon after our meeting at the theater, Dad and Jenna moved permanently to the hut in Korovkino. For many years afterwards, he rarely ever left the village.

Dad's life trajectory—from gifted poet, to alcoholic dissident, to psychiatric patient, to rural recluse—was not as singular as you might think. Many men and women of his generation, finding no government-sanctioned outlet for their talents, descended into substance abuse and eventually burned out. Those who could emigrate did so. Those who could not died slow or quick deaths in their apartments.

Although my family was of the firm opinion that I was nothing like my dad, either in talent or in temperament, I couldn't help but wonder sometimes, *Is this what my life is going to be like? Is that going to be my choice—to either sell out or stay true to myself and drop out of society altogether? Are those the only two options for a Soviet citizen with brains?*

CHAPTER 20

BAD PERESTROIKA

A factory head manager calls his secretary into his office and starts kissing her.

"Ivan Petrovich," she whispers as he unbuttons her blouse, "please close the door!"

"Can't do, Anya. People might think we're drinking in here."

WHILE MY FATHER'S life was falling apart, so was the country.

Gorbachev's fight against alcohol was not going well. Vodka sales were curtailed, and prices were substantially increased. However, people didn't decrease their consumption of hard liquor. Instead, they began distilling their own. In villages and small towns, people knew better than to spend their hard-earned rubles on astronomically expensive vodka. So instead, they started buying sugar and yeast and making *samogon*, Russian moonshine.

Urban alcoholics had it worse. Stuck in the big city with no access to an illegal distillery, they resorted to drinking various disinfection liquids and colognes. The most popular brand of cologne was Troynoy, which came in elegant 250-milliliter bottles, contained 64 percent ethanol, and cost only one ruble—a total bargain! Naturally, it was toxic, but not as immediately so as some of the other alcohol surrogates used by the proletariat to quench their thirst, such as brake fluid, antifreeze, and even varnish. I have never tried Troynoy or any other cologne, but I was told it tastes absolutely vile. People tried to neutralize this flavor by dunking a red-hot metal nail into the bottle before draining it. On the bright side, this beverage left one not only with a buzz but also with a pleasantly manly scent.

Eventually, in 1987, the anti-alcohol program had to be rolled back. Moonshine had become endemic in the countryside. In the cities, people were dying from methanol poisoning or slowly deteriorating from cologne-induced organ failure. The government had to acknowledge defeat: Russian men would rather die than quit drinking. But there was also another reason. The failure of Gorbachev's program of acceleration, in combination with abysmal oil prices, meant another large budget shortfall. The government needed money, and in Russia, selling vodka had always been the fastest way to get it.

* * *

In 1986, as Lenin's hardbacks and Brezhnev's memoirs were disappearing from bookstores and getting pulped, the floodgates for all other literature were beginning to open.

Two years into the official start of the glasnost policy, people were finally starting to realize that if they said something out of line with the party, no one was coming anymore to arrest them for "anti-Soviet propaganda." Previously forbidden books began to trickle into print, even though the runs were still very limited. The literary heavyweights were first in line for publication. Boris Pasternak's *Doctor Zhivago*, the novel that got him hounded by the Soviet authorities and won him the 1958 Nobel Prize for Literature, finally appeared in bookstores. Ivan Bunin's *From the Other Shore* also emerged from the shadows. And a new name had emerged that was previously known only to literary experts and never published in Russia: Vladimir Nabokov.

Then an altogether incredible thing happened: Solzhenitsyn was officially rehabilitated in the eyes of the Soviet state, and his works were authorized for publication in installments in magazines. A part of me still couldn't quite believe this sudden bounty. It was hard to credit that this was the new normal, that the new leader's permissiveness was genuine, and that he wouldn't suddenly change his mind and turn back the clock. At the same time, many people read the appearance of Solzhenitsyn's writings in print as the writing on the wall for the grand Soviet project.

Limits on magazine subscriptions were lifted. Whereas most families used to be restricted in their reading material, suddenly anyone could subscribe to any magazine or newspapers they wished to read. Everyone wanted to know the truth about the country they lived in, after decades of being lied to.

Nineteen eighty-seven became the year when everyone subscribed to everything. Gone were the days of mandatory subscriptions to *Pravda*, which moldered unread in the recycling corner. That year, our household was receiving no fewer than fifteen magazines and newspapers, and it was still not enough. It was the same for most people all over the country. By the time the USSR was on the threshold of dissolving, it was the best-read country in the world. The *Argumenty i Fakty* weekly digest entered the *Guinness Book of World Records* as the newspaper with the most subscribers in the world: 33.5

million. People were hungrier for knowledge than they were for actual food.

My dad, a man of letters, was in a semipermanent state of ecstatic shock. He had lived his entire life knowing that some books were simply forbidden, the way one knows that the sky is blue. Seeing them being distributed by Soviet publishing houses to anyone who showed up with cash blew his mind. "I thought I would never live to see Nabokov or Solzhenitsyn printed in the USSR!" he would say to me every time we saw each other. Of course, he also subscribed to every newspaper and magazine that we read, and more besides.

Glasnost meant more than just the freedom to curse the government out in the streets rather than in one's kitchen, with the faucet running and the radio blaring. It meant that the media, which until then was largely restricted to propaganda, could now investigate corruption, resource mismanagement, poor harvests, and other structural problems that plagued the Soviet economy. Magazines and newspapers scrambled for real news reports, hard-hitting editorials, legitimate experts, and thorough analysis. The truth was finally being told about Stalin's purges, the Gulag labor camps, Khrushchev's agricultural failures, and the war in Afghanistan. Finally, the magnifying glass was turned on the October Revolution and Lenin himself. They were discussed with diminished fervor at first, then with neutrality, then with barely concealed hostility. The sacred cows were off to the slaughterhouse.

The inert TV programming of my childhood was beginning to crumble. Old shows were going off the air, and new ones were taking their place. By the end of the '80s, the TV guide read like a thriller: "Which show got axed this week? What's going to take its place?" The evening news was becoming unrecognizable. Before glasnost, Soviet anchormen had

only two intonations: breathless approbation, for narrating over
the footage of Soviet heads of state; and condemnation, for anything and everything happening in the West. But in 1987, I
remember watching a news report on the weekly *International
Panorama* roundup, where the topic was America. For the first
time ever, the reporting was purely informative rather than
inflammatory. I can't recall the exact subject matter—it was covering either some arts exhibition or the latest scientific development. But I do recall that there was no vilification, no usual tu
quoque attempts to denounce the living conditions of America's
exploited working class, no comments on imperialism or war-
mongering. For the first time ever, it was just the facts.

When Gorbachev had his summit meetings with Reagan in
Iceland, our TV screens started showing altogether unthinkable
things: a Soviet general secretary and an American president
were smiling at each other and shaking hands enthusiastically.
At some point, Reagan even made an appearance on Soviet
television, and he was actually permitted to address the Soviet
people directly! When I saw the wrinkled leader of the rotten
and corrupt imperialist world beam at me from the television
set, I almost choked on my meatball.

The film industry, too, underwent tremendous changes.
Soviet films began to depict things no one had ever seen on the
big screen before: the misery of everyday life; the toll of alcoholism; the lives of veterans, both old and those fresh out of
Afghanistan; increasing drug use; suicide; the spread of AIDS;
and, most importantly to movie connoisseurs like my young
self, boobies.

Despite the newly acquired freedoms, living during perestroika felt rather like being on a wild and exhilarating roller
coaster ride—it was unsettling, disorienting, and sometimes
terrifying. Moreover, years passed and the ride just kept

accelerating. By 1988, everyone on board was getting heartily sick of it, and more and more people were clamoring to be let off.

Gorbachev welcomed the complaining. He reasoned that if we could just air everyone's grievances and establish a feedback system between the government and the people, then we could all pull together to scrape the rust off the Soviet economic engine and get it purring again. Sadly, he was wrong. By the time he came along, both the engine and the car itself had long rusted all the way through.

His policies were quickly losing support. The liberalization of the media and the flood of Western films were welcome, but many of his other undertakings had distinctly negative consequences. For instance, his attempt to liberalize the economy by permitting private companies, while well intentioned, was not well implemented. The state banking system was not equipped to support Russia's budding capitalists, so funding for the first companies and cooperatives often had to be provided by loan sharks. The judiciary and the police were also not equipped to resolve the inevitable problems brought about by such arrangements; to the extent that there was ever organized crime in the USSR, it was usually an intra-party issue of corruption and was dealt with by the KGB, not the police. To cover the gap in contract enforcement, a new breed of "problem solvers" sprung up in the USSR almost overnight. These thugs, outfitted in tracksuits and armed with baseball bats and lead pipes, ended up functioning as informal regulators and middlemen across almost all sectors of the new liberalized economy.

By 1988, the USSR was experiencing severe food shortages. But it was not the food scarcity of my childhood, where one had to stand in line for sausages or oranges for hours. Gorbachev's reforms had dismantled essential components of the state's supply apparatus before the emerging free market could pick up the slack. Suddenly, every grocery item became "in deficit." Older folks began to grumble that they'd seen all this before, during the war.

In Leningrad, rationing cards came back into effect for the first time since the end of the Second World War. These were numbered sheets of pink paper with blue stamps and clippable coupons for the various rationed items: pasta, salt, matches, soap, sugar, tea, vegetable oil, butter, flour, et cetera. Each of the items now had a monthly allowance: one could not buy more than 500 grams of sausage, 400 grams of butter, 250 grams of cheese, 100 grams of tea, 1 kilo of sugar, and so forth, per person per month.

Yet the one coupon to rule them all was the one for vodka: one half-liter bottle per person per month. Every member of the household was allotted these coupons, not just those who could legally drink. Even a newborn infant, provided he was a registered and legal resident of the city, was issued pink sheets with a vodka coupon. Welcome to the big wide world, little Maksimka boy! Have a drink—you'll need it.

People no longer said they went out to shop; now, they went to "redeem coupons." Families turned into hunter-gatherer groups, eagerly exchanging information about which store had what in stock, and where certain coupons could be redeemed. This store had run out of everything but salt; that one still had some butter and flour. Hurry!

The market economy didn't really take hold and start growing until after the final year of the Soviet Union. Soon, the government admitted that it could no longer control prices, and allowed them to be raised across the board. Sensing what was coming next, people desperately tried to spend every ruble they had on any object of value they could lay their hands on: shoes, socks, underwear . . . Soon the stores were entirely bare. It took another year before the economy finally began to rebound, and privately owned stores stocked with imported goods began to pop up all over the city like mushrooms after a warm summer rain.

But this was still in the future. For now, all we could do was hang on to our rationing cards and watch as the old world collapsed around us.

CHAPTER 21

THE EMPIRE RETURNS THE BLOW

A Soviet and an American chicken lie on a supermarket shelf. The American chicken is rosy, plump, and fresh. The Soviet one is gray, thin, and covered in feathers and mud.

The American chicken says, "Look at yourself! You are all blue and skinny and ugly. Just look how beautiful and appetizing I am!"

The Soviet chicken replies, "That's great and all. But unlike you, I got to die a natural death!"

IN EARLY JUNE 1987, I received an important word from the universe. It was when the city authorities organized a two-week American film festival in our local Leningrad movie theater.

I was sixteen and had just finished school exams, with very decent results, and was enjoying some well-deserved downtime before university entrance assessments were to start. All my friends were elsewhere. Vova was away staying at a village, and Vasya Bazanov never woke up before 11 a.m. on days when he didn't have to go to school, so I didn't even bother calling him. For a working-class boy, he was almost pathologically lazy. Whenever I would visit him after school and ask if he could come and hang out, his homework was almost never done.

"What have you been doing after school?" I'd ask. "It's already six!"

He would shrug. "I bit my nails for an hour. Then I played piano for an hour. Then I burped for an hour."

It was safe to assume, therefore, that Vasya would still be asleep. So the movie festival was mine to enjoy alone.

Every morning that week, I had breakfast and left at 9 a.m. to stand in line for an hour or two to get a ticket to whatever festival film was still available that day. It was a bit of a lottery—the names of American movies meant nothing. I always had a book with me. All Soviet intelligentsia kids like myself carried a book with them when they went out. You just never knew when there was some sort of an interesting line to stand in, maybe for cheese, or maybe for imported Romanian shoes. Or, now that perestroika was chugging along full speed, for American film festival tickets.

The book I had with me this time was George Orwell's *Nineteen Eighty-Four*, borrowed from my dad. He had only given it to me for a few days, so I had to finish it quickly. The book was still forbidden in the Soviet Union, and it was a foreign-made *tamizdat* edition. Despite there being almost no risk of getting in trouble, I still wrapped the book's outer cover in a newspaper to hide the title, out of ingrained habit. I could not say that I was particularly excited about the novel itself—life under Big Brother's eye may have been quaint and thought-provoking to Western readers, but for someone like me, who had spent all his life in a very similar setting, it was everyday. So I just enjoyed the fact of reading a forbidden book.

The line was substantial. I read for about forty minutes before my turn came. In the box office window there was a small handwritten note informing cinemagoers that the only tickets available were for "*The Empire Returns the Blow*: color, science fiction, 1980, USA." I just shrugged. There was a decent seat still available for the 11 a.m. screening, in the auditorium with the biggest screen, no less—the biggest in town, in fact. And I've always liked science fiction. All right. "One for *The Empire*, please."

I still had some time to kill before the show. So I went to the Tauride Gardens nearby, sat down on a bench next to the iron statue of Lenin, lit a Marlborough (admittedly, a total waste of a perfect show-off item that should have been saved), pulled out *Nineteen Eighty-Four*, and looked around.

For a while, I entertained the thought of reading the book out loud to the statue of Lenin. But I quashed the impulse. There are some renowned lines by Russia's most prominent poet, Alexander Pushkin, that go

> Dear friend, have faith: the wakeful skies
> Presage a dawn of wonder—Russia
> Shall from her age-old sleep arise,
> And despotism impatient crushing,
> Upon its ruins our names incise!

In those days, people told each other a parody of these lines that reflected everyone's deep-seated suspicions about the authorities' true intentions:

> Dear friend, have faith: this too shall pass
> This time of freedom and of glasnost
> While fellows from GosBezopasnost*
> Will meanwhile all our names amass.

*State security, or KGB

So I read quietly until it was time to go in for the film.

There were no previews or commercials in Soviet cinema. The lights went off, and the movie started abruptly with a burst of loud classical music and slowly floating yellow titles.

Then various flying saucers began to hover on the screen. That was cool. Then some kangaroo-like creatures carrying spacemen started to hop around on a snowy planet. That was even better. But by the time the elephantine AT-ATs began to clomp across the screen toward the rebel base, my coolness receptors went into overload. From that moment, my jaw dropped and remained in that position for the entire duration of the film.

I had no idea who any of these characters were—after all, *The Empire Strikes Back* was the sequel. But I didn't care. Everything about this film was just great and like nothing I'd seen or experienced before: the wide-screen visuals of space battles; the tricky, morally ambivalent characters with dark secrets; the limitless variety of alien creatures; and, most importantly, the incredible sense of adventure, future, and hope—the feeling that the world was vast and full of wonders, and that everything was possible.

Many American boys probably felt the same way after first watching *Star Wars*, but imagine how much more intense the experience was for an innocent Soviet teenager who'd never had any exposure to such amazing special effects and who'd never owned any electronic gadgets.

The ending really got to me, too. When Luke, Leia, and the two robots stood there looking out at the spaceships ahead, it was obvious that there must be a third part, which I probably wouldn't get to see. (Little did I know, it had been released four years before.)

All movies are essentially escapes from reality, and sci-fi space operas even more so, but in this case, the divide between the magic on the screen and the dead, gray routine of real life was simply too much to bear.

The Soviet Union had always excused its sad state of poverty and dilapidation with its striving for Communism; it seems unreasonable to expect things to be clean, attractive, and in good order during such a monumental transition.

All Soviet citizens were born, grew up, worked, gave birth, and died under an all-encompassing implied sign: "Pardon Our Dust, Work in Progress." But in the last years, it had been dawning on people more and more that there was no actual work being done—there was only dust. The USSR was not decrepit and poor because it was putting all its effort into building a bright, shiny tomorrow for all the people, with limitless food, free toys for all children, vacations on Mars, and a room for every person to themselves, in a separate apartment without endless lines for the toilet. It was that way because construction had long stopped. Moreover, the foreman, even though he had every intention of finishing the high-rise he was tasked with in time and under budget, was never given any blueprints and was making things up on the fly. Half the workers were drunk on the job, and the other half were scouring the site for things to steal. And worst of all, even if the tech crew ever got people over to Mars on one of their hundreds of flying saucers that seemed to consume all resources and talent, the only thing one could imagine them doing there was sitting in on party meetings (albeit perhaps in space suits) and eating the same meatballs with the same cockroaches, which would surely survive the trip even better than the human travelers.

And all the while, somewhere else, people really were dreaming big, and having grand visions of cosmic proportions, and inspiring each other to strive for the forces of light in the face of all adversity. These people, one just knew, could never be appeased with a promise of a bright tomorrow without asking for a good-faith down payment on it today.

I came out of the movie theater knowing that I was a Westerner at heart, a member of the rebellion, and nothing would ever change that. I wanted to see the third part. In fact, I wanted to live in a place where such films got made. Soviet propaganda talked a lot in my childhood about how Western propaganda wanted to pervert Soviet youth and instill anti-Soviet values in them.

Well, *Star Wars* put the final nail in the coffin of my Soviet ideals. I had to fight the Empire and escape my homeland, but I had no idea how to do it. I only knew that I had to figure it out soon.

August 21, 2011

I saw Grandma's body for the first time in the cemetery church, an ugly wooden structure constructed in a hurry in the late '80s, possibly the year I saw *The Empire Returns the Blow*. Grandma looked the same as when I'd seen her a few months before—weak, pale, and distant.

About twenty relatives and family friends were in attendance. They didn't give me, Alyosha, or Mom much of the usual funeral blather about how tragic or how untimely her passing away was. Everyone knew that it was time.

The unremarkable priest sang for his supper well but without enthusiasm. After he had finished commending Grandma to the Almighty, Alyosha, myself, and another two distant relatives carried the coffin for some three hundred meters to the grave under the birch tree.

It was all over in half an hour.

Russian funerals are followed by not one but three memorials: on the third, ninth, and fortieth days since the death. This tradition encompasses all elements of the Russian spiritual experience: pagan, Russian Orthodox, and Soviet. At a typical memorial, a lot of emphasis is made on the person's achievements, their good relationships, their standing within the community—in short, the materialistic side of their existence. The Orthodox faith survives in the funeral service and in the votive candles lit before the photograph of the deceased by their relatives. But these more contemporary traditions are buoyed by a strong pagan undercurrent. Besides the veiling of mirrors in the dead person's house, there are blini, the sine qua non of every memorial spread. These round, thin crepe-style pancakes symbolize the sun and promise eternal life in the otherworldly realm to the departed soul. Food is also offered, symbolically, to the soul of the deceased, placed on little saucers in front of the photograph with the votive candles, as well as on the grave itself.

We held Grandma's first memorial after the funeral, at a small restaurant not far from her apartment. It was the same place where we'd celebrated her ninetieth birthday. She was still hale and hearty then, enjoying herself thoroughly and even tipping back a shot or two.

But this day we placed her picture from that very ninetieth birthday on a small table in the corner of the restaurant room, with a piece of rye bread, a shot of vodka, and a lit candle next to it.

The same twenty people attended. One after another, they stood up and said all the right things about how important she was to all of us, how much she had accomplished in her long life, how much she would be missed.

"I'm not good with toasts or speeches," I said when my turn came, "but now that she's gone, it feels like a true end of an era. We lost the head of the clan that was keeping us together for decades."

I was not exaggerating. Grandma had been the family matriarch, the rock of our dynasty. Up until her last days, everyone had always consulted her on all key life decisions. Even my dad, who wasn't strictly speaking even a relation of hers after his and Mom's divorce back in the early 1970s, continued to run all his plans by Grandma.

We drank without clinking glasses—another funerary custom.

After the memorial, everyone went their separate ways. Mom went home. Alyosha and his wife went back to their hotel. I was left all to myself.

It was an August evening, and it was still light in Saint Petersburg. I decided to hold a memorial of my own, not just for Grandma but for all the things she represented to me, chief among them my childhood. . .

CHAPTER 22

DANGEROUS LIAISONS

"Excuse me, do you know where Comrade Ivanov lives?"

"If you are referring to the Ivanov who used to live opposite the city prison and who was recently visited by his American relatives, he now lives opposite his old house."

STOP ME IF you've heard this one before. A young girl receives news that an elderly relation of hers, whom she'd never known, has died abroad in a faraway land and left her a substantial fortune, which transforms her life forever.

It may sound like something out of a paperback novel, but this actually happened to my mother when she was ten years old. Or rather, it's what could have happened. What happened instead was a quintessentially Soviet story.

Before the Revolution, Saint Petersburg was a truly cosmopolitan metropolis. Many expats made their home there. It was a sort of Singapore or Dubai of its time. Foreigners moved there to get a shot at making money and maybe even gaining a title of nobility. My mother's side of the family hails from that motley crowd.

Grandma was for a large part Greek. Her father, Nikolai Klado, was a nobleman and part of a long-standing family tradition of military service. (Most famously, his great-grandfather Angelo Klado, during his service in the imperial guard, was the first to address Tsar Paul I, the son of Catherine the Great, as "Your Imperial Majesty" straight after his mother's fatal stroke. His timely assertiveness worked—the new tsar instantly promoted him by two ranks.)

My grandpa Roman Brosset was for a large part French. He traced his ancestry to an adventurous nineteenth-century academic and hyperpolyglot by the unlikely name Marie-Félicité Brosset. Supposedly, he received this name at the insistence of his grandmother. That's right: our family had its very own version of Johnny Cash's song "A Boy Named Sue." In preparation for a life in the priesthood, Marie-Félicité attended a seminary and learned ancient Hebrew and Arabic. He became so interested in the Far East that he quit the seminary. After learning Chinese, Tibetan, and Manchu, he became interested in Georgian. Since most materials about this language were published in Russian, he learned Russian as well. In 1837, he moved with his family to Saint Petersburg to become an adjunct in the Academy of Sciences. He soon became a top scholarly authority on Georgia. (One of the central streets of Tbilisi, the capital of Georgia, is named after him.) He returned to France toward the end of his life, but his children and grandchildren remained in Russia, working mostly for the government.

One of them, my great-grandfather Theodore Brosset, was a diplomat. He was appointed as the envoy to Sweden after the tsar's abdication in March 1917. When the Bolshevik Revolution took place several months later in October, Theodore was recalled. He must have had a pretty good idea of what the Bolsheviks were all about, because he chose to stay put in Sweden. Of course, that meant he was now out of a job—a real problem since he had spent his entire life in diplomatic service and knew no other trade. To feed himself and his new family in Sweden, he opened a bakery. Just imagine the time this pedigreed blue blood from Saint Petersburg's most refined social circles must have had trying to master the humble art of baking! (Though, family lore has it that he soon repositioned himself as the strategist and finance executive of the enterprise, focusing on client relationships and cash flow and leaving the actual process of bread making to his family's nannies and servants, who had also stayed in Sweden with them.)

It all sounds rather comical in retrospect, but Theodore's decision, the same agonizing choice made by so many Russian émigrés at the time of the 1917 Revolution, split the Brosset family. My grandfather Roman and his sister, Natalia, remained in Saint Petersburg, whereas their father, stepmother, and two younger brothers never returned from Sweden. In 1918, Natalia managed to escape Soviet Russia and move to China, where she soon married Jean-Paul de Viaud, a French diplomat who was stationed there. She spent most of the 1920s and 1930s in Shanghai and the post-war years in Guangzhou, where Jean-Paul headed the French consulate.

So, Grandpa Roman's family was scattered all over the globe. The new Soviet state mostly left him alone. It imprisoned him only once for just six months after discovering that he had belonged to the Boy Scouts as a kid—Cheka was checking if he was secretly a Western spy. But his background proved to have one major advantage: it kept him from getting drafted during World War II. Being both noble-born and of foreign heritage, he was considered too untrustworthy to be sent into battle. Instead, he worked through the war as a low-ranking engineer at a military factory, which had been evacuated in

1941 from Leningrad to the Ural Mountains, far from the invading German troops. His mother and his first wife were not allowed to join him, and they had to stay behind in Leningrad. In 1942, during the three-year siege of the city, they starved to death two months apart. They were buried somewhere in the mass graves of Piskarevskoe Cemetery, along with half a million other residents of Leningrad whose lives ended in the same way. One can only imagine how Grandpa Roman felt when he returned from the evacuation to find his home empty.

In 1946, he married Grandma and they had a daughter, my mother. Unfortunately, Grandpa Roman didn't live to see her grow up. When he was just fifty-four, and Mom was only five, he died of a heart attack right before her eyes. His death has haunted Mom ever since.

She also never got a chance to learn anything from him about his family. She did not know that she had an aunt and two uncles abroad until she was an adult.

In December 1958, Grandma received a notice that a piece of registered mail had arrived for her at the Leningrad central post office. Her first thought was that her ever-extravagant brother, Nikolai, must have sent her a box of fruit and treats from sunny Tajikistan for the New Year.

But it was something very different—a letter from France from someone called Jean-Paul de Viaud. Grandma examined the envelope. It was obvious that it had been opened and resealed before, and that she would not be the first person reading it. This did not surprise her in the least; it was well-known that all incoming and outgoing international correspondence in the Soviet Union was perlustrated.

The letter, typed neatly in Russian, delivered a bombshell. In it, Jean-Paul explained that he was the husband of Natalia de Viaud, née Brosset, who had passed away that year in Paris. He spoke of how all her life, Natalia regretted leaving her brother

Roman behind in Leningrad and was saddened that she'd never been able to see him or write to him again. Jean-Paul continued that he and Natalia had no children of their own, and so, using various diplomatic channels available to him, he'd obtained information for Natalia about Vera Brosset, Roman's only child. As the only woman among the four siblings, Natalia had been the bearer of all the family heirloom jewels, and she had willed them to her only niece, young Vera.

The letter concluded with practical instructions: how Grandma should confirm her guardianship over Vera, how to contact the French embassy in Moscow to prepare the necessary paperwork, and so on. A photo of Natalia was also included.

Grandma's reaction was swift. That same evening, she dashed off and mailed a letter to Jean-Paul, or rather to the KGB officers monitoring her correspondence. In her reply, she politely explained that the Soviet Union provided for all of her and Vera's needs; that they had everything they desired; and that they were very happy. Therefore, they would not be accepting any gifts from an unknown émigré relative from a foreign capitalist country.

As for Mom, Grandma had concluded that a ten-year-old Soviet girl with a strange, foreign last name was better off not knowing about such things. God forbid she might let something slip at school about it! And so she told Mom nothing. She also threw away Jean-Paul's letter. It was safer that way. The only thing she kept was Natalia's portrait. I still have it. In it, Roman's sister looks like a beautiful, gracefully aging Hollywood star, diamond earrings sparkling in her ears and two diamond clasps adorning her sleeveless evening dress.

Grandma knew what she was doing. One of her most vivid childhood memories was of being awakened in the middle of the night by armed sailors, the unofficial militia forces of the Bolshevik revolutionary government. The sailors ransacked her family's apartment in search of valuables, even taking mattresses off the children's beds and ripping them open in case there were jewels or money hidden in them. Her brother, Nikolai, was arrested in 1930 and sent into internal exile in the city of Vologda; he later fled to Tajikistan. Her elder sister, Tatiana, a meteorologist, was arrested in 1935 for corresponding with distant relatives abroad. She spent the next twelve years in Siberia.

* * *

In 1987, Grandpa Roman's younger brother, Alexis Brosset, who had stayed behind with his father, the diplomat-turned-baker, in Sweden, returned to Leningrad for the first time since 1917. Although Roman had died decades earlier, Alexis, by then in his late seventies, somehow found out Mom's address and wrote to her. He wanted to see her and the rest of his involuntarily estranged family. By then, perestroika was in the air and contact with foreign relatives was no longer forbidden. And so, a visit was arranged.

It was an emotional meeting. After all the hugging and crying was done, we all sat down to a big family dinner. It was a tremendous moment for everyone, but most especially for Mom and her uncle. She could hardly take her eyes off him. He looked strikingly similar to long-dead Grandpa Roman.

Naturally, there was vodka on the table. Uncle Alexis would sip it and say in Russian with a slight accent, "Oh, what a tasty vodka!" It was such a weird thing to say, I thought. How can vodka be tasty? And why is he sipping it? The Russian way of drinking vodka was to throw it back and nibble on something right away afterwards, to kill the aftertaste, or at least sniff something strong smelling. These foreign relatives sure were a strange bunch. . .

* * *

My mother may have missed her chance at enrichment through our foreign relations back in 1958, but my brother and I lived in a different time and got luckier: Great-Uncle Alexis gave us ten dollars each! To us, this was a big-time payday.

In the USSR, every large city had a handful of special shops called Beryozka (Little Birch Tree), which accepted special government checks issued for Western currency. They mainly served the few lucky Soviet citizens who worked abroad in exciting places like Iran, Vietnam, Egypt, or Cuba—the USSR did an excellent job of sticking its fingers into many pies all over the globe. Such personnel were paid in these checks. Obviously, they were a hot ticket on the black market; illegally traded checks usually went for double the official rate at two rubles to one check.

When I was thirteen, I took some saved-up gift money and bought ten checks for sixteen rubles from one of Mom's girl-friends, who had just returned from working in Bulgaria—a good deal!

Mom, a consummate networker, had a small army of girl-friends who often visited her to gossip about their marital or extramarital relationship issues. Mom would listen, nod with understanding, feed them tea and cookies—or Armenian Cognac, depending on how dire things were—and say things like, "Oh, dear . . . No! Are you joking? He hasn't—he couldn't have! I understand all too well. He doesn't deserve you, really. He doesn't . . . I know, I know . . . Oh, I know . . ." And she would pat the woman's hand, and pour her more tea, and give her a handkerchief to blow her nose and blot her running mascara. On one such evening, with newly acquired checks in hand, I left them to their usual therapy and traveled across town to Vasilyevsky Island to the sole check-accepting Beryozka in Leningrad. At the door, I was stopped by the security guard.

"Show me the checks," he said.

Heart in my mouth, I opened my wallet and revealed the banknote. He stepped aside and let me in.

It felt like a trip to a parallel universe. For the first time in my life, I saw a store chock full of shiny foreign stuff: German jeans and sneakers, Japanese tape recorders, TVs and washing machines—everything I knew must have existed somewhere outside our stuffy, closed-off universe but could never quite imagine. Alas, the vast majority of these things were far beyond my means. For a long time, I walked around the store, just absorbing the novelty and abundance of it all. My final selection was a belt for nine checks. It was bright orange and made of nylon. The peacock in me thought that it was sure to be a hit with the ladies. Soviet clothing was universally dark and bleak, so choosing an orange accent was the way to go for the cool, dissident Western convert like me. I wore it every day during my last three years at school.

* * *

But now, with real green money from Great-Uncle Alexis in our pockets, Alyosha and I knew that our dreams were about to come true. We were going to a different kind of Beryozka: the kind that accepted only real foreign currency, like dollars, pounds, and deutschmarks. This shop catered exclusively to foreign tourists, selling them Western goods to help them feel a bit more at home in the USSR. It also had a guard at the door; his job was to check the entering customers. Anyone who looked Soviet was not allowed on the premises. That was the store we took our great-uncle to.

Our expedition was not without risk. Perestroika might have been in effect, but owning any hard foreign currency was still a crime, punishable by three years in prison. Still, we decided to venture into the store as a family. Since our great-uncle was western European, and thus had every right to shop at the hard currency Beryozka, we just rode his coattails inside.

We bought a Mars bar, a few cups of yogurt, and something else entirely new to us: a few cans of some Scandinavian soda. The USSR did not sell any drinks in aluminum cans with tabs.

"Check it out," I whispered to Alyosha low enough so that the shop assistants wouldn't hear that we were speaking Russian. "It's the same type of cans as in American movies!"

"Awesome!" he whispered back. "How many can we get? I also want this Tic Tac candy in a plastic box."

All these things completely blew our minds. Especially the yogurts, with their nifty plastic packaging, thin colorful foil on top, and cherry chunks. Oh, and the Mars bar, which we shared immediately. It was no Red October Chocolate Factory bar, that's for certain. It clearly took decades of capitalist inventiveness to come up with such a mix of flavors and textures.

Also, while Uncle Alexis had his back turned, I got something else: with my remaining seventy cents I picked up a pack of filterless GI-style Camel cigarettes. It was an item of ultimate alternative understatement. Subsequently, it worked wonders to attract the attention of some curious girls.

On balance, I was probably more excited about the food than I was about meeting our long-lost relative.

But I also had one more cynical thought.

Back in the '70s, the Soviet Union ceded a little to American pressure and began to allow some of its citizens to emigrate to Israel. People quickly caught on that the emigrants would be allowed to bring their immediate families. A popular joke, refashioned from a slogan about automobiles, stated that a Jewish wife is not a luxury, but rather a means of transportation.

Now I found myself thinking, *So, I have a genuine passport-carrying western European great-uncle. How do I turn him into a means of transportation? Can I ask to visit him in Sweden? Will Soviet authorities issue me an exit visa? Will Sweden give me an entry visa? Can I go to study there without speaking Swedish? Would it be too much to ask my great-uncle?*

It was a chaos of questions and no answers. But an exit plan had begun to form in my mind. Still, I would need several other elements to make it work.

CHAPTER 23

WHEN IT'S TIME TO MOVE ON

The son of the director of a Leningrad meat-processing factory is taking university entrance exams.

"Your answers so far were impeccable," says the examiner. "Now for the last and most challenging question: Which two countries took part in the Russo-Japanese war?"

AFTER THE YOUNG Pioneers, the next organization a young Soviet had to join was the Communist Youth Union, abbreviated Komsomol. This was the last stepping-stone to being a full-fledged member of the Communist Party, which was important for many prestigious career tracks. (By the time the USSR collapsed, there were 20 million card-carrying members of the Communist Party out of a population of 240 million.)

Membership in Komsomol was also a requirement for admission to many universities and technical colleges. The only soul I personally knew who had never been in Komsomol was Dad's wife, Jenna, and even that was only because of some odd circumstances involving moving between Moscow and Leningrad.

Two factors affected how and when you would be admitted into Komsomol. The first was your age: you had to be over fourteen. The second was your merit: your grades, community activism, et cetera. Your school's Komsomol organization had to recommend you for membership. Usually, people who didn't get in immediately had to try again six months later.

Though I was a good student and the president of the International Friendship Club, I was the youngest in my class, so I was a bit concerned about my chances of getting in on the first go. My friend and soup-tossing guru Sasha Lesman was ten months older than me, but he was a relatively poor student, scraping by on 3s and 4s (i.e., "passing"). So we ended up going through the admission process around the same time, in eighth grade.

After we both got our school recommendations, we went to the district Komsomol headquarters by the Chernyshevskaya metro station to have our talks. We met with two serious comrades, and they interviewed us at the same time, two on two. They asked mostly formulaic questions about our grades and "the political situation in the world." As my homeroom's coordinator of *politinformatziya*, I knew my official propaganda lines faultlessly.

Sasha Lesman had a worse time of it. The situation with his grades was not ideal, either. After Sasha admitted that he had only a 3 in Soviet literature, one of the interviewers asked, "All right, just tell us then, who wrote the novel *Virgin Soil Upturned*?"

This grand opus was penned by Mikhail Sholokhov, the only recipient of the Nobel Prize for Literature whom the Soviet government permitted to accept it. Sasha, who didn't know the correct answer but caught on that he ought to show his loyalty to the Communist cause, said that the author was Leonid Ilyich Brezhnev. The interviewers fell off their chairs with laughter. Now that Brezhnev was gone, it was okay to laugh. Sasha was admitted.

Upon admission into Komsomol, you were given yet another lapel pin, with yet another Lenin. My first day at school with a Komsomol lapel pin and without that Young Pioneer red tie was glorious. The class shitmunchers and ne'er-do-wells who hadn't been admitted yet watched me arrive with envy: I may have still had a high-pitched voice and no facial hair, but they still had to wear that stupid bloody tie, despite being already long in the tooth.

Komsomol members had to pay membership dues: two kopecks a month. A monthly stamp went into the membership book, testifying that you were up-to-date on these dues. As to what Komsomol actually did, that remained a mystery. There were occasional assemblies: a Komsomol homeroom meeting once a quarter and an all-school Komsomol meeting once every six months. No one ever did anything at those gatherings; people just doodled in their notebooks or did homework for the next day. I myself would stay in the back row and read a book. By the time I was in the union, everything about Komsomol was all complete pro forma bullshit.

* * *

The bigger problem was what I would study in college. In the USSR, young people didn't just apply to a university; they applied to a particular department. I needed a subject that would get me out of the country, one that I showed some faculty for and that wouldn't absolutely bore me to death.

That summer, with one year of school left ahead of me, I was constantly lectured by Grandma to make up my mind about my academic future. There were no career or guidance counselors in the USSR; everything was left entirely to the children and their parents.

At first, I toyed with the idea of majoring in math. Despite my failure at the big-time egghead math club, I was still pretty good at it, and had the top grades in my class. But then I went to a prospective student day at the Applied Math department of Leningrad State, to scope things out, and realized that these were not my people. They were the real deal, with thick glasses, faraway gazes, and brains the size of planets. The same exact guys that dominated the math club were now dominating on a much higher, more intense level. I knew that my self-esteem would not survive being around this crowd for the next five years. On a more mundane note, I also realized that I didn't want to commute all the way to the math campus in Peterhof every day by train.

Much to their credit, none of my guardians tried to exert any kind of pressure on me, despite their varying vested interests in different subject areas. Mom sometimes floated the idea of my applying to the economics department, mainly because it was very close to our house. I rejected this idea out of hand, reasoning that to have a successful career in the field of economics in the Soviet Union, I'd first have to become a member of the Communist Party, and that was never going to happen. Mom realized that her anti-Soviet, freedom-loving son was right, and let the matter drop. This was happening in 1986, when the idea of the Communist Party losing power in the USSR, let alone of the country itself falling apart, was still utterly beyond comprehension.

Then Tolya voiced the idea of me applying to the physics department, where he himself was the dean. Again, I had the grades for it, and connections being everything in the USSR, a spot there would have been granted to me without a doubt. But I despaired I would end up studying something related to military technology or avionics or other restricted fields and be stuck in the Soviet Union forever.

My parents' ideas thus exhausted, I was left to fend for admission on my own.

Then, on the evening of September 5, 1986, when I was skateboarding on Kalyaeva Street with my pals, I made the final decision: to apply to the Oriental department of Leningrad State University.

I can't pinpoint when and where my fascination with the Far East began. Perhaps it was with Granddad introducing me to Zen Buddhism. Or perhaps Grandma's strict upbringing instilled in me an affinity for a Confucian, rule-oriented, elder-honoring worldview. Regardless, somewhere along the way—nurtured by Vova's books about Atlantis and Schliemann's discovery of Troy, the Hermitage Museum club, and the Archaeological Society at the Young Pioneer Palace—I had turned into a thorough Orientalist.

I also knew one boy who had just started at the Japanese department that year and was already raving about it: my "god-brother" (i.e., my godmother's son), Andrei Mikhailov. We had been friends for most of our lives—or rather, my mom and his mom, Julia, had been. At family events and parties, they would have fun together, and we would just sort of hang out, making small talk until the parents were worn-out by merrymaking and it was time for everyone to go home.

After I picked my future department, I further narrowed my choice to the Japanese and the Chinese Studies divisions. On balance, my odds were better with the Chinese. Since Japan was pro-Western, competition to get into the Japanese section was much stiffer. And there was another reason: I could study abroad.

After the USSR shot down the South Korean airliner in 1983, all study trips to Japan were halted. By contrast, Sino-Soviet relations were improving steadily, and the Chinese Studies department was starting to organize study-abroad programs in China. I had never been outside the Soviet Union, and even though another Communist country didn't strike me as the most exciting of destinations, it was better than not getting to go anywhere at all.

Decision now made, I began to apply myself extra hard that school year. Even though I attended one of the top schools in Leningrad and did well there, and despite the fact that both of my stepparents worked at the university of my choice, my family and I were taking no chances. It was assumed that I would do my utmost to be admitted on my own merits.

Therefore, I had tutors. In fact, I had two sets of tutors: paid and unpaid. The unpaid ones were Grandma and Dad, who helped me with English and Russian literature.

Grandma was not the best conversationalist—she and I could never have the same kind of tête-à-tête that I could have with progressive foreign visitors to our school. But when it came to English grammar, her authority was unquestionable. In her university teaching years, she even coauthored an English grammar book that is still being reprinted and used in universities across Russia today.

So every Friday afternoon, Grandma would sit with me at her desk and drain my brains with grammar exercises: aligning verb conjugations, switching from past continuous to present indefinite, and restructuring sentences into the conditional or imperative mood. I was bored to death, but I knew that I had to do it. English exams in Russia were 80 percent about correct grammar.

Still, a part of me relished the fact that, thanks to my ongoing role as host for foreign visitors at my school, my knowledge of contemporary English beat Grandma's stodgy book learning by a mile.

"How would you put this sentence into the imperative?" she would ask, then write down, "We are going to the public house."

I would laugh. "Gran, nobody even knows what a 'public house' is anymore! Charles Dickens has been dead for a hundred years, you know. It's just *pub* nowadays. *Pub!*"

Grandma accepted *pub*, under protestation, but she drew the line at *chuffed*, *tosh*, and even *awesome*.

Almost invariably, our lessons devolved into bickering. Eventually, she decided to pawn me and my smart mouth off on an old friend of hers so that I might grate on her nerves instead.

My new English tutor was a little old Jewish lady named Eugenia Isaakovna. Back in the overtly and aggressively anti-Semitic 1950s, Grandma helped her get a teaching job at school, and Eugenia Isaakovna never stopped being grateful to her. Our lessons quickly settled into a comforting routine. Every Monday, I would come home from school, eat some leftovers, and then take the same trolleybus number fifteen to her huge communal apartment on the Fontanka River.

Eugenia Isaakovna's approach to teaching English was through great works of literature. She would make me learn by heart excerpts from works by Oscar Wilde, Lewis Carroll, and Robert Burns so that I could improve not just my grammar but my sense of style as well: "High above the city, on a tall column, stood the statue of the Happy Prince . . ." Naturally, she and I did not quarrel about word choice. It was one thing for me to argue with Grandma, but who could argue with Oscar Wilde?

I also had Russian language tutors. They, too, were elderly, a married couple both well over eighty who lived in a big, untidy apartment on the Petrograd Side. Grandma called them "cat parents," because they had twelve cats. I am desperately allergic to all things cute and furry, so the three hours a week that I spent at their place were mostly taken up with me constantly blowing my stuffed nose.

Paying for these lessons was a surprisingly tricky matter in terms of sheer mechanics. Grandma considered it tasteless to ever speak about money, even when the situation called for it. When she herself gave English lessons, her pupils did not pay her straight up. Instead, at the end of the month, they would bring her a box of sweets or chocolates, and they would place an envelope with the money for that month's worth of lessons inside. Grandma would accept the box with effusive gratitude, as though it were a gift, then immediately hide the envelope out of sight, as though it contained something dreadfully compromising.

The "cat parents," on the other hand, had no such hangups. They preferred to be paid per lesson rather than once a month. So every time I came to see them, I brought an envelope containing ten rubles. They took out the money in my presence and returned the envelope to me. This greatly offended Grandma's aristocratic sensibilities.

"How can anyone do that?" she'd ask rhetorically. "It's like they're selling cucumbers at a farmers market!"

That year, Dad was spending the winter months away from the icy hardships of his village hut in Korovkino, which gave him the opportunity to tutor me in Russian literature. Today I wonder if his temporary move to the city that year was actually driven by his wish to help me out. Having spent most of his life in snobbish and self-absorbed aloofness, perhaps he was starting to realize that besides his poetry and articles, I would be his only material connection to eternity.

Every Saturday afternoon, I would ride the subway to Dad and Jenna's tiny room in a miniature communal apartment near Zvezdnaya station, far away from the city center. We would have coffee with pastries and cigarettes (Dad was the only adult around whom I felt free to smoke openly), and then we would dive into the world of nineteenth- or early twentieth-century Russian poetry and prose. Dad knew exactly what professors expected to hear about each of the books on the required reading list, and what sort of character analysis would jibe the best with the official party line. I took diligent notes.

When we covered enough ground and it would be time for another coffee and cigarette, Dad would lean back and say, "Now that I told you all that crap you'll need for the exam, I should say that, honestly, a lot of Pushkin's poetry is simplistic, sex-obsessed drivel. . ." Or, "The real drama of Mayakovski's poetry was that he was a gifted prostitute who was desperate to sell himself to the Bolsheviks, but the Bolsheviks wouldn't buy him. . ." Or even, "The only Nobel Prize winner in Soviet Literature, Mikhail Sholokhov, is probably a fake. Many alternative historians believe he nicked *And Quiet Flows the Don* from a dead writer. I also cannot imagine how a son of a peasant, who spent most of his youth as a soldier, would at the age of twenty-two miraculously produce a three-volume book, which, no offense to Tolstoy, is better written than *War and Peace*."

* * *

June 1987 was devoted entirely to preparing for our final school exams.

June, without a doubt, is the most charming time of the year in Leningrad. Around the middle of the month, the white nights begin, when the sun barely sets and the sky remains twilit through the night. My friends and I took advantage of these extra-long days by cramming for hours on end through the night. I would cram from 11 p.m. till 7 a.m., then head to school, take my exam, return home, and sleep for the rest of the day. Thankfully, there was always a full day off between tests.

There was no single results day, with all the grades announced at once. Instead, we got our grades either on the spot for verbal exams or the next day for written papers. I left school with 5s on all my exams and mostly the same for the final marks entered into my transcript. My friends also performed well.

On June 30, 1987, we graduated from Leningrad City Secondary School Number 185 with In-Depth English Language Instruction. We had our individual pictures and a class photo taken, and then went to celebrate at a nearby café called Elegia with our teachers.

Our proud parents later catered quite an extravagant dinner to celebrate the occasion, with a great deal of "deficit" food. However, the extravagance was partially due to the fact that we were joined by about twenty students from the United States. This was at the beginning of perestroika, and contact with foreigners was no longer proscribed, so our English teacher arranged for us to be visited by a group of schoolkids from Seattle. They were the students of an American teacher she had encountered on one of those Soviet-American teleconferences. Having real live American teenagers around was such an exciting idea that our teachers didn't even stop to think or to check whether our class might want to keep our graduation dinner a more intimate occasion. After all, we were saying goodbye to one another after ten years of growing and learning side by side. Now, our little celebration was turned into a party with total strangers, and was very crowded, very noisy, and, naturally, alcohol-free.

The American kids were a year or two older than us, probably high school seniors. They were all dressed pretty casually—but, to our eyes, astonishingly fashionably—wearing jeans, sneakers, brand-name T-shirts, Swatch watches, and so on. As for us, we were in formal gear; for instance, I wore a suit. The Americans didn't look too excited to be there and spoke mostly to one another. Which was understandable; their teacher had just dragged them to some local Communist kids' party, where everyone was all dressed up like little comrade grandmas and grandpas, and looking at them funny to boot.

As perennial president of the International Friendship Club, I had much more experience than the others at speaking with foreigners, so I eventually broke the ice with one of the Yankee party crashers. He was a very tall Egyptian American named Kamal. I had no idea people like him existed in America. The idea that there were Americans who spoke perfect American English and yet were neither Anglo-Saxon nor African American had never really occurred to me. Soviet media taught us that America was a rigid caste society with only two kinds of people: evil white capitalists who controlled all the means of production, and poor oppressed workers and farmers, most of whom were black and frequently subjected to lynching and other nasty KKK ceremonies.

Around 9 p.m., the Americans went back to their hotel, and most of our class went home to change into casual clothes. Meanwhile, Olya Moskvina took a bunch of us, including Kamal, back to her place. This was my idea. My cunning plan was to use Olya's apartment, which was easily more opulent than 99.99 percent of all Soviet apartments, as a propaganda piece, to show that the Soviet Union actually provided a very high quality of life. Predictably, Kamal was quite stunned to see the stratospheric living standards of the first Soviet home he had ever been to. "This is really nice," he kept saying. "Not what I expected."

After I put him in a taxi back to his hotel, I joined everyone for the traditional ramble. We all met up once more by the school, all thirty of us, and went to stroll along the banks of the Neva River.

Leningrad is located between Lake Ladoga and the Gulf of Finland, which are connected by the short, broad, and deep Neva River. Its bridges are built low to the water and get raised at night to let boat traffic through. This scene is very picturesque, especially when the weather is clear. Tradition has it that kids graduating school take one last walk together along the river as classmates, to say their symbolic goodbyes to their childhood as they head out into the metaphorical open waters of adulthood. For the rest of the night, we walked along the riverbank, watching the ships pass in the June twilight. It was our last time together as a group.

* * *

A month after graduation, those of us who were intending to go on to university submitted our application documents to our chosen institutions. My case was somewhat more complicated than most. The Oriental department at Leningrad State was an "ideological department." People who studied Asian languages and cultures were assumed to be preparing for work abroad, which meant prolonged contact with foreigners. It was therefore imperative that these privileged individuals be ideologically reliable standard-bearers of the Soviet ideals, ready and eager to spread the gospel of socialism wherever they ended up, or at the very least to set a positive example to the rest of the world.

Even at the undergraduate level, all applicants were subjected to extensive background checks. Mine was a tricky case. Sure, my stepfather, Tolya, was a high-level university official, and for a couple of years he even chaired the party organization on the Peterhof campus. However, my mother's name was Brosset, and she had two uncles in capitalist Sweden. And if that wasn't bad enough, my dad was a dissident and was friends with other dissidents, some of whom had criminal convictions; his poems had been published abroad, and to top it all off, he had spent a year in an insane asylum. I included none of this in my application. However, the university's "first department" (i.e., its KGB representatives) would have no trouble establishing all these facts. That was very worrying.

Beyond that, an application to an ideological department required a personal recommendation from the local and regional Komsomol organizations. The first one I got without any problem. Character references were basically form letters, and school authorities did not spend much time coming up with creative ways to describe their charges.

Here is what was on the signed and stamped yellowish sheet of paper I received in the principal's office:

> *Sergey Grechishkin, born January 12, 1971, has attended the Leningrad City Secondary School Number 185 with In-Depth English Language Instruction from 1977 to 1987. He has been a member of Komsomol since 1985. Diligent; approaches his studies responsibly; active in class and school activities; showed initiative with regards to the school International Friendship Club, of which he was head from 1984 to 1986.*

Sergey is respected by his peers and teachers. He is ideologically and politically mature. The teachers' body and the Komsomol organization of School Number 185 recommends Sergey Grechishkin as a candidate for matriculation at the Oriental department of Leningrad State University named after A. A. Zhdanov.

With the letter from my school's Komsomol chapter now in hand, I had to knock on some doors in the city's central Komsomol office to get an endorsement from the higher-up chapter as well. This took a solid day of walking from office to office and from interview to interview, answering questions about the global political situation and various aspects of Soviet political ideology. Fortunately, I knew perfectly well what my interrogators expected to hear.

This all being done, I was ready for the university entrance exams.

* * *

The Chinese Studies section of the Oriental department received about 140 applications each year and accepted only 10—about 7 percent, not dissimilar to that of an American Ivy League institution. There were three entrance exams: a four-hour essay on Russian literature, an oral history exam, and an oral English test.

For the essay, together with hundreds of other applicants, we were taken into a huge auditorium, given two subjects to choose from, and told to write a ten- to fifteen-page essay off the cuff. Though I was well prepared by my school, my dad, and my tutors, I was still very nervous. A ton of things could go wrong. I could get completely unexpected topics; I could make spelling mistakes from sheer nervousness; I could misquote or misattribute an author or a critic (we were supposed to know a bunch of quotes by heart); or, more prosaically, I could run out of time, ink, or paper.

My topic ended up being "A Poet's Place in the Ranks of Workers," a line by Vladimir Mayakovski, a futurist poet who at first supported the new Soviet regime, then shot himself dead after the regime stopped supporting him. The future-oriented Communists turned out to have paradoxically old-fashioned and bourgeois artistic sensibilities.

I wrote a rough draft, then went to the restroom, checked a smuggled crib sheet for appropriate quotations, then came back and inserted them into the text.

Meanwhile, the older central Asian guy who was sitting in front of me was totally lost. He looked "fresh off the boat"—or the train, rather—as though he had just arrived in Leningrad from Tajikistan or Uzbekistan. In the time it took me to write my entire rough draft, he had only managed five or six lines. I felt somewhat bad for him when I left the lecture hall.

I finished on time, confident in my quotations and with my pen adequately inked. However, I could not fall asleep for hours and hours that night. Visions of potentially misplaced commas danced in my head. And what if I didn't develop the essay theme properly? And what if there were spelling mistakes?

"I know I'm going to get a 3," I thought finally, dozing off at around 4 a.m. "It's going to be a total fucking disaster."

But I ended up getting a 5 for content and a 4 for grammar and style. I must've left off a comma or two somewhere, after all. Or perhaps they just didn't feel like giving me two 5s. There was no point in appealing the grade. The admissions committees were notoriously stingy. Whenever anyone appealed their grade, the instructors would simply sprinkle in some excess punctuation in a similar-colored pen to justify their decisions. Also, the very act of appealing was entered into your record as a strike against your character.

I was equally nervous about my second exam, Russian history. For one, I did not have any tutoring in this subject, so I had to rely only on my own preparation and memory. All day and night before the test, I stayed up filling final crib sheets, summarizing the dates of reign of all the Russian tsars, the countless circumstances of the three Russian Revolutions (one in 1905, two in 1917), and the numbers of divisions on both sides during the main battles of the Great Patriotic War. Exhausted, I went to the test without having been to bed, leaving the crib sheets at home so as not to be tempted to use them.

Luckily, it all went well: I got another 5.

That left just English, which I knew far better than most kids being tested and possibly some of the instructors. There was, however, one terrifying snafu. In the confusion of so many different exams being administered simultaneously, I was accidentally sent to the wrong exam room. Tolya, who had been keeping track of my progress through the university grapevine, was flying off on a work trip that day. Before his flight, he rang up his connection in the admissions office from the airport to ask how I was getting on.

"You won't believe it," the connection told him, "but your Sergey was sent to the wrong room, and he still got a top grade! The instructor didn't even know that he was your kid! So he's definitely in."

You'd think that her supposition was pretty well justified. After all, I did just get three 5s on my entrance exams, and I had excellent school grades, plus all those character references and Komsomol endorsements! Well, yes—but so did many others applying for the same spots. That was the dirty open secret of the game: once you cleared all the required hurdles, the remaining contenders were sifted mostly on the basis of connections. There's no telling if I'd have been selected were it not for Tolya's position at the university. I later discovered that all my new university friends who ended up getting in also had something or someone in their corner.

But what a tremendous relief when I knew that I'd made it! Soon I would be a student of the Oriental department of Leningrad State University named after A. A. Zhdanov! And that meant that if all went well—knock on wood—for the first time in my life, I would be leaving the Soviet Union.

CHAPTER 24

IN HIGHER EDUCATION

A *Pravda* reporter asks a newly admitted university student, "You are part of the class of 1980. As a citizen of the coming Communist future, what are your plans for the new millennium?"

"They are quite modest, really. For most of it, I will be dead."

LIKE ALL SCHOOLS across the USSR, universities rang in the new academic year on September 1. On that day in 1987, my future fellow students and I showed up to the main city campus of Leningrad State University.

The Oriental department was small. It took in only fifty-five students each year, and just ten of those were admitted to pursue Chinese studies.

I knew only two people in the entire department: Andrei, a year ahead of me, and Olya Bezverhova, my infamous Amazonian ex-classmate. She had also managed to get into the Japanese group. (It might or might not have had something to do with her father being a senior KGB officer.)

The old university campus was located right in the heart of Leningrad, on the embankment of the Neva River and almost opposite the Winter Palace, the former tsars' residence. It was made up of a collection of scruffy eighteenth-century academic buildings in the classical style and in various stages of decay. One of them housed the Philology department and the Oriental department—our new academic home. Despite their close geographical proximity, the two departments had very different reputations.

The Oriental department was an acknowledged nest of nerds and highfliers, as well as narcs, who cast a watchful eye over the other two.

The Philology department, or *Filfak* (short for *Filologicheski fakultet*), on the other hand, was considered to be a very happening place. All fashionable Leningrad girls wanted to get into *Filfak*, to study European languages. For one thing, that meant that they might someday be able to travel to the West, and for another, there was a nonzero chance of meeting a foreigner, catching his eye, and acquiring a much coveted "Mrs. degree," with the foreign visa that entailed. It was, by all accounts, an easy ride academically and a good party scene, and had a reputation best expressed in the popular slogan, "If you want to feel and fuck, come and join us at Filfak!"

The building itself was remarkably shabby and run-down, with sadly outdated paraphernalia. Nevertheless, there was still in it an atmosphere of daring intellectual inquiry, and our courses were taught by renowned luminaries of linguistics and anthropology. For example, we heard lectures by Lev Gumilev, a historian famous for his highly unorthodox theories of ethnogenesis. (He also happened to be the son of two of Russia's most famous twentieth-century poets, Nikolaj Gumilev and Anna Akhmatova, which certainly added to his charisma.) It also pleased me to think that I was walking in my father's footsteps—quite literally, since he, too, walked these halls as a Russian lit student twenty years before me.

* * *

On the third day of our classes, as we sat there diligently repeating basic Chinese sounds after our instructor, a Komsomol administrator came into our lecture hall and informed us that tomorrow we were all heading out to the potato fields for one month to help with the harvest. Naturally, neither students nor professors were invited to express their views on whether it was a good idea for the students to break for a month just days into their very first semester.

He also asked us all to relinquish our internal passports (nobody had passports for international travel, since there was no free international travel). Apparently, the potato fields were located within ten kilometers of the Finnish border, and the vigilant fellows in the Big House would need to collect our information before we could be allowed to go. We gathered our passports, and the next day we were off to dig up potatoes within a stone's throw of Finland.

On the train, a surprise awaited me: I ran into my poor bemused central Asian fellow from the Russian literature exam. It turned out that Ulukbek (that was his name) had been accepted into the Arabic department. Apparently, he had some stellar nonacademic credentials: he had been a member of the Communist Party since he was eighteen, and he was a veteran who had just returned from a two-year tour of duty in Afghanistan. He also qualified for the Soviet equivalent of affirmative action, which set aside some university spots for applicants from central Asian republics.

Ulukbek was the oldest in our year, so the authorities put him in charge of keeping us young'uns in line. He used to psych us up for potato digging by instructing us, in archaic Russian flavored with a strong Uzbek accent, without a hint of irony: "Be ye therefore bold, men, and spare not yer lives for your motherland!" If Master Yoda could speak Russian, he would probably sound like Ulukbek.

On the fields, each day resembled the last. We got up at 8 a.m., ate a bowlful of some unidentifiable nasty slop, then boarded the bus that took us to the fields. Our job was to gather spuds into buckets and then to schlep them to the tractor. Again and again and again, rain or shine.

At midday, great big kettles with more slop were trucked into the fields for our refreshment. It was amusing to think that the up-and-coming intellectual elite of the USSR, who had beaten a one-in-twelve acceptance rate, were greeting this new stage of their lives in conditions not too far removed from those of prisoners in Siberian labor camps.

At least our evenings were free. Since we had all just met each other, and since everyone was young and upbeat, we all became friends very quickly. Some bright sparks brought vodka with them. Our bodies still being relatively young and innocent of strong drink, one bottle split ten ways sufficed to get us all gloriously drunk.

My "godbrother" Andrei even managed to sneak in some pot with him. In hindsight, he was playing with real fire—if busted, he would be kicked out of both Komsomol and our ideological and morally upstanding Oriental department in the blink of an eye.

In the barracks where we lived, there was an old TV set. It had no working sound but was remarkable in another way: it showed Finnish TV, which couldn't be jammed this close to the border. So, for a few evenings, after sharing a joint in the boiler room (the first in my life—the apex of my countercultural drive to live dangerously), we would amuse ourselves watching Finnish TV on mute and without the slightest idea of what was going on, dubbing the programs in different silly voices. Every time we did it, I came close to wetting myself with laughter.

One evening, I was heading to a nearby village in search of booze with one of my newly made friends, Sasha. (His claim to fame was that his mother had been a girlfriend of Rudolf Nureyev before the latter escaped to the West and came out of the closet.) A fellow at the store told us, "Wait two hours, guys. We're about to get a shipment of vanilla liquor." Having no other real options, we stuck around, and soon we were walking back to our barracks with eight bottles. This sugary dreck kept us in good spirits for the next week; we were not greedy children. However, I haven't been able to stomach vanilla-flavored liquor ever since.

Naturally, we had chaperones—no one was going to send a bunch of college kids alone into the rural wilderness, especially within sight of the Finnish border. Young professors took turns supervising us in weeklong shifts. We soon noticed that they were all of them young men from the Arab or Iranian Studies departments. Moreover, they were all gloomy and muscular, and had little patience for rule breaking. There was a definite whiff of the military about them. Later I found out that our chaperones were so-called downed pilots: special ops or intelligence officers who had been on assignment in the Middle East and whose positions had become in some way compromised. They would return to the USSR and change careers, often choosing to instruct the next generation in Arabic or Farsi, or teaching courses on the histories and cultures of the countries they used to infiltrate.

One evening, after helping himself to a healthy quantity of the infamous vanilla liquor, one of them told us stories of his life and times in war-torn Yemen. He used to be a military instructor to local Soviet-friendly insurgents, spreading the gospel of Karl Marx and the AK-47. I remember him telling us of how one day, he was standing and speaking with a local militia man in a village square when someone passed behind the guy and, suddenly, a massive bloody dagger emerged from his interlocutor's chest.

There was also one girl who attracted my attention. She was in my year at the Arabic department. Her name was Dilya, and she had a very unusual, downright exotic look about her. Later I learned that her mother was Russian and her father was Tajik, practically Iranian. She had what one used to call Oriental features (which in the USSR meant either Middle Eastern or central Asian) and a beautiful smile. But I was sixteen and still shy, so I kept out of her way and never tried to speak to her.

* * *

After we came back from our month-long heroic potato farming and finally got down to the business of studying, I was surprised to see that Komsomol was still an active presence in our academic lives. Perestroika was raging, and at my old school, all Komsomol activity had by now become entirely perfunctory. Here at the university, however, there were meetings and mandatory seminars held by various Komsomol administrators and lecturers.

One day in October, our Komsomol leaders told us that all the youth of Leningrad was to gather in Palace Square to celebrate some Komsomol anniversary or other. This square was the epicenter of the Great October Socialist Revolution and basically Leningrad's analogue of the Red Square; all the parades took place there. That evening, our entire class, and indeed most of the university, along with a good chunk of the rest of Leningrad's politically disciplined youth, crowded into the square. It was a pleasantly warm evening, and the sheer crowd numbers inspired one with a sense of belonging to a larger movement—a sense that by 1987 was of course entirely illusory.

Nevertheless, we felt young and happy, and paradoxically free.

At the end of the rally, our department headed to the subway. I found myself walking next to Dilya, and we got to talking: about who she was, who I was, where she was from, what I liked to do for fun, that sort of thing. It was a new and exciting experience.

A few days later, I happened to wake up early and, instead of waiting at home, headed to the university thirty minutes or so before the start of the class, just because. All the department offices and cafeterias were still closed; there was hardly anybody around. I walked aimlessly up and down the hallways and suddenly saw Dilya, who was sitting on a windowsill. She'd caught a ride with her dad and also ended up there early. We fell to talking and almost ended up being late to our first classes.

The next morning, I came early once again, and found Dilya on the same windowsill. The same thing happened the next morning, and the next, until it became our thing. We talked a lot, about everything. I told her that I would probably be leaving for China the next year, or at least that's what the administration was promising us. She confessed that she wouldn't like for me to leave. From that point on, it gradually dawned on me that there was something going on between us.

Life in the Chinese department was rather peculiar. For the first two months, we covered nothing but syllables, working on hearing and pronouncing distinct Mandarin tonemes. Since the meanings of Mandarin syllables change depending on their tone, mastering those distinctions was crucial:

Mā mà mǎ: Mother is scolding the horse.
Mǎ mà mā: The horse is scolding Mother.

After that, we moved on to our first logograms, or written characters.

That was how my first year largely passed: endless hours in the language lab, listening to and repeating after audio recordings of syllables, and an avalanche of flash cards with Chinese characters on them. I woke up to flash cards; I studied them on the bus; I looked through them while waiting to cross the street, like people do today with their phones.

Besides Mandarin, we studied Chinese history, Chinese literature, and the history of the Communist Party of the Soviet Union.

If that last one seems like the odd man in the lineup, recall that it was still 1987 and this nonsense was still compulsory. Our professor was very strict and still utterly committed to his subject matter, swirling though it was around the drain of history. He also happened to be completely blind, but his hearing was so excellent that he could hear paper rustle from a mile away. He conducted his exams in the form of oral Q and A sessions, interrogating two people at once. We would sit down across from him, place our hands on the desk in front, and answer his questions.

Although we respected the professor's professional integrity, we had no respect whatsoever for the material itself. Cheating on his exams was not just a matter of sport; it was a matter of honor. Some guys in our class came up with the idea of taking a standard soft-cover notebook and wetting it. Soggy paper didn't rustle. This way people could take the notebook with them to the exam table and read text off it. But my friend Sasha did them one better. Wary of relying on paper, which tore and disintegrated easily, he wrote out a summary of the entire course on an old bedsheet in water-resistant pen. Then he sewed the sheet into a book and wet it. He and I took our exam together and aced it. But the hardest part of it for me was suppressing laughter as Sasha, with perfect seriousness, placed his cloth book right under the professor's nose and began to read all the answers straight out of it, hemming and hawing a bit here and there for verisimilitude.

In the meantime, my social life finally blossomed. Dilya and I started seeing more and more of each other. Our morning meetings were not enough, so we would arrange to meet up after classes, usually at the Grileta café behind the campus, where we would have coffee and a grilled cheese sandwich, if there were any for sale. (That was becoming less and less reliable as perestroika marched on through the land.) At some point, I started walking Dilya home.

One day after school, we both had audio assignments in the language lab, and all of the audio rooms were taken except one. Dilya suggested that we share it. We took our tape reels and squeezed into a small space. First, I spent half an hour listening to my tapes and repeating them back. My exercises provoked gales of giggles in Dilya. I couldn't blame her: one rather often-encountered syllable in Chinese, *hui*, is a perfect homophone of the Russian curse word designating a lynchpin piece of masculine anatomy.

After I was done with my tapes, she put in her own Arabic ones and started repeating after them. Pretty soon, however, she stopped. The tape played on, but she remained silent.

"Dilya," I asked, "are you listening?"

"No," she said.

"Can I kiss you?" I ventured.

"Yes," she said.

For the next three months, I was crazy in love and completely consumed by this entirely new experience. I was drowning, I was flying; I thought of nothing else but Dilya. Some part of me, however—the sensible, Granny's boy part, no doubt—still managed to keep up with all my schoolwork, learn hundreds of character cards, and not mix up whether the mother was scolding the horse or the other way around.

Dilya and I took long strolls, went out to cafés, and talked, talked, talked. At my place, our telephone had a long cord, and I would drag it over to my and Alyosha's room, after he was already asleep, and hide the phone under the bedcovers. Thus concealed, I could talk to Dilya at night for hours on end—three hours, four hours—about anything and everything. I made her mix tapes with Western music that I was into at the time; I wrote her horribly naive and clumsy poetry; I introduced her to all my friends, to Grandma, and to my numerous parents.

In three short months, she became a complete part of my life.

* * *

One day, Olya Bezverhova took me aside in the courtyard of our department building, lit up a cigarette, and told me with an assured air, "You better keep an eye out, because Dilya is a dish and super popular, and there are a lot of fellows hovering in the wings. They're older than you and more experienced. And she seems to be an explorer, too."

I rolled my eyes at her warnings. *What a bunch of bunk,* I thought.

In January I was turning seventeen, and was feeling myself to be quite the adult. I arranged for my parents to "clear the area" and go visit their friends the Mikhailovs, Andrei's parents. Grandma at the time had a part-time job as a front desk person at the dormitory next door. Alyosha agreed to go and hang at his friend's house for the evening. Thus, I had the apartment to myself. My parents made no comment when I dragged home two boxes of red wine. Grandma cast an appreciative eye over this haul and said, "Young man, you will clearly go far in life."

I invited both my new and my old friends to the birthday bash, including my new college buddies Olya, Sasha, Anton, Andrei, and, of course, Dilya—about twenty people altogether. We cooked a couple of large, thick pizza pies (the ultimate debauchery in terms of Western consumption) and made a bucket of mulled wine. We lit the fireplace, danced, and smoked brazenly in the kitchen. A few people puked in the toilet and in the stairwell. In short, it was a successful party.

A week or so later, Dilya told me not to walk her home that day, because she was going to be working on some group assignment in the library with her classmates. This happened again the next week, then a couple of times the week after, and then more and more often. I didn't say anything and just looked forward to the next time we could hang out after classes.

One day, I was riding the bus home from the university alone, as was becoming the norm. I was standing near the back window, flipping as always through my Chinese flash cards. For a split second, my eyes flicked to the window to look out onto Nevsky Prospect.

That split second was enough for me to see Dilya walking hand in hand with Andrei.

The world faded out for a second. Then it faded back in, but it was a different world.

That afternoon, I bought a bottle of beer and some cigarettes and began to shamble around my neighborhood like a
zombie. After a while, I broke a ruble at a nearby store into
a jingly mess of two-kopeck coins and started walking from
phone booth to phone booth dialing Dilya's house. Time after
time, her mother or her sister would answer the phone, saying
she was not home. At ten at night, I finally reached Dilya herself. She was quite annoyed with me calling her house every
half an hour. Hurt and quite tipsy, I babbled out a whole
bunch of tearful nonsense to her. She deflected by saying we
would talk about it the next day, at the university. But we did
not talk about it the next day, or about anything ever again.

To say that the next several months were hard is to say
nothing. I lived in perpetual darkness. Nothing could take my
thoughts off Dilya and the mess we were in—not my buddies,
not my books, not my character flash cards with their quarrel-
some horses and mothers, not even alcohol.

Although I never told anyone what had happened, everyone just sort of knew. The pain on my face must've made it
obvious. Occasionally, Grandma would ask me, "Are you over
it all yet?" I didn't know what to tell her.

I desperately needed a change of scenery. I desperately
needed to go to China.

My salvation would come not from the West but from the
East.

CHAPTER 25

SHOULD I STAY OR SHOULD I GO?

A lecture is announced in the university science club. It's titled, "When Will We Be Able to Go on Holidays to the Moon?"

A student raises his hand.

"Professor, could you please first tell us when we will be able to go on holidays to Spain or Greece?"

IN THE SUMMER of 1989, one of the largest squares in the world, Beijing's Tiananmen, meaning "Gate of Heavenly Peace," was neither heavenly nor peaceful. For months, Chinese students protested there for a more open and democratic society and faster liberalization of the country. And for months, the Chinese government deliberated on how to handle these protests, which were growing, gaining momentum, and spreading to other cities.

In the end, party hard-liners won the debate and on the night of June 4, tanks and bullets rolled in. Thousands of students were slaughtered by the army that night. In the aftermath, the government conducted widespread arrests of protesters and their supporters, kicked out foreign journalists, strengthened the security forces, and purged all officials and professors deemed sympathetic to the protests.

Expectedly, the Chinese government was condemned and heavily criticized by Western countries, which immediately imposed sanctions and embargoes. However, the USSR was somewhat at a loss for what the proper reaction should be. Gorbachev neither denounced the Chinese government nor voiced support.

At the end of June, three of my classmates and I, who were on the list to go to China, were called to the university international affairs office. There a senior admin lady with a robotic, stone-cold face told us, "Given the situation in China, the Ministry of Education of the USSR is in constant consultations with the Ministry of Foreign Affairs of the USSR. At present, we do not know whether there will be student exchange programs between China and the Soviet Union anymore. You should proceed with your applications to receive permits to exit the Soviet Union. However, you should be aware that you might not get to use them. We will notify you as soon as we have more information."

For the second time in just a few months, my world was upended.

Still heartbroken and now also despondent over my dwindling odds of getting out, I took a bus to Korovkino to stay with Dad. Spending time away from the city in intellectual conversations with him, as well as listening to foreign radio and reading books, I thought, would do me a world of good.

Days went by, and still there was no word about China.

Every morning, while Dad was asleep (he usually went to bed around four in the morning and got up around two in the afternoon), I would put on my boots, take a walking stick, and go for a hike in the woods on the long island between the canals. It was impossible to get lost, so I could confidently walk for hours, breathing in the cool Lake Ladoga breeze, all alone save for the forest birds. (Fortunately, they were not in competition with me for mushrooms.)

By the beginning of August, hope was beginning to desert me. By the middle of August, it was completely gone. My morning constitutionals were turning into dispirited rambles.

I was not going to China. I was going to stay here, in the USSR, all my life, until I died and was put into the ground. And I would rot in that ground, and my bones would mix with it, and then this fucking country would finally have consumed me entirely.

* * *

On August 21, a biker dinged and clanged his way up to our hut. It was Uncle Lesha. He had brought a telegram from Grandma. When I read it, I whooped like a man possessed. She wrote that on August 25, our group was scheduled to depart for China—from Moscow. And we had to be in Moscow by the twenty-third.

Dizzy with the news, I hopped on the bus back to Leningrad, threw my stuff into one suitcase and one backpack, and took the overnight train to Moscow. Grandma decided to come with me, but Mom and Tolya stayed in Leningrad; they had a wedding to attend.

On August 24, all the students departing for China gathered at the central office of the Ministry of Education. Besides the four of us from Leningrad, there were also twenty or so kids from Moscow, from the Institute of Asian and African Countries, the Institute of International Relations, and the Institute of Military Translators—all the places that taught

Chinese in the Soviet Union, bar a couple of smaller schools in the Far East.

A casually dressed middle-aged gentleman from the KGB told us that perestroika or no perestroika, we were all still Soviet citizens, and that we must conduct ourselves abroad as befits ambassadors for the Soviet way of life. We were also told that we had to be extra attentive, because everyone in the great wide world outside the USSR was seeking to corrupt us, or was a suspected spy out to recruit us. For the first time, we would be interacting with foreigners daily, and we had to follow very strict rules. We were not to speak to Americans or western Europeans under any circumstances, and if such circumstances arose despite our best efforts, we were to relay our conversations in their entirety to a special person at the embassy. We were not allowed to cross the Chinese border, and we were to check in as frequently as possible with the embassy in Beijing.

We all stared at him, struggling not to roll our eyes. By now, all this tired claptrap was fit for the rubbish heap of history, and we all knew it. In the Q and A section that followed, all the questions were purely practical:

"Is it better to bring a bicycle from the Soviet Union or to buy one in China?"

"Do we need to receive approval from the embassy to travel between cities in China?"

"Can we travel to Tibet without a special permit?"

"Is there a place in Beijing where one can buy black rye bread?"

"How much salami are you allowed to carry with you to China on a train?"

The last question came from an energetic girl with short brown hair wearing a denim jacket, who sat in the row in front of me. Everyone laughed, including her and her girlfriends.

We were told which universities we were going to. A few folks from Moscow and I were assigned to the Institute of Foreign Languages in Tianjin. This city was relatively unknown to me despite being just one hundred miles south of Beijing and having over eleven million people. But I didn't care—it was not in the USSR.

After lunch, we waited to be given various official papers to sign and our first batch of foreign currency. The Soviet bureaucratic machine still chugged along, churning out the required forms, passes, and certificates. In the best Soviet tradition, we had to queue for each document, each official stamp, each signature or sign-off, to a myriad of office doors.

As I stood in line for my travel money, I saw that girl in the denim jacket just in front of me. One could tell she was from Moscow: she and her friends were very assured and clearly at home, whereas we Leningrad guys were somewhat subdued in this bureaucratic maelstrom. Now, I could see her face. She was really cute: dimples, freckles, and sweet laughing eyes.

Suddenly she turned to me.

"You're going to Tianjin, too, aren't you? My name is Ira. What's your name?"

She was addressing me formally, in the form similar to the French *vous* or the Italian *lei*, as though I were her elder. I found it amusing and I decided to be witty.

"Vova," I said.

She looked puzzled and turned back around without continuing this conversation.

*   *   *

The train departed from Moscow's Yaroslavsky station at midnight on August 25. Grandma and I were staying with relatives just a couple of subway stops away. Before leaving for the station, I made all the final good-bye calls to my friends and relatives in Leningrad.

Alyosha and my buddies from school and university were all very happy for me and wished me the best of luck. Dad, who returned from the village to say good-bye to me on the phone, was in one of his dramatic moods.

"You realize that you are leaving forever, don't you?" he said.

"No, I'm not," I replied.

When I spoke to Mom and Tolya, they'd just returned home from the wedding. Mom said, "The whole party was totally strange. Both Mikhailovs were very nervous; Andrei didn't know how to behave; and Dilya's father brought about fifty relatives from Tajikistan. They are such different people. I have no idea how they're going to live together. You are so lucky."

Funny, I didn't feel lucky.

*   *   *

That night Yaroslavsky train station was sticky, hot, crowded, chaotic, and messy. And our car was even more so, what with the endless backpacks, boxes, bicycles, and all types of electrical appliances that people decided they just couldn't do without in China.

Ira the Moscow girl seemed to have more stuff than anybody else. As her parents carried box after box into the compartment next to ours, she noticed me watching her.

"Hi, Sergey." Her smile dimpled her lovely freckled face.

I blushed. "Hi, Ira. Boy, that sure is a lot of salami. . ."

"Just twenty-seven sticks," she said with a straight face, cracking her knuckles. "It should get me through September. . ."

Slowly, the train took off. I watched through the window as Grandma waved good-bye to me from the platform and wiped away her tears.

I fell back onto my top bunk and put my hands behind my head. I thought about Dilya getting married, about Grandma, about Dad, and about this new girl, Ira. She was funny. I liked her.

Soon, I was falling asleep, lulled by the clatter of train wheels. Our trans-Siberian journey was to last six days. The USSR still stretched, huge and mighty and utterly permanent, across one-sixth of the world's surface. But for once, I would not be a part of it.

And as I lay there, finally leaving my homeland, I pondered the extent and nature of my newfound freedom. Across the thin compartment wall from me, mere inches away, was Ira—my future wife and the mother of our children: Mike, Alex, and Zoya. She was probably dreaming of salami.

August 21, 2011

After Grandma's memorial, I bought a bottle of wine in a paper bag and went for a stroll around my old neighborhood.

The streets had changed their names, but everything around seemed the same. The only substantial change was the new parking lot in the place of the old green promenade by the Big House where my friends and I spent so many pleasant evenings. Now instead of children and dogs, it was packed with the latest BMW and Mercedes models belonging to the tireless, stealth defenders of the motherland.

I went to see my old school, Number 185. The courtyard had not changed one bit in the twenty-five years since my graduation. It had the same dusty gravel; misshapen, stinking trash cans; and amorous stray cats. It was as if time had stopped there. I turned and headed down the now-renamed Voinov Street, in the direction of "home"—our old place on Kalyaeva Street. Or rather, Zahar'evskaya Street.

In our own courtyard, there were not many changes, either. A few new benches had been installed and a few windows replaced, but other than that, everything was the same, just shabbier. The house itself had not been repainted since I'd last seen it. The subway vent still stuck out of the ground like a demented doghouse, belching creosote-scented air. There was even the very same clumsily painted sign, "No Parking!" on the wall.

I looked at the windows of our old apartment. A bell tower now rose above them; the building next to us was once more a church, and the bell ringing had recommenced along with the services. Who lived there now? I wondered.

Suddenly I realized that I could find out. Phone numbers for landlines remained the same regardless of who lived in the apartment: like the serfs of old, they were attached to the real estate.

I took out my cell phone and dialed my old number, which I still remembered by heart. A middle-aged-sounding man picked up. I apologized to him, introduced myself, and began to wax poetically, in the way of sentimental drunks everywhere, about how for the past fifteen years, I had been living in London but that I had spent my childhood in flat number 44, which he now called home. I was in town for just that one day, I said, and would he by any chance let me in for just a few minutes? Predictably, he declined, saying that he was busy.

"Please!" I whined into the phone. "I'm down in the courtyard; can I just come up for a minute? You can look out of the window and see that I'm not a freak." (In what way seeing me was supposed to reassure him was unclear.)

"No!" said the unknown resident, now with more than a trace of alarm, and hung up.

Denied reentry into my childhood, I went on wandering around the neighborhood. I shambled past our gastronom, which also hadn't changed a bit (though presumably the food inside now sported far more brand names and disposable packaging); past the Kolobok café, where a few furnishings had been updated—and hopefully the meatball recipe; past all the shops where I had spent so much of my childhood standing in lines.

The store where I used to buy school supplies now sold haute couture shoes. The store where I spent three fruitless hours queuing for bananas was now an Italian restaurant. I quashed an absurd desire to knock on its door and demand the two bunches of bananas I was still owed.

As I passed the stop of trolleybus number fifteen, tears, which had eluded me since I had received news of Grandma's passing, suddenly ambushed me. I walked down Tchaikovsky Street toward the former Leningrad cinema, making no effort to wipe the tears away. Passersby gave the strange crying foreigner a wide berth.

I made it to the park, sat down on the same bench where I'd killed time before seeing *The Empire Returns the Blow*, and had a smoke. This time it was Marlborough again.

After a while, I finished my bottle and decided that this was quite enough of sad drunken Russian nostalgia for the day. Also, I was getting hungry.

The small bar on Vosstaniya Street was practically empty—there were only two guys and two girls inside, all in their late twenties or early thirties.

I spent an hour chewing on bar snacks, having a few more drinks, and senselessly surfing Facebook. Then I decided to strike up a conversation with them.

"So, are you guys from around here?" I asked.

"No, we are from Kolpino. We just like to come here," said one of the girls.

I moved to their table and we talked for a few hours. Or rather, I did most of the talking, and they mostly asked me questions, about what life was like in China, in France, Italy, London, and all the other places I'd lived; about being a banker and the great recession of 2008, which at that time was still unfolding; about my family and raising three children away from Russia . . .

The five of us ended up shambling out of the bar around midnight and heading out for a stroll around town. My flight back was at six in the morning, and the thought crossed my mind that it would be wiser to go back to my hotel and catch a few hours of sleep, but the call of the white night was too strong. Eventually we dropped into another bar, had a round there, then another one, and then went to watch the bridges get raised for the night. As with Jonas and his girlfriend before, I was awash in a wondrous feeling of universal comradeship.

When we finally called it quits at four o'clock in the morning, one of the guys called me a taxi—my Blackberry had died long ago. We exchanged phone numbers and Facebook names, I hugged all my new besties good-bye, then checked out of my hotel and went to the airport. Predictably, we never connected again.

When the Lufthansa crew closed the door in preparation for departure, I was already nodding off. The funeral arrangements, the ceremony itself, and my mild-mannered attempts at debauchery afterwards were all catching up with me.

As my eyes closed, I remembered how in 2001 I talked Grandma into visiting my family in London. She was eighty-five and would be crossing the border of Russia for the first time in her life. It would also be only her second time on an airplane, exactly sixty years after her first and only flight. When the Germans laid siege to Leningrad in 1941, one of Grandma's friends managed to get her on the last cargo plane leaving the city. It had no seats or seat belts—just some hay and blankets on the floor. As the plane took off, the pilot had to go through a storm while dodging German antiaircraft fire. The crew got the passengers safely to their destination in southern Russia, but the experience stayed with Grandma for the rest of her life. Knowing she was terrified of flying, I came back to Saint Petersburg to accompany her. We both steeled ourselves for the worst, but to my astonishment, she didn't even notice our plane taking off. There was no noise, no turbulence, no sudden lurches or drops in altitude. It didn't feel like any kind of flying she'd experienced. When we landed, she was thrilled.

She spent most of her two weeks in London walking in Hyde Park with our boys, even though by that time she was already quite old and frail. She had never been a master of generalizations and so she did not share much of her impressions of seeing the West for the first time. The only thing she kept repeating every time we visited a "place of interest" in London like Piccadilly Circus, the Tower of London, or Westminster Abbey—all the attractions she knew so well from teaching English—was "It doesn't feel real, it doesn't. . ."

My life, too, had turned out to be totally unreal and amazingly different from anything I could've made up as a child. Living in London and Tuscany? Zigzagging nonstop across the globe? Being able to eat anything I wanted, in any restaurant? Having three children who speak English to one another? All of this was completely unimaginable.

But as history teaches us, the only predictable thing about life is its unpredictability.

Was I happy with my upbringing? Did I have a happy childhood?

Well, it was what it was. From a nutritional and a relationship standpoint, it wasn't particularly great. But it also wasn't awful or tragic. It was, when I look back on it now, normal.

But my kids' childhoods couldn't be more different from mine. For starters, they avoided divorces and the bizarre upbringing arrangements that I grew up with. Unlike me, they never experienced any shortages—be it of love, of food, or of entertainment. They were never taught to lie or to keep their mouths shut. If I grew up looking through a tiny peephole in the Iron Curtain at the big world outside, imagining what was happening in it, my children have been the true citizens of that big world from the get-go. And that is, unquestionably, the most meaningful achievement of my life.

While waiting for my next flight, over a breakfast of Alaskan crab salad and white wine in a caviar bar, I reflected on all of this for the last time.

Memories aside, there was nothing left to tie me to Russia or to my childhood in it. I knew where I was from, but I didn't know who I was anymore. My national identity had been totally erased. I'd had enough of my love-hate relationship with Russia, and I wanted to get away from this bond as strongly as I wanted to escape the country when I was a boy.

I thought about how the last two decades of Russian history were marked by a scuffle between my generation's attempts to flee the USSR, both physically and metaphorically, and the previous generations' efforts to rebuild it again. I had to admit, my team wasn't winning. It still isn't today.

Russia, where are you racing to? I thought. *Give answer!* But she gives no answer. . .

I was now incontrovertibly a grown-up. The first part of my life was over. Like my homeland, Grandma would no longer loom over me. The burden of guilt at leaving her behind was gone. I felt relieved and free.

An hour later, I boarded my flight to Florence, where my Westernized family was waiting for me.

Soon, very soon, I was surrounded by the whispering hills and roaring cicadas of my dear and so beloved inner Tuscany.

ACKNOWLEDGMENTS

My deepest duty of gratitude goes to all of my friends who took a leap of faith (and took out their credit cards) and made preorders. This book would not be possible without you.

This book wouldn't be anything at all without Rebecca Winfield, who made me believe in its feasibility, and Anna Zaigraeva, who helped me immeasurably at every stage of this project.

This book also wouldn't be possible without the wonderful Inkshares team—Matt Harry, Adam Gomolin, Avalon Radys, Angela Melamud, Elena Stofle, and Jessica Gardner. Another huge thank-you goes to the team of cover designers at CoverKitchen.

I also need to thank my incredible children—Mike, Alex, and Zoya—for whom, ultimately, I wrote this book. And, of course, I need to thank my amazing wife, Ira, who has always supported all my projects, however nonsensical they were.

And, finally, the very last thank-you goes to the Flying Spaghetti Monster.

GRAND PATRONS

Aleksey Levchenko
Alex Tolchinsky
Alexander Gutin
Alexander Klachin
Alexander Savin
Alexander Vinokurov
Alexandra Von Sauber
Alexey Belov
Alexey Khavin
Alexey Mikaylovskiy
Alexey Trusov
Alina Sycheva
Andrei Taskin
Andrey Leonovich
Anna Pankratova
Anton Rushakov
Anya Goldin
Craig Lindahl
Daniel Attia
David Goldberg
Delia Salikhova

Denis Bugrov
Dmitry Krukov
Dr. Olga Vienna
Egor Sirota
Ekaterina Tokareva
Elena Plotkina
Evgeny Astakhov
Evgeny Borisov
Gleb Filshtinsky
Helen McKeon
Igor Pesin
Igor Semenyuk
Ilona Kitain
Ilya Epishchev
Iouri Chliaifchtein
Irina and Dima Leshchinskii
Irina Gofman
Jacqui Castle
John Cavanagh
Julia Bliss
Katherine Sauter

Konstantin Kroll
Lado Gurgenidze
Michael Madden
Mikhail Kazarin
Mikhail Noskov
Nikolai Sitnikov
Oleg Pavlov
Oleg Tinkov
Pavel Malyi
Rashad Azizov
Ravi Ruparel
Robert Dennewald
Sergei Mamotov
Steve Hacking
Timour Boudkeev
Vassilina Bindley
Vladimir Nikonorovich Zhuchkov
Vladislav Tersh
Vladislav Zabelin
Vsevolod Rozanov
Yermolai Solzhenitsyn
Yiannis Demopoulos
Yulia Korneva
Yury Titarenko

INKSHARES

INKSHARES is a reader-driven publisher and producer based in Oakland, California. Our books are selected not by a group of editors, but by readers worldwide.

While we've published books by established writers like *Big Fish* author Daniel Wallace and *Star Wars: Rogue One* scribe Gary Whitta, our aim remains surfacing and developing the new author voices of tomorrow.

Previously unknown Inkshares authors have received starred reviews and been featured in the *New York Times*. Their books are on the front tables of Barnes & Noble and hundreds of independents nationwide, and many have been licensed by publishers in other major markets. They are also being adapted by Oscar-winning screenwriters at the biggest studios and networks.

Interested in making your own story a reality? Visit Inkshares.com to start your own project or find other great books.

Printed in the USA
CPSIA information can be obtained
at www.ICGtesting.com
JSHW022208140824
68134JS00018B/926

9 781942 645900